Canada: The State of the Federation 2011

The Changing Federal Environment: Rebalancing Roles?

Edited by
Nadia Verrelli

Institute of Intergovernmental Relations
Queen's Policy Studies Series
School of Policy Studies, Queen's University
McGill-Queen's University Press
Montreal & Kingston • London • Ithaca

The Institute of Intergovernmental Relations

The Institute is the only academic organization in Canada whose mandate is solely to promote research and communication on the challenges facing the federal system.

Current research interests include fiscal federalism, health policy, the reform of federal political institutions and the machinery of federal-provincial relations, Canadian federalism and the global economy, and comparative federalism.

The Institute pursues these objectives through research conducted by its own associates and other scholars, through its publication program, and through seminars and conferences.

The Institute links academics and practitioners of federalism in federal, provincial, and territorial governments and the private sector.

The Institute of Intergovernmental Relations receives ongoing financial support from the J. A. Corry Memorial Endowment Fund, the Royal Bank of Canada Endowment Fund, and the governments of Manitoba and Ontario. We are grateful for this support, which enables the Institute to sustain its program of research, publication, and related activities.

L'Institut des relations intergouvernementales

L'Institut est le seul organisme universitaire canadien à se consacrer exclusivement à la recherche et aux échanges sur les enjeux du fédéralisme.

Les priorités de recherche de l'Institut portent présentement sur le fédéralisme fiscal, la santé, la modification des institutions politiques fédérales, les mécanismes des relations fédérales-provinciales, le fédéralisme canadien dans l'économie mondiale et le fédéralisme comparatif.

L'Institut réalise ses objectifs par le biais de recherches effectuées par des chercheurs de l'Université Queen's et d'ailleurs, de même que par des congrès et des colloques.

L'Institut sert de lien entre les universitaires, les fonctionnaires fédéraux, provinciaux et territoriaux et le secteur privé.

L'Institut des relations intergouvernementales reçoit l'appui financier du J. A. Corry Memorial Endowment Fund, de la Fondation de la Banque Royale du Canada, et des gouvernements du Manitoba et de l'Ontario. Nous les remercions de cet appui qui permet à l'Institut de poursuivre son programme de recherche et de publication ainsi que ses activités connexes.

ISSN 0827-0708
ISBN 978-1-55339-207-1 (pbk.)
ISBN 978-1-55339-208-8 (epub)
ISBN 978-1-55339-209-5 (pdf)

CONTENTS

v   *Preface*

vii   *Contributors*

1   1.   Introduction
        Nadia Verrelli

I   The Changing Federal Environment: Initial Observations

9   2.   Embracing Imperfection: How Canada Fares in the Comparative
        Federalism Literature
        Thomas O. Hueglin

27   3.   The Size of the Federal and Provincial Governments in Canada:
        Some Quantitative Evidence
        François Vaillancourt

II The Implications of the 2011 Federal Election

45   4.   The West in Canada: Assessing the West's Role in the Post-2011
        Federal System
        Loleen Berdahl

65   5.   The Orange Wave: A (Re)Canadianization of the Quebec
        Electorate?
        François Rocher

83   6.   Institutional Reform
        David E. Smith

III Health Policy, Economic Federalism: Who Is in Charge?

95   7.   Never More than a Step from Paradise: Canadian Provinces and
        the Public Funding of Health Care Services
        Pierre-Gerlier Forest

111   8. Federalism and Securities Regulation in Canada
           Eric Spink

153   9. Canadian Federalism and International Trade: A Small Step While
           Waiting for the Giant Leap
           Patrick Fafard and Patrick Leblond

IV The Provinces and the North: Growing in Importance?

171   10. Something Old or Something New? Territorial Development and
           Influence within the Canadian Federation
           George Braden, Christopher Alcantara, and Michael Morden

195   11. On the Relative Neglect of Horizontal Intergovernmental Relations
           in Canada
           Éric Montpetit and Martial Foucault

215   12. From Old Canada, the New East: Adjusting to the Changing
           Federal Environment
           Christopher Dunn

PREFACE

This volume is the first of three State of the Federation books under the full responsibility of former IIGR director André Juneau. During 2011 it became clear to him that the relative roles of the federal and provincial governments were changing, or at least it was worth asking the question of whether they really were changing or whether, as Roger Gibbins put it, we had seen this movie before. Mr Gibbins, then president of the Canada West Foundation, was one of four informal advisors Mr Juneau had enlisted to assist him in refining this theme of changing relative roles, and their advice proved to be invaluable in developing the scope and structure of the conference that is the basis for this book. The other advisors were André Pratte from L'Idée fédérale, Matthew Mendelsohn from the Mowat Centre, and Elizabeth Beale from the Atlantic Provinces Economic Council. Such a theme was a departure from recent State of the Federation volumes, which had been devoted to more specific topics, such as the New Ontario or environmental federalism. The advisors, and Mr Gibbins in particular, believed that it was opportune to attempt a broader review, literally, of the state of the federation. Mr Juneau wishes to thank them all for their support.

The conference was held in Montreal, which contributed to recreating some of the ties the IIGR has had with Quebec scholars.

The Institute and Mr Juneau wish to thank CIBC and COGECO for their generous financial contributions, as well as the Forum of Federations and the National Round Table on the Environment and the Economy for their support for the conference.

Above all, the Institute wishes to thank Professor Nadia Verrelli, a research associate at IIGR, who worked with the emerging theme, put it into final shape with Mr Juneau, organized most aspects of the conference, and edited the present volume.

We also wish to thank Maureen Garvie, our conscientious copy editor, Valerie Jarus, and Mark Howes of the Publications Unit of the School of Policy Studies and, as always, Mary Kennedy, the indispensable administrative assistant at the Institute.

John R. Allan
Director, IIGR

*The Institute of Intergovernmental Relations thanks its
sponsors and partners for the 2011 State of the Federation conference,
"The Changing Federal Environment: Rebalancing Roles?"*

The Institute is grateful for the financial support of:

The Institute thanks the hosts for two of the panels:

NATIONAL ROUND TABLE TABLE RONDE NATIONALE
ON THE ENVIRONMENT SUR L'ENVIRONNEMENT
AND THE ECONOMY ET L'ÉCONOMIE

The Institute is pleased to acknowledge the following partners:

ATLANTIC CONSEIL
PROVINCES ÉCONOMIQUE
ECONOMIC DES PROVINCES
COUNCIL DE L'ATLANTIQUE

L'IDÉE FÉDÉRALE • THE FEDERAL IDEA

CONTRIBUTORS

Christopher Alcantara

Christopher Alcantara is associate professor of political science at Wilfrid Laurier University. His main research areas are Indigenous-settler relations and the political and constitutional development of the Canadian territorial North. He is the author or co-author of two books (one of which, *Beyond the Indian Act: Restoring Aboriginal Property Rights*, with Tom Flanagan and André Le Dressay, was shortlisted for the Donner Prize), and numerous scholarly articles. His latest research projects, both funded by SSHRC, examine the evolution of Inuit self-government in Canada and the intergovernmental relationships that are emerging between municipal and Aboriginal governments.

Loleen Berdahl

Loleen Berdahl is an associate professor in the Department of Political Studies at the University of Saskatchewan. She earned her PhD in political science from the University of Calgary in 1998 and is a past Fulbright Graduate Scholar. Her research interests include regionalism, public policy attitudes, political behaviour, and internal trade policy. She is the co-author of four books, including *Western Visions, Western Futures* (with Roger Gibbins) and *Explorations: Conducting Empirical Research in Canadian Political Science* (with Keith Archer). She is the project leader for the new survey and focus group research facility at the University of Saskatchewan, funded by the Canada Foundation for Innovation. She is also a co-investigator on two SSHRC-funded research projects examining political behaviour in Canada.

George Braden

George Braden is a graduate of Sir John Franklin High School in Yellowknife and holds degrees in political science from the University of Alberta (BA) and Dalhousie University (MA). During his professional career, he has served in a variety of positions with a focus on the political, constitutional, and economic development of the Northwest Territories, prior to and following the establishment of Nunavut. Since 2005 he has operated an Ottawa-based firm specializing in monitoring and analyzing national, territorial, and international media from a northern-issues perspective. In October 2009 he was appointed as a policy advisor to the Hon. Dennis Patterson, senator for Nunavut.

Christopher Dunn

Christopher Dunn is a professor of Political Science at Memorial University of Newfoundland. He received his undergraduate education from the University of Manitoba and his MA and PhD (1990) from the University of Toronto. He came to teaching after time as an education consultant and a provincial cabinet–level planner. His teaching and publishing areas include Canadian politics, the Constitution, federalism, public policy, and public administration. He has been a member of the board of directors of the Association for Canadian Studies, the Humanities and Social Sciences Federation of Canada, the Canadian Political Science Association, and the Canadian Federation for the Humanities and Social Sciences. He was a member of the Green Commission on Constituency Allowances and Related Matters and also contributed research pieces to two other commissions of enquiry, the Macdonald Commission (1985) and Renewing and Strengthening our Place in Canada (2003).

Patrick Fafard

Patrick Fafard is a political scientist with a special interest in Canadian health policy and issues of federalism and intergovernmental relations. He is an associate professor in the Graduate School of Public and International Affairs at the University of Ottawa. He holds a PhD in political studies from Queen's University and is the author and co-editor of several publications dealing with health policy, federalism, and environmental policy. He has also enjoyed an extensive career in government and most recently served as director general, Strategic Policy and Research, in the Intergovernmental Affairs Secretariat of the Privy Council Office. Before joining the Government of Canada he worked for the governments of Alberta, Ontario, and Saskatchewan and served as the executive director of Saskatechewan's Commission on Medicare.

Pierre-Gerlier Forest

Pierre-Gerlier Forest is a professor with the Department of Health Policy and Management at the Bloomberg School of Public Health and the director of the Institute for Health and Social Policy, Johns Hopkins University. From 2006 to 2013, he was the president of the Pierre Elliott Trudeau Foundation, a national institution fostering innovation in applied social and policy research. He has served as assistant deputy minister with Health Canada, where he was first appointed to the G.D.W. Cameron Chair (2003) before becoming chief scientist (2004–06). Well known for his work in the areas of health policy and the governance of health-care organizations, he also held the position of director of research for the Commission of the Future of Health Care in Canada (Romanow Commission). He spent the first part of his academic career at Université Laval, where he was professor of policy analysis and public management with the Department of Political Science (1990–2007). He holds adjunct professorships with the National School of Public Administration (Quebec) and the Faculty of Medicine, Université de Montréal.

Martial Foucault

Martial Foucault (PhD, economics, Université Paris 1 Panthéon-Sorbonne) is full professor of political science at Sciences Po Paris and director of the Centre for Political Research at Sciences Po, CEVIPOF (CNRS). Between 2006 and 2013, he was associate professor at Université de Montréal. He is also an associate editor of the journals *Canadian Public Policy* and *French Politics*. His research interests range from political economy to political behaviour as well as public policies, fiscal policies, and statistical methods. His current research interests include decentralization in Africa and the nature of local governments. His most recent publications appear in the *British Journal of Political Science*, *Electoral Studies*, *American Journal of Political Science*, *West European Politics*, and *PS: Politics and Political Science*.

Thomas O. Hueglin

Thomas O. Hueglin is professor of political science at Wilfrid Laurier University in Canada, where he was the 2009–10 University Research Professor. He received degrees from St Gall University, Switzerland (PhD) and Konstanz University, Germany (Habilitation). His most recent book publications are *Comparative Federalism: A Systematic Inquiry* (2006, with Alan Fenna; 2nd edition forthcoming 2015), *Classical Debates for the 21st Century: Rethinking Political Thought* (2008), and *We All Giggled: A Bourgeois Family Memoir* (2011). His current research is focused on federalism and political theories of diversity and governance.

Patrick Leblond

Patrick Leblond is associate professor in the Graduate School of Public and International Affairs at the University of Ottawa as well as research associate at CIRANO (Montreal). He is also affiliated professor of International Business at HEC Montreal and visiting professor at the World Trade Institute (Bern, Switzerland) and the University of Barcelona (IELPO LLM program). He is a member of Statistics Canada's International Trade Advisory Committee and an advisor to the Canada-Europe Roundtable for Business. He has applied his expertise in business, economics, and international relations to questions relating to global economic governance and international and comparative political economy, more specifically those that deal with international finance, international economic integration, and business-government relations. His regional expertise focuses mainly on Europe and

North America but includes North America's relations with Asia. Before moving to Ottawa, he taught international business at HEC Montreal and was director of the Réseau économie internationale (REI) at the Centre d'études et de recherches internationales de l'Université de Montréal (CERIUM). He also spent some time at the Institute for Research on Public Policy (IRPP) in Montreal as visiting scholar. He holds degrees from Columbia University (PhD), Cambridge University (M.Phil), Lund University (MBA), and HEC Montreal (BBA).

Éric Montpetit

Éric Montpetit is professor and chair of the political science department at the Université de Montréal. He completed a PhD in comparative and Canadian public policy at McMaster University in 1999. His current research centres on policy in domains requiring scientific knowledge (notably biotechnology) in North America and Europe, on the role of experts in these domains, on policy learning, and, more generally, on disagreements generated by the making of policy choices. His past research included environmental policy comparisons. His recent work has been published or is to appear in the *Canadian Journal of Political Science*, *West European Politics*, *Political Studies*, and the *Journal of European Public Policy*.

Michael Morden

Michael Morden is a PhD candidate in the Department of Political Science at the University of Toronto. His dissertation research looks at the rise of Indigenous direct action and the dynamics of conflict that follow flash-point protest events. His other research interests include the form and function of the Indian Act, anglo-French relations in Canada, and nationalism and ethnic conflict in theory.

François Rocher

François Rocher is professor of Political Science at the School of Political Studies, University of Ottawa. His research interests focus on broad issues that inform the Canadian political dynamic, including the constitutional debate, Canadian federalism, Quebec nationalism, and the politics of management of ethnocultural diversity. He has published extensively in academic journals and edited books. Recently, he co-edited *La dynamique confiance / méfiance dans les démocraties multinationales* (2012), *The State in Transition: Challenges for Canadian Federalism* (2011), and *Essential Readings in Canadian Politics and Government* (2010) and is co-author of *Immigration, diversité et sécurité: les associations arabo-musulmanes face à l'État au Canada et au Québec* (2009).

David E. Smith

Currently distinguished visiting professor at Ryerson University, David E. Smith holds degrees from the University of Western Ontario (BA), Duke University (MA and PhD), and the University of Saskatchewan (DLitt). He is the author of several books on Canadian political parties and a trilogy of studies on the Canadian Parliament. His most recent work is *Federalism and the Constitution of Canada* (2010). He was book review editor of *Canadian Journal of Political Studies* (1979–84) and chair of the Publications Program of the Aid to Scholarly Publications Committee (Social Science and Humanities Federation of Canada), 1990–94. He has sat on numerous committees of the Social Sciences and Humanities Research Council and was Saskatchewan member of the Historic Sites and Monuments Board of Canada between 1975 and 1990. He also appears frequently as an expert witness before committees of the Parliament of Canada.

Eric Spink

Eric Spink is a lawyer in private practice in Edmonton. From 2006 to 2010 he was an executive director with Alberta Finance, where he helped develop and implement the "passport system" of securities regulation. Director of enforcement at the Alberta Securities Commission from 1988–90, he also served as a member and vice chair of the commission from 1995 to 2003. He was a member of the Canadian delegation to the Hague Conference on Private International Law, which produced the 2002 Hague Securities Convention. He led a major property-law reform project that produced harmonized Securities Transfer Acts first enacted by Alberta and Ontario in 2006. In 2010 he wrote four reports that were filed in evidence by Alberta in the references to the Quebec and Alberta Courts of Appeal and the Supreme Court of Canada regarding the constitutionality of the proposed federal Securities Act.

François Vaillancourt

François Vaillancourt holds a PhD from Queen's University at Kingston. He is a member of the Royal Society of Canada, a fellow at CIRANO, and a retired professor in the Département de sciences économiques, Université de Montréal (1976–2010). He has published extensively in the area of public policy, particularly fiscal federalism, taxation, and language policy. In the 1990s, he was visiting scholar at the Institut d'Études Européennes (Université Libre de Bruxelles, 1994), the Shastri visiting lecturer in economics (India,1993), a visiting scholar at the Federalism Research Centre, Australian National University (1991) and the visiting professor of Policy Modeling, Institute for Policy Analysis, University of Toronto (1991). He was also research coordinator, Income Distribution and Economic Security, Economic Research, Royal Commission on the Economic Union and Development Prospects for Canada (1983–85) and associate editor of *Canadian Public Policy* (1985–95). He was the Fulbright Canadian Research Scholar at Kennesaw in 2007, visiting professor at the Andrew Young School of Policy Studies in Atlanta in 2007 and 2009, visiting professor at FUCaM (Mons, Belgium, 2006), and visiting professor at the École Normale Supérieure de Cachan in Paris (2006 and 2008). As a consultant for various bodies, he has worked on domestic finance issues (taxation, transfers) in 21 countries.

Nadia Verrelli

Nadia Verrelli holds a PhD from Carleton University. She is an assistant professor of political science at Lakehead University and an ongoing research associate at the Institute for Intergovernmental Relations at Queen's University. Her area of study includes the Supreme Court of Canada, Canadian federalism and constitutionalism, and Quebec politics. She has published on Canadian federalism, the Canadian Senate and the Supreme Court. Her latest publication is "The 'Cents' and Nonsense of the Federal Spending Power," *Journal of Parliamentary and Political Law* (2013). Currently she is exploring the role of the SCC in shaping Canadian federalism. She is also looking into the Clarity ethos in comparing Quebec and Scottish nationalism, for which she received a grant from the Secrétariat aux affaires intergouvernementales canadiennes (SAIC), Government of Quebec.

1

INTRODUCTION

Nadia Verrelli

In the past decade, Canadians have witnessed a change in the Canadian federal environment. The creation of the Council of the Federation in 2003, the strength of the resource sector, the growing attention paid to the North, changes to the equalization formula and the readjustments of fiscal arrangements, the "new" Ontario, the changing partisan landscape in Canada, the potentially diminishing influence and power of Quebec in the federation, and the proclamation of "open federalism" (and its actual practice) — all are manifestations of this change. More specific illustrations include Saskatchewan's stance on foreign investment in potash, regional initiatives on climate change, new provincial demands for a larger role in international trade negotiations, widespread opposition (with the important exception of Ontario) to a national securities regulator, attempts at institutional reform of the Senate and the House of Commons, and the positions taken by Newfoundland and Labrador, Nova Scotia, and Quebec on the Lower Churchill project. Provincial governments are not hesitating to assert themselves in protecting their interests.

In light of these changes, the Institute of Intergovernmental Relations invited experts from academia and government to explore this "new" Canadian federal environment at our State of the Federation conference, held in Montreal in December 2011. Participants were asked to discuss the role of the provinces and the territories in the federation and consider whether we are witnessing a redefinition, a change, and/or a rebalancing of the relationship between the central government and the provincial and territorial governments. We focused on three overarching research questions that capture the idea of Canada's changing federal environment.

The first of these was whether the power base in Canada was changing and how, if such change was occurring, governments were responding. In particular, authors were asked to consider how the provinces were asserting or reasserting themselves. For example, are the provinces attempting to enlarge or redefine their role or powers in the federation? If they are, what are the manifestations of these enlargements or redefinitions? What role are provincial institutions (e.g., the Council of the

Federation) playing in these processes? Are they effective, or should provinces seek other avenues of cooperation and coordination? In short, has the proclamation of the era of "open federalism" resulted in substantive change?

The second major issue authors were asked to consider were the implications of the changing environment and redefinition of roles for Canadian unity, federal-provincial/territorial relations, and interprovincialism.

These questions are largely cast in the traditional terms of the relationships between provinces, regions, and the federal government. It was important, therefore, to ask, as the third major theme, whether there are underlying forces—for example, economic or technological change, or demands for citizen engagement—that are pushing some at least of the provinces or regions to more forcibly assert themselves in the global community.

These and related issues generated two days of lively debate and the papers that resulted are presented in this volume.

THE CHANGING FEDERAL ENVIRONMENT: INITIAL OBSERVATIONS

In the book's opening chapter, Thomas Hueglin offers a comparative look at Canadian federalism. Reviewing the growing body of comparative federalism literature, he demonstrates that the world of federalism is changing in both theory and practice. Belgium and Spain have added to the asymmetrical and multinational dimension of federalism; the European Union has been recognized as a case of treaty federalism. According to Hueglin, despite such changes, the perception of Canadian federalism remains negative. While Canada continues to be taken seriously as a model of cooperative federalism, the American model is still the prevalent one when studying federalism from a comparative perspective. This bias precludes a full understanding and appreciation of Canadian interstate federalism.

Focusing on the evolution of the roles of the federal and provincial governments between 1989 and 2009, François Vaillancourt argues that the importance of the federal government has declined, while that of Western Canada has increased. Bringing together data on five indicators—expenditures, revenues, debt, public employment, and private output—regulated by each level of governments, he examines how provinces and the central government have changed relative to each other. These changes, he maintains, are weakening central Canada through "Dutch disease"[1] and turning Canada back into a staples economy. Vaillancourt concludes

---

[1] The term "Dutch disease" is understood as the surge in the processing of natural resources accompanied by a fall in employment in the manufacturing sector. The term originated from the discoveries of vast natural gas deposits in the North Sea in the 1960s that caused the Dutch guilder to rise, making its manufactured goods less competitive in world markets.

by offering ways in which to deal with this challenge, which in his view must be addressed in the next decade.

These chapters lay the groundwork for the papers that follow. In the next sections, the authors explore how Canadian federalism, used by the two orders of government, could, as Hueglin suggests, "figure more prominently as an adequate response to the complexities of governments, societies, and economies."

IMPLICATIONS OF THE 2011 FEDERAL ELECTIONS

In this spirit, the book's second section examines the 2011 federal election and its implications for the dynamics of the federation. The 2011 election of a Conservative majority government seemed to mark the political ascendancy of Western Canada. Further, it saw a decline in the support for the Bloc Québécois and an increase in support for the New Democratic Party. But did those results really mean a large change for the West's role in the federation and a recommitment to Canadian federalism by Quebec? Further, how does the quest for institutional reform play out in the current federal environment?

Loleen Berdahl and François Rocher explore the potential impact of a majority government based on a West–Ontario coalition with Quebec in the opposition, on relations between Quebec and the rest of Canada, and on the changing roles in the federation of Ontario, Quebec, and the West. The two authors provide a foundation to help the reader explore whether the 2011 election result reflects a realignment of the party system. Is the West in and Quebec out? If so, what are the implications of the new makeup of the House of Commons, not only on day-to-day politics but on Canadian federalism? If not, what do the election results tell us about regionalism in Canada?

Berdahl considers the "change" for the West by discussing the implications of the 2011 election for government and public policy: political institutions (specifically, the House of Commons and the Senate), intergovernmental relations, and western regionalism. While the West is generally understood to encompass British Columbia, Alberta, Saskatchewan, and Manitoba, she appreciates that this concept is not without problems. She outlines the reasons for the 2011 election result, marking a new chapter for the West but not substantially altering the West's role in the federation.

François Rocher, focusing on the implications of the election results for Quebec and that province's role in the federation, examines whether Quebec has in fact recommitted to Canadian federalism. He analyzes critically the overall post-election image of the Bloc Québécois by looking at the press response, Quebec's views of Canadian federalism, and issues that are faced by federal parties. He reminds readers that the NDP's electoral status in Quebec is fragile, and that the enduring divide between Quebec and the federal government cannot disappear overnight.

This political reality is reflected in Quebecers' weak identification with Canada and loyalty to their provincial government.

As David Smith points out in his contribution, a further consequence of the 2011 election is that the subject of the prerogative power of the Crown has disappeared from the daily news, although by no means for good. Looking at institutional reform in the current political environment, Smith discusses the prerogative power of the Crown that is normally exercised on advice of the first minister. This power remains significant in two areas of public policy: foreign relations, and what is called the "condition of Parliament." In exploring the latter, Smith looks specifically at the summoning, dissolution, and prorogation of Parliament. He also addresses the possibility of institutional reforms as they apply to the House of Commons, asking the key question: Does the House have a future?

HEALTH POLICY, ECONOMIC FEDERALISM: WHO IS IN CHARGE?

The volume's third section considers the role of the provinces in key policy sectors: health policy, national securities, and international trade policy. Which order of government is or ought to be the leading force? How much cooperation between the two is desirable? What are the implications of the relationship between the two orders on the overall dynamics between the central government and the provinces?

Pierre-Gerlier Forest explores Canada's health care system and the growth of health care spending. Multiple factors, including an eroding provincial tax base and changing demographics, have contributed to an increase in the proportion of provincial budgets dedicated to health care expenditures. Most public debate in Canada is focused on mechanisms to increase funding (public or private) or to improve efficiency, followed by concerns about the trade-offs between health care spending and the public financing of other essential public goods. Forest argues that, despite all the talk about health care reform, what has been accomplished to date amounts to little more than tinkering, to the neglect of important considerations crucial to true reform. This oversight, he maintains, comes at great cost to the long-term health of Canada's medicare system and, potentially, to the welfare of society.

Eric Spink addresses the possible implications of the Supreme Court of Canada's recent decision on a national securities regulator, in which it opined that the federal government's proposed national securities regulator is *ultra vires*. According to Spink, the federal and provincial governments hold contradictory visions of Canadian federalism, reflected in constitutional decisions of the court that may present a constitutional risk. Outlining the securities references decisions and the treatment of the contradictory evidence, he argues that the securities references seem to disguise constitutional proposals as policy proposals. A more transparent process, he argues, could reduce constitutional risk.

In their paper Patrick Fafard and Patrick Leblond discuss international trade policy and the role of the provinces in Canada and abroad. In the twenty-first century, trade relations between countries have shifted from tariffs and associated non-tariffs barriers to "second-generation" trade agreements. These agreements seek to address a wider range of issues that fall (fully or partially) under the constitutional jurisdiction of provincial and territorial governments. In light of this shift, one would expect to see greater involvement of the provinces in the negotiations of second-generation trade agreements. Indeed, the authors do observe this trend with respect to negotiations relating to the Canada-European Union (EU) Comprehensive Economic Trade Agreement (CETA). According to Fafard and Leblond, the provincial involvement in CETA could potentially represent a giant leap forward in Canadian trade policy; however, their analysis shows that CETA is in fact only a small step on the road of involving the provinces in Canada's trade negotiations.

THE PROVINCES AND THE NORTH: GROWING IN IMPORTANCE?

The book's fourth and final section explores the growing importance of the North and the changing dynamics among the provinces and the central government. Both issues serve as a backdrop for the authors' consideration of potential implications of these changes on Canadian federalism and interprovincialism.

George Braden, Christopher Alcantara, and Michael Morden discuss how the North is affected and is a potential player in the emerging "new" Canadian federal environment. The "new" Canadian federal environment, they argue, has had positive and negative effects on the development and influence of territorial governments in the Canadian federation. According to the authors, there are political and structural reasons for why politicians, policy-makers, and the Canadian public have all demonstrated increased interest in the North. The authors analyze recent trends in the territorial North, how these have contributed to the sense that a new Canadian federal environment has emerged, and how they have shaped the governance structures and processes of devolution for the territorial governments. Assessing the ability of the territorial governments to exert their influence in an effective manner within a variety of intergovernmental forums, the authors demonstrate that territorial governments have made progress vis-à-vis intergovernmental forums; however, each territory continues to face challenges in its own right.

Next, Éric Montpetit and Martial Foucault examine horizontal intergovernmental relations using data on policy priority. Fully acknowledging that this method is vulnerable to criticism, they maintain that measuring intergovernmental relations comprehensively is a worthwhile goal; the results produced in this paper have been consistent with the qualitative knowledge of scholars of vertical intergovernmental relations and have raised significant questions about scholarly neglect of horizontal

intergovernmental relations. Beginning with a definition of intergovernmental relations understood as the relationship between Canadian governments on matters
of policy development, the authors look at the correspondence between policy
priorities and intergovernmental relations. They examine speeches from the throne
as a method for governments to express their policy priorities, while also offering an analysis of vertical intergovernmental relations. Finally the authors take a
measurement of horizontal intergovernmental relations within Canada, finding
that between 1960 and 2010, horizontal relations have been no less important, and
possibly more so, than vertical ones.

In the final chapter, Christopher Dunn examines the shared political, social,
and economic characteristics of "Old Canada" or the "New East," comprising
Quebec, New Brunswick, Nova Scotia, Prince Edward Island, and Newfoundland
and Labrador. When all the provinces in Old Canada do not work together, he
maintains, the region does not work as a whole. Nonetheless, he argues that it may
hold the key to a more creative interprovincialism and federalism in Canada. He
goes on to discuss the Quebec–Atlantic Canada relationship to determine if the
tensions between the two can be overcome to form a model of cooperation and
interprovincialism similar to that already evident in Atlantic Canada. Dunn concludes by arguing in favour of the New East and offers recommendations on how
it can become a reality. According to Dunn, at certain points in Canadian history
it becomes more useful to cast regionalism in larger, more functional categories
that share beneficial commonalities and possibilities.

CONCLUSION

The authors in this volume all explore different issues as they relate to the changing
federal environment. Admittedly, the conference and the subsequent publication
of its proceedings do not cover the whole gambit of factors affecting the Canadian
federal environment. Notably missing is how the growing political role and actions of Indigenous peoples affect Canadian federalism in general and the role
of the central and provincial governments specifically. This area, increasingly
important in light of the Idle No More movement and other actions undertaken by
leaders and actors in the Indigenous community, will be explored in the Institute
of Intergovernmental Relations' 2013 State of the Federation conference and subsequent volume. I urge readers to seek this out when it becomes available. In the
meantime, this volume represents a significant addition to the current literature on
Canadian federalism and its continuing evolution. We believe the book as a whole
advances the discussion on how and why the Canadian federal environment is
changing and how governments have responded to the changes. In light of this,
we hope that this collection demonstrates that Canada, while lauded as an example
of cooperative federalism, should also be better understood and appreciated as an
example of intrastate federalism.

I

THE CHANGING FEDERAL ENVIRONMENT: INITIAL OBSERVATIONS

EMBRACING IMPERFECTION: HOW CANADA FARES IN THE COMPARATIVE FEDERALISM LITERATURE

Thomas O. Hueglin

According to some, comparative federalism has in recent years become a growth industry (Erk 2007). It therefore seems to be a good idea to take a look at the new comparative federalism literature to find out whether the perception of Canadian federalism has changed over time.

Traditionally, that perception has mainly been a negative one. Canada is a quasi-federation at best (Wheare 1964), and a potential case of federal failure at worst, according to Friedrich (1968). Canadians themselves did not really help the cause, putting their own assessments under labels such as "Must Canada Fail?" (Simeon 1977) or "And No One Cheered" (Banting and Simeon 1983). Admittedly, these gloomy titles stem from a period in Canadian history particularly mired in constitutional and political crisis. Yet decades later, Gerald Baier, in his comparison of Canadian federalism and the (ultimately ill-fated) European Constitutional Treaty, still thought it necessary to caution his readers, "In terms of federalism there may presently be more to learn from Canada's pathologies than from its good example" (2005, 207). No wonder, then, that when Richard Simeon summoned the academic home front to compile an assessment of how Canada was faring in the comparative political science literature as a "giver," Alan Cairns summed up the collective effort in his conclusion as providing a "somewhat bleak picture" (2008, 244).

Yet it seems reasonable to assume that there should be a new and more positive interest in Canadian federalism, and mainly so because the world of federalism has greatly changed. Spain and Belgium have been added to the federal family, for instance, pushing the balance on the comparative continuum from symmetrical and homogeneous federalism towards asymmetrical and multinational. The European Union has been recognized, at least in some quarters, as a novel type of confederal or treaty federalism (Hueglin and Fenna 2006, 13-14). Already in 1972, Simeon had mused whether what was then called the Common Market did not provide the most obvious comparative vantage point for the Canadian practice of federal-provincial diplomacy (Simeon 2006, 300). And federal solutions to ethnic conflict are being explored almost everywhere, from Iraq, Sri Lanka, and Cyprus all the way to Bolivia, Nepal, and possibly post-Gaddafi Libya.

In such a diverse comparative federalism environment, it would seem that the comparative interest in Canada's messy, unorthodox, intergovernmental, multinational, and asymmetrical federalism ought to be on the rise. As Leibfried, Castles, and Obinger put it, "Canada arguably provides the most dramatic example of the temporal variability and mix-and-match nature of federal arrangements," and its on-going debates therefore "seem destined for repetition in nations such as Belgium, Spain, Italy—and even the territorially devolving United Kingdom" (2008, 319, 345).

Yet a closer look at the literature yields ambivalent results. On the one hand, there is evidence that Canadian federalism is indeed taken more seriously in its own right, and as a comparative yardstick for other and similar cases. On the other hand, misperceptions and misrepresentations still permeate much of the literature for a variety of methodological reasons. Both are explored in this chapter. However, given the new breadth of the comparative federalism field, there is no pretence of being comprehensive. Rather, the intention is to single out selectively what may be typical or symptomatic.

In doing so, this investigation leaves aside the kind of large-N studies in which the specificities of the Canadian case tend to get lost in generalization. Gerring, Thacker, and Moreno, for instance, seek to correlate degrees of centralization with democratic success in 77 countries. Canada gets mentioned once, alongside India, Switzerland, and the United States, as a case of federal design chosen to accom-modate populations that are "fractious and diverse" (2005, 578). Similarly, Feeley and Rubin (2008) want to demonstrate that federalism inevitably is a suboptimal tragedy because a clean democratic solution to the majority/minority conundrum is not possible, and especially not when it is compounded by "two or more regions that contain separate majority and minority populations." In this instance, Canada appears side by side with, inter alia, Russia, China, Sri Lanka, and Algeria (2008, 46). This is not to argue that such studies cannot make valid points. But they hardly provide the kind of "exacting level of sensitivity to the specific character and ex-perience" (Fenna 2011, 178) that would allow one to explore whether a substantive change in the perception of Canadian federalism has occurred over time.

TOO NARROW: THE AMERICAN MODEL

The main methodological reason for Canada's ambivalent place in comparative federalism is easy to see. Still primarily relying on the classical American model, the conceptual understanding of federalism has not kept pace with changing federal reality. American federalism is judicial federalism based on the constitutional division of powers (LaCroix 2010, 172). It almost entirely lacks the two fundamental dimensions of federalism described in Canadian parlance as intrastate and interstate federalism (Smiley and Watts 1985, 4). Intrastate federalism means that the constituent members of a federation participate in federal legislation. The classical model for this is the American Senate. The directly elected American senators, however, represent the interests of their constituencies, follow partisan loyalties, or, on occasion, may defend whatever is considered to be the national interest. They hardly if ever represent state interests. As has been shown for Switzerland in particular, voting patterns in such upper chamber senates do not typically differ from those in lower parliamentary chambers (Linder and Vatter 2001, 99).

Because Canada does not have an elected, equal, and effective senate, so goes the argument, Canadian federalism had to turn to interstate federalism, a development facilitated by Canada's parliamentary system of federalism (e.g., Baier 2005, 12). In order to achieve cooperation and coordination within and across contested and overlapping power domains, the two levels of government engage in an unloved and much criticized process of intergovernmental negotiations known as "executive federalism" (Brock 1995).

American federalism is routinely described in terms of intergovernmental relations as well. Yet it almost entirely lacks the interstate dimension that is so typical for Canada. Indeed, what is singled out to be "among the most important vehicles" for the advancement of state interests, the National Governors Association, or the National Conference of State Legislatures, appear only, according to one of the most prominent experts of American federalism, to "occasionally testify at congressional hearings or draft letters to congressional leaders expressing state concerns" (Dinan 2011, 400)—and not much more. Canadian provincial premiers would only scoff at the suggestion of having intergovernmental relations reduced to lobbying and letter writing. What constitutes intergovernmental relations in the United States, then, is for the most part administrative cooperation after the fact, when Congressional legislation has already happened unilaterally and the states scramble for ways of complying with federal regulations in order to get grant money (see Kincaid 2011).

Obviously, when the intergovernmental or executive dimension of federalism is excluded from the definition, a meaningful comparative perspective on Canadian federalism can hardly emerge. Thus Feeley and Rubin, who define federalism as "a means of governing a polity that grants partial autonomy to geographically defined subdivisions of the polity" (2008, 12), dismiss the entire literature on what they call "process federalism" as functionalist "intellectual mush" (70-6). They have a point insofar as what goes for intergovernmental relations in the United States does not exactly live up to the "formalist structure of a truly federal regime" (76), but in order to make this point, they throw out the entire European tradition of procedural or consociational federalism based on negotiated agreement, which is in fact older than the American constitutional tradition, and which lives on in just about every federation with the exception of the United States (Hueglin and Fenna 2006, 86-97).

As a consequence, the Feeley and Rubin study can contribute little to an adequate comparative understanding of Canadian federalism. The authors duly note that Canadian federalism is driven by a duality of overlapping identities, which they wrongly seem to attribute to French Canada only (2008, 50). Based on their assumption that separate identities "are likely to generate true normative conflicts" (52), they see federalism as a "compromise between unity and dissociation," the outcome dependent on "a variety of complex factors" (50). What those factors are in the case of Canadian federalism remains unsaid because the procedural dimension of federalism is dismissed a priori. But apparently, no matter what the outcome, since it will be based on compromise, it must inevitably be tragic. However, the real tragedy here is not that federalism is based on compromise but that Feeley and Rubin appear to believe that compromise cannot be democratic.

Still grounded in the American-centred tradition of conceptualizing federalism, Jacob Levy asserts that "real federalism is marked by a very high level of stability" provided by "constitutional rigidity" and "fixed constitutional allocation" of powers at "only two" levels of authority. But he admits that constitutional power allocations can be and are "bargained around" (2007, 462-3). Starting from the credible premise that such bargaining will happen when "ethnocultural and linguistic cleavages" are "stacked with provincial ones" (468), Levy briefly turns to Canada, where he notes that one such province, Quebec, by negotiating "for additional authority," may pull along "the other provinces whose voters and leaders dislike the asymmetry," thus protecting the "whole system of provincial autonomy" (470).

Levy makes the point that cultural-linguistic loyalty anchored in Quebec has been a major factor for the decentralized state of the Canadian federation as a whole. He even ventures to suggest, at least unintentionally arguing against the compact theory of federalism popular in Quebec, that the lone francophone province is better off in the symmetry of ten equal provinces than in the asymmetry of Quebec versus the rest of Canada: "facing a federated majority" allows for more flexibility than being confronted with "a unified one" (470). Yet at the same time Levy's account of how Canadian federalism actually works remains bloodless and inaccurate. It conveys no real sense of Canada's regime of interstate federalism with its elaborate quid-pro-quo of national agenda setting, cost-sharing, and de facto asymmetrical opting out.

In fact, the only example Levy provides for bargaining around the constitution is a 1987 US Supreme Court case, *South Dakota v. Dole*, in which Chief Justice Rehnquist delivered the majority opinion that it did not violate the limits of the Congressional spending power to withhold federal highway funds from a state deviating from a uniform minimum drinking age (463). If that state wanted to get those funds, in other words, it had to give up its autonomy in regulating the minimum drinking age as it saw fit. At least from a Canadian perspective, to call this bargaining in the sense of process federalism raises the suspicion of conceptual mush. It much more appropriately falls into the category of what John Kincaid has labelled "coercive federalism" (2011).

TOO BROAD: COMPARATIVE INTERGOVERNMENTALISM

In order to appreciate the distinctiveness of Canadian federalism from a comparative perspective, then, one obviously needs to get away from the classical American model of constitutional federalism with judicial reinterpretation as the only means of adjusting power allocations according to time and circumstance. Widening the perspective requires a more critical assessment of the role constitutions play in federal systems. Constitutions are "incomplete" original contracts, as Jonathan Rodden has pointed out, and they are therefore "important not because they solve the assignment problem, but because they structure the ongoing intergovernmental contracting process" (2006, 37-8). Canadian federalism provides the prime example for Rodden because, in his words, "the Canadian federal and provincial governments are clearly locked into an ongoing process of intergovernmental contracting that takes place primarily outside of central government institutions" (36-7). For Rodden, this process is not an aberrant feature of Canadian federalism owing to the lack of a legitimately functioning senate but a significant interstate variation of shared rule, which can also be observed in other federal systems.

Rodden is not alone. From a broad comparative perspective, Michael Burgess unsurprisingly notes that "executive federalism" is a key feature of Canadian federalism characterized by "regular formal meetings between federal and provincial ministers and their respective civil servants" (2006, 138). What does come as a bit of a surprise, however, is his concluding suggestion of a "symbiotic association in both legislative and public policy terms along the lines stipulated in their constitutions" that makes Canada comparable "to Australia and even to the German model" (138).

Turning to Australia first, there is indeed some comparability insofar as Australian intergovernmental relations rely on mechanisms that have developed "largely outside the constitution," most notably COAG, the Council of Australian Governments (Saunders 2012, 417), which indeed may be seen as comparable to First Ministers' Conferences or Meetings in Canada. However, the comparability ends here, almost before it has begun. Australian intergovernmental relations are entirely overshadowed by the Commonwealth's "dominance of financial resources," and they generally operate under the assumption of "uniformity" as the "objective of cooperation" (417). The directional dynamic of both federations, in other words, is situated at opposite ends. As Brian Galligan puts it, "Australia does not have the same decentralizing drivers as Canada" (2012, 338).

Burgess is right, of course, that much is to be gained from a comparative perspective on intergovernmental relations in these federal systems, but the comparison has to be systematic and accurate. Thus, a comparison between German and Canadian federalism is particularly instructive not for symbiotic similarities but because it points to a fundamental difference in the way in which the two systems manoeuvre about what is indeed one of the central tenets of most if not all federal systems operating outside the American model: negotiating legislative compromise between the two levels of government. While Germany constitutes the strongest possible case of intrastate federalism, with the Länder governments directly participating in central legislation, Canada, in its reliance on extra-constitutional and rather informal mechanisms of reaching intergovernmental compromise, is a unique case of interstate federalism among classical federal states.

A "symbiotic association" is not what comes to mind in any of the three cases. Central financial dominance and policy prescription put Australian federalism more in the vicinity of American coercive federalism (Fenna 2007, 299). Germany perhaps comes closest to something resembling intergovernmental symbiosis because obstructionist rivalries based on partisanship are often muted by the country's longstanding tradition of administrative federalism whereby the Länder are in charge of administering most federal legislation. As Fritz Scharpf puts it, even Länder governed by the opposition "cannot be interested in a standstill of legislation, in general and over longer periods of time, the consequences of which, in the relationship between state and citizens, they then have to administer themselves" (2009, 51). As for Canada, finally, to speak of symbiosis in a country simultaneously struggling with Quebec separatism and Western alienation is a stretch. It is more appropriate to characterize the intergovernmental relationship as an "uneasy embrace" (Banting 2008, 158).

Burgess ends his brief discussion of intergovernmental relations with an old question: do institutions matter? (2006, 138). This question is about whether the stability of a federation can be sustained by clever design alone, whether it depends on how this design reflects societal cleavages, and/or whether the most telling explanation for the design and performance of a federal system is rooted in its historical origins. These are questions that have resurfaced in a number of recent contributions to the comparative field.

TOO ONE-SIDED: DESIGN, SOCIOLOGY, OR HISTORY?

Jenna Bednar considers "principles of design" that sustain a "robust federation" (2009). Her argument is quite simple, although not explicitly stated: the stability of a federal system requires maintaining constitutional and political balance between the two levels of government. Yet, so Bednar assumes, governments will always try for opportunistic reasons to change that balance in their favour. She lists three strategies for doing so: the constituent units of a federation will try to "shirk on their responsibilities to the federation" and/or "shift the burden of making the union work" horizontally onto other constituent members; the federal government in turn will try to encroach upon the member units' jurisdiction (68-9). Bednar then suggests four "safeguards" against this kind of opportunism: "structural" checks and balances at the federal level of government; "popular" accountability, which presumably requires a "vibrant relationship between citizens and the governments at both levels"; a "political" balance mainly provided by "party organizations at the local and national level"; and judicial review (95-125).

So far so good. One can easily find illustrations for Bednar's opportunism/safeguards scenario in the comparative federalism field. American federalism is the most obvious case of federal checks and balances, although this has hardly prevented federal encroachment. In Germany, the tendency of the electorate to vote for parties at the Länder level that are in opposition at the federal level points to some degree of popular astuteness regarding the balance of powers; in the Swiss grand coalition scheme, parties are the main transmission belt of federal balance. Judicial review more generally belongs to the key characteristics of federal stability.

However, Bednar aligns her argument more to a historical exegesis of the *Federalist Papers* than with comparative evidence. And when it comes to Canada, her account rather runs aground. Given that Canada's system of parliamentary government almost entirely lacks intrastate checks and balances, and does not have a strong national party system as a vehicle for either popular or political balance, Canadian federalism should figure prominently as a prime case of federal encroachment. Yet Canada is arguably one of the most decentralized federations on record. Bednar's explanation resorts to the old tale of the colonial arbiter in all things constitutional, the Judicial Committee of the Privy Council (JCPC) in Britain, as a defender of provincial rights. Yet there is considerable evidence that the judges in London only went with the political flow as presented by the Canadians appearing before them. According to Richard Gwyn (2011), they were swayed in particular by Canada's "best legal mind" at the time, Liberal leader Edward Blake, who defended Ontario's interests against federal unilateralism in favour of other provinces in several cases before the JCPC, and who was also first to come up with the idea of Confederation as a "compact" among provinces (68-70).

With the JCPC out of the way after 1949, Bednar then argues, the provinces, led by Quebec, countered political and judicial encroachment tendencies by populist strategies of "raising public suspicion of Ottawa's greed for power" (2009, 140-3). While Alan Cairns (1977) would have told the story of the governments and societies of Canadian federalism by and large in the same way, this perspective leaves out far more than it tells. Too much preoccupied with mathematical modelling of intergovernmental utility and compliance games, Bednar gives short shrift to the extent to which such games are embedded in historical and sociological contingencies that defy rational simplifications.

The compact theory of Canadian federalism as embraced by Quebec has always oscillated between two versions (McMenemy 1995, 41). According to one, Confederation was a treaty among provinces that could only be altered with provincial consent; according to the other, it was a treaty between English and French Canada that put Quebec on an equal footing with the rest of Canada and its federal government. For Levy, common sense rather than rational choice would suggest that Quebec is much better off playing games in a pool of ten provinces than going *mano a mano* with a unified English Canadian bloc—let alone going sovereign in English-speaking North America. Yet the second version of the compact theory as a deal between two equal partners has endured in Quebec, and separatism as an option remains on the low burner. The reason for this obviously is grounded in Quebec's historicist sociocultural self-understanding as a defeated nation.

The classical locus of the sociological perspective on federalism has been William Livingston's "Note on the Nature of Federalism" (1952), which contended that the institutions of federalism are only "surface manifestations" of the "deeper federal quality" embedded in society (84). His contention spawned a rich debate about the nature of Canadian federalism that focused on regional political economy as much as on cultural and linguistic differences without ever ignoring the role that governments played in the process. However, this multi-causal perspective all too soon gave way to a narrower, government-centred view of executive federalism (Smiley 1979). The sociological perspective was rejected because it allegedly paid "inadequate attention to the capacity of government to make society responsive to its demands" (Cairns 1977, 695).

As a consequence, much of Canadian scholarship on federalism returned to institutional design as the main variable for the explanation of political dynamic and change. There are probably several reasons for this other than the traditional institutionalist focus on federalism as a system of divided government. During much of the 1980s and '90s, Canadian federalism was indeed in the throes of an institutionalist crisis occasioned by Prime Minister Pierre Trudeau's "magnificent obsession" with constitutional patriation (Clarkson and McCall 1990). At the same time, the rise of neoliberal triumphalism reduced much of political science to the analysis of allegedly rational market choices. In so doing, it all but eclipsed from the research agenda sociological investigations seeking "to delineate the major perceptions of society which underlie political activity affecting the federal form of government" (Black 1975, vi).

Here is where Ian Erk begs to differ. Detecting a "new institutionalist logic" in much of the recent comparative federalism literature, he wants to show instead that Livingston was right after all (2008, 4-5). His comparative analysis of continuity and change in federal systems is based on five case studies, with Canada alongside Austria, Belgium, Germany, and Switzerland. Erk finds that "the written constitution of the Canadian federation is of limited use in explaining how the federal system works" (55). Instead, his analysis proceeds to examine two public policy domains that he thinks display "the greatest degree of disparity between the letter of the law and the true workings of the system": namely, the media and education (55). On the basis of this analysis, he concludes that Canadian federalism is primarily driven by "the underlying ethno-linguistic duality of the Canadian social structure" (55). And he comes to the general and comparative conclusion that, as in the other cases examined, the most cogent factor explaining the true workings of federalism is the congruence between political institutions and society.

Put simply, Erk identifies two clusters of federal systems—those that do not show significant levels of ethno-linguistic diversity, such as Austria and Germany, and are therefore characterized by a centralizing dynamic, and those that do, such as Canada, Belgium, and Switzerland, and therefore find themselves on a decentralist trajectory. Erk's comparative analysis is compelling to a point. Canadian federalism is moved away from the comparative straightjacket of American judicial constitutionalism and towards the much more congenial bi- or multi-cultural neighbourhood of Belgium and Switzerland. But his argument also has serious shortcomings.

By treating English Canada as one homogeneous bloc in his bipolar ethno-linguistic scenario, Erk ignores socioeconomic regional diversity within English Canada and thus unduly trims down the complexity of Canadian federalism—perhaps deliberately so, in order to make a limited comparative point more strongly. Moreover, it is not entirely clear what role the mass media and education play in the "system"—if that is meant to be the "federal system." To be sure, francophone Quebecers read French newspapers, and their children probably hear more about the Plains of Abraham in school than do their English counterparts. There is also clear asymmetry in the de facto power allocation of media and educational policy. But do these factors have a significant impact on the way Canadian intergovernmental or executive federalism works, that is, in those policy areas that are overlapping as well as contentious?

From a broader comparative perspective, there is also a nagging question about how far the explanatory value of Erk's analysis reaches. Rejecting what he sees as a new institutionalist logic in comparative federalism, Erk claims that centripetal German federalism as established in 1949 "has not socialized the German nation into a federal society" (2008, 5). This generalization appears to be wrong at least in part. The German tradition of administrative federalism goes back much farther than 1949. While there may not be a deep division of cultural identities between the German Länder, there is a Länder-based political identity dating back to the foundation of the quasi-federal Bismarck Empire in 1871 when the Länder were compensated for the loss of most legislative powers to Berlin by their retention of administrative and cultural autonomy (Lehmbruch 2000, 60). These political identities survived the centralized Nazi state, and, as became clear during the process of German reunification after 1989, they also survived 40 years of unitary communism in East Germany when "territorial identities thought to be lost" quickly advanced to the top of the democratic reform agenda (127).

These political identities are not just a matter of governments and political leaders. As mentioned above, Germans often vote for different party majorities at different levels of government, thus making political use of the federal form by means of "vertical balancing" (Bednar 2009, 111). With his exclusive focus on sociocultural cleavages as the explanatory variable for the dynamic of federal systems (form follows function), Erk is missing out on the possibility that institutional practice may bring forth a political culture as important for a comparative understanding of continuity and change in federal systems as their underlying societal foundations (function follows form). Aroney, Prasser, and Taylor make a similar point about Australia (2012, 297-8).

One reason why Erk dismisses the federal form as an explanatory variable in its own right is his explicit ambition to "show the shortcomings of neo-institutionalist approaches" (2008, x). In his view, the main shortcoming is the assumption of institutional continuity and its imprint upon societal interests. "Interests," he argues, thus come to be seen as "nested in prevailing institutional arrangements" (5). However, as at least the German case suggests, institutional continuity may indeed be an important explanatory variable, and the new brand of "historical institutionalism" cannot be dismissed so easily.

Jörg Broschek, for instance, has contributed a comparative historical institutionalist analysis of Germany and Canada that attempts to explain continuity as well as change in these federal systems. According to Broschek, historical institutionalism "emphasizes that early events causally influence later developments" (2012, 663). He then describes the earlier events as critical junctures that lead to the formation of a particular federal arrangement, and presents later developments as contingent upon a path-dependent framework or trajectory. In the German case, the critical juncture was the unification of Germany in the Bismarck Empire. Prussian hegemony was combined with a Bundesrat, in which the governing Länder princes "ensured that state [read: Länder] executives and their bureaucracies were able to sustain an important role for federal legislation" (672). For Broschek, path dependency rather than social homogeneity then explains why and how contemporary German federalism still maintains this emphasis on intrastate federalism as the main mechanism for political accommodation and compromise.

In the Canadian case, according to Broschek, the critical juncture was provided by the period of 1844–67 under the impact of the American Civil War and the joint-decision trap that had deadlocked the United Province of Canada. Because of the latter issue, Confederation "constituted a deliberate effort of disentanglement." The result was a "dualistic scheme" of "separating rather than distributing authority." Because of its deliberate ambiguities, "the dualistic allocation of competences" almost immediately became "subject to power-based reinforcement" by both levels of government, leading to province-building as well as federal encroachment (674). This dualistic dynamic further delegitimized the already weak intrastate mechanisms for political accommodation and compromise in the Senate and Cabinet, and instead put Canada on a path-dependent trajectory of interstate federalism.

On can quibble with the details of Broschek's view, and one can take issue with the disentanglement thesis as somewhat reductionist in light of Confederation as a grand effort at constructing Canadian unity. Canadian scholars of federalism may also point out that the theoretical apparatus of critical junctures and path-dependent frameworks essentially does not yield much that would go beyond a solidly descriptive historical narrative. One may even venture to speculate—somewhat nastily, perhaps—that historical institutionalism is but an attempt to battle against the dominance of the rational-choice approach in social science by dressing up historical description in more scientific clothes. The undeniable value of historical institutionalism, however, with its methodological focus on the trajectory of "institutional inheritance" (Ziblatt 2006, 16), lies in the comparative perspective by offering a compelling and systematic explanation for the kind of structural variations outlined above.

Both federal systems have at their core a mechanism of negotiating compromise without which federal stability and the effectiveness of federal governance cannot be sustained. But there are significant differences in the choice of mechanism: Germany relies predominantly on an intrastate mechanism of political accommodation; in Canada, interstate federalism is the name of the game. Broschek's analysis in this way also sheds some light on the theme for the 2011 State of the Federation conference, namely, the redefinition of roles in the federation. The dualistic nature of the original design inevitably resulted in a path-dependent "sequence of decentralizing and re-centralizing trends." Thus, Broschek contends, Canada's interstate mechanisms provide a "scope for creative recombinations" that is "considerably larger" than is the case with Germany's intrastate federalism, establishing "an institutional environment more conducive to entrepreneurial politics" (2012, 678-9).

The views of Canadian federalism emerging from these different comparative approaches are, taken together, partial and complementary rather than mutually exclusive. Bednar's account of governmental populism drumming up support for intergovernmental battle hardly explains in full the institutional as well as sociocultural contingencies shaping the intergovernmental bargaining game. But it adds one piece to the puzzle of what sustains balance and stability in a federal system: "Intergovernmental retaliation requires democratic support" (2009, 218). How far that support goes is not just a matter of populist strategies, as Quebec sovereigntists have found out. It is also a matter of "federal culture," a "common perception about the boundaries of authority" (218). Erk's sociocultural explanation of federalism in turn may well explain where on the centralization-decentralization continuum that common perception may come to be located. But it is not sufficient to explain "the uncodified workings of the federal system" (2008, 55). These workings, identified as the interstate process of bargaining, compromise, and agreement with or without opting out, are better explained by Broschek's analysis of path-dependent continuity and change.

A MODEL IN ITS OWN RIGHT?

Alas, all of the above may do little to improve Canada's image as an aberrant federation, let alone elevate Canada to the status as a new model of federalism from which much may be learned in comparative perspective. Neither will moving it closer to volatile Belgium or to glacial Switzerland necessarily improve its comparative image, nor will its path-dependent reliance on interstate federalism do so, as long as comparative federalism — in Canada itself as elsewhere — remains wedded to formal schemes of power division and bicameralism as the sine qua non of federalist legitimacy. But then again, the American Political Science Association's tribute to Richard Simeon's classical analysis of Canadian federalism as a regime of federal-provincial diplomacy (2006) as being of "lasting significance in federalism and intergovernmental relations" may give pause for thought.

Fame and fortune often come by association. As mentioned at the outset of this chapter, Simeon had suggested that it might be worth comparing Canada's intergovernmental federalism with governance in the European Union (2006, 300). And in one of his last contributions to the field, Daniel Elazar (2001) suggested that the European Union rather than the United States might be the appropriate federal model for a new post-modern epoch. As it happens, Peter Katzenstein has had similar praise for Canada, calling it "arguably the first post-modern state par excellence" (cited in Clarkson 2000).

At a moment when the European Union finds itself in the midst of an unprecedented financial crisis, such fame by postmodern association may not go very far. Moreover, institutional differences of EU governance are so significant that a comparison with Canadian federalism must appear far-fetched indeed. The constituent units of the Union are sovereign member states, not provinces; the European Commission hardly qualifies as a federal government; the Council of Ministers is not an informal intergovernmental mechanism outside the constitutional framework but the legislative centre of the Union's institutional design in which decisions are formally assigned to qualified majority voting. Moreover, the direction of the intergovernmental process is horizontal, among member states, rather than vertical, as between the two levels of government in Canadian federalism.

The comparability of Canadian and European Union federalism lies elsewhere, in the reliance on procedural rather than constitutional mechanisms for making decisions about the allocation of authority (Hueglin 2013). We are back to executive federalism, the "ongoing process of intergovernmental contracting that takes place primarily outside of central government institutions" (Rodden 2006, 36-7). Executive federalism is what makes Canada an aberrant case of federalism, and it is also what Canadians themselves see as the principal problem of democratic accountability in their federal system. The comparison with European Union governance, however, suggests that this kind of intergovernmental bargaining may in fact be a singularly appropriate form of governance for complex and divided societies characterized by a weak national or common identity. In such cases, even qualified majority rule will not provide stability in matters of concurrent or conflicting jurisdiction. Constitutional federalism then inevitably becomes treaty federalism (Hueglin and Fenna 2006).

In the case of the European Union, a distinction must be made between the European Council, where treaty-changing decisions are made unanimously by the heads of state or government, and the Council of Ministers, where decisions are made by means of qualified majority rule. But even the Council of Ministers, aided by COREPER (the committee of the member states' permanent representatives), tries in its ongoing negotiations to avoid majority decisions, except as a threat in order to reach agreement at least among the important players (Lewis 2010, 151). The more recent adoption of the so-called Open Method of Coordination, a largely informal intergovernmental practice of comparative policy learning through benchmarking and the identification of best practices, etc., points in the same direction: cooperation and adjustment rely on intergovernmental "consensus-forming" (Hodson and Maher 2001, 723).

The problem with a consensus-seeking machinery behind closed doors is accountability, the suspicion that intergovernmental agreements often amount to not much more than politically expedient horse-trading rather than pursuit of a common good. The problem is not just one of transparency and responsible government but goes to the heart of intergovernmental decision-making: how should authority be distributed among the two levels of government in a federal system when a clear constitutional division of powers is neither possible nor desirable for the effective delivery of a common good.

In the European Union, the principle of subsidiarity provides an answer to this question. Subsidiarity ultimately is a procedural guideline that avoids final constitutional allocation of powers and instead provides the intergovernmental process with principles about who should do how much of what in a federation. Under the premise that decisions should be taken as closely as possible to the citizens affected by them, the subsidiarity principle compels all Union acts within the field of concurrent jurisdiction to a broad process of consultation, deliberation, and decision-making among all governmental stakeholders. Moreover, the eventual result can be appealed before the European Court of Justice (Hueglin 2007).

From a Canadian federalism perspective, this process may sound outlandish. However, the Supreme Court of Canada has based a string of its recent decisions on the principle of subsidiarity (Arban 2013). Already in the 1998 *Secession Reference*, it had stated that while the constitutional division of powers is the "primary textual expression of the principle of federalism," the overall purpose of Canadian federalism is that it "facilitates democratic participation by distributing power to the government thought to be the most suited to achieving the particular societal objective" (2 SCR 217, 47, 58). It then held, in the 2007 *Canadian Western Bank* decision, that "interjurisidictional immunity" in the strict constitutional sense would be "incompatible with the flexibility of contemporary Canadian federalism" (SCC 22, 45). And in the 2001 *Spraytech* decision it had already elaborated explicitly that "matters of governance are often examined through the lens of subsidiarity. This is the proposition that law-making and implementation is often best achieved at the level of government that is not only effective, but also closest to the citizens affected and thus most responsive to their needs, to local distinctiveness, and to population diversity" (SCC 40, 3).

By adopting a language very close to the European stipulations of subsidiarity, the Supreme Court of Canada did not so much open up a new perspective of Canadian federalism in comparative perspective as it affirmed what have been its guiding principles all along. But in doing so, it has given the comparative federalism literature new impulses of situating the Canadian case in the context of procedural rather than constitutional federalism.

EMBRACING IMPERFECTION

What all this amounts to for the study of comparative federalism more generally, therefore, postmodern or not, is that "institutional tidiness," as the great champion of European integration theory, Ernst Haas, once put it (1975), can no longer be expected in complex and diverse social systems. Jenna Bednar, after her book-length search for structural safeguards maintaining a robust federation, seems to come to a similar conclusion. What ultimately holds a federation together, she muses, must be a public "federal culture" upholding "respect for the union" (2009, 218). But what that federal culture implies, in the end, is not a constant struggle for institutional and legal certainty; on the contrary, it is "embracing imperfection" within a context of institutional and procedural "redundancy" (174).

The federal culture Bednar has in mind is a result of many factors emerging from this recent body of comparative federalism literature: the history of the original institutional design and its path-dependent trajectory of continuity and change as well as the underlying societal culture, which does not exhaust itself in regional or linguistic cleavages but extends the way that both governments and societies learn from it and adapt to it. In the case of Canadian federalism this federal culture of redundancy is anchored in the three intertwined models of federalism that Keith Banting has identified (2008): a classical model based on the constitutional division of powers; a shared-cost model that comes closest to the principle of subsidiarity in its allocation of particular provincial policy powers under the umbrella of general national objectives; and a joint-decision model most closely approximating council governance on the basis of mutual agreement.

From a comparative federalism perspective, then, this model complexity suggests that Canadian federalism ought to figure much more prominently as an adequate response to the complexity of governments, societies, and economies, and that it should be embraced much more assertively by Canadians themselves. Unfortunately, this is not on the agenda of the current federal government. Prime Minister Stephen Harper has steadfastly asserted that he wants to turn Canadian federalism back to the classical model of divided jurisdiction (Behiels and Talbot 2011). It remains to be seen if Broschek's historical institutionalist analysis proves to be correct and the Harper government will find it impossible to break out of a path-dependent trajectory that remains embedded in continuity. For now, it is the Supreme Court of Canada that seems to have a better grasp of what that continuity must entail: "Cooperation is the animating force," it admonished the Harper government in its recent *Securities* decision, and concluded, "The federalism principle upon which Canada's constitutional framework rests demands nothing less" (2011 SCC 66, 133).

REFERENCES

Arban, E. 2013. "La subsidiarité en droit européen et canadien : Une comparaison." *Canadian Public Administration* 56 (2): 219-34.

Aroney, N., S. Prasser, and A. Taylor. 2012. "Federal Diversity in Australia: A Counter-Narrative." In *The Future of Australian Federalism*, edited by G. Appleby, N. Aroney, and T. John, 272-300. Cambridge, UK: Cambridge University.

Baier, G. 2005. "The EU's Constitutional Treaty: Federalism and Intergovernmental Relations – Lessons from Canada." *Regional and Federal Studies* 15 (2): 205-23.

Banting, K. 2008. "The Three Federalisms: Social Policy and Intergovernmental Decision-Making." In *Canadian Federalism*, edited by H. Bakvis and G. Skogstad, 137-60. Don Mills, ON: Oxford University Press.

Banting, K., and R. Simeon. 1983. *And No One Cheered*. Toronto: Methuen.

Bednar, J. 2009. *The Robust Federation*. Cambridge, UK: Cambridge University Press.

Behiels, M., and R. Talbot. 2011. "Stephen Harper and Canadian Federalism: Theory and Practice, 1987–2011." In *Challenges for Canadian Federalism*, edited by M. Behiels and F. Rocher, 15-86. Ottawa: Invenire Books.

Black, E.R. 1975. *Divided Loyalties*. Kingston and Montreal: McGill-Queen's University Press.

Brock, K.L. 1995. "The End of Executive Federalism?" In *New Trends in Canadian Federalism*, edited by F. Rocher and M. Smith, 91-108. Peterborough: Broadview Press.

Broschek, J. 2012. "Historical Insitutionalism and the Varieties of Federalism in Germany and Canada." *Publius: The Journal of Federalism* 42 (4): 662-87

Burgess, M. 2006. *Comparative Federalism: Theory and Practice*. London: Routledge.

Cairns, A.C. 1977. "The Governments and Societies of Canadian Federalism." *Canadian Journal of Political Science* 10 (4): 695-725.

—. 2008. "Conclusion: Are We on the Right Track?" In *The Comparative Turn in Canadian Politics*, edited by L.A. White, R. Simeon, R. Vipond, and J. Wallner, 238-51. Vancouver: UBC Press.

Clarkson, S. 2000. "The Multi-Level State: Canada in the Semi-Periphery of Both Continentalism and Globalization." Paper, University of Toronto.

Clarkson, S., and C. McCall. 1990. *Trudeau and Our Times*. Toronto: McClelland & Stewart.

Dinan, J. 2011. "Shaping Health Care Reform: State Government Influence in the Patient Protection and Affordable Care Act." *Journal of Federalism* 41 (3): 395-420.

Elazar, D.J. 2001. "The United States and the European Union: Models for Their Epochs." In *The Federal Vision*, by K. Nicolaidis and R. Howse, 31-53. Oxford: Oxford University Press.

Erk, J. 2007 "Comparative Federalism as Growth Industry." *Publius: The Journal of Federalism* 37 (2): 262-78.

—. 2008 *Explaining Federalism*. London: Routledge.

Feeley, M.M, and E. Rubin. 2008. *Federalism: Political Identity and Tragic Compromise*. Ann Arbor: University of Michigan Press.

Fenna, A. 2007. "The Malaise of Federalism: Comparative Reflections on Commonwealth-State Relations." *Australian Journal of Public Administration* 66 (3): 298-306.

—. 2011. "Form and Function in Federal Systems." *Australian Journal of Political Science* 46 (1): 167-79.

Galligan, B. 2012. "Fiscal Federalism: Then and Now." In *The Future of Australian Federalism*, edited by G. Appleby, N. Aroney, and T. John, 320-38. Cambridge, UK: Cambridge University Press.

Gerring, J., S.C. Thacker, and C. Moreno. 2005. "Centripetal Democratic Governance: A Theory and Global Inquiry." *American Political Science Review* 99 (4): 567-81.

Gwyn, R. 2011. *Nation Maker*. Toronto: Random House.

Hass, E. 1975. "Turbulent Fields and the Theory of Regional Integration." *International Organization* 30: 173-212.

Hodson, D., and I. Maher. 2001. "The Open Method as a New Mode of Governance: The Case of Soft Economic Policy Co-ordination." *Journal of Common Market Studies* 39 (4): 719-46.

Hueglin, T.O. 2007. "The Principle of Subsidiarity: Tradition – Practice – Relevance." In *Constructing Tommorow's Federalism*, edited by I. Peach, 201-18. Regina: University of Manitoba Press.

—. 2013. "Treaty Federalism as a Model of Policy Making: Comparing Canada and the European Union." *Canadian Public Administration* 56 (2): 185-202.

Hueglin, T.O., and A. Fenna. 2006. *Comparative Federalism: A Systematic Inquiry*. Peterborough, ON: Broadview Press; Toronto: University of Toronto Press.

Kincaid, J. 2011. "Political Coercion and Administrative Cooperation in U.S. Intergovernmental Relations. In *Varieties of Federal Governance*, edited by Rekha Saxena, 37-53. New Delhi: Cambridge University Press.

LaCroix, A. L. 2010. *The Ideological Origins of American Federalism*. Cambridge, MA: Harvard University Press.

Lehmbruch, G. 2000. *Parteienwettbewerb im Bundesstaat*. Wiesbaden: Westdeutscher Verlag.

Leibfried, S.F., G. Castles, and H. Obinger. 2005. "'Old' and 'New' Politics in Federal Welfare States." In *Federalism and the Welfare State*, edited by H. Obinger, S. Leibfried, and F.G. Castles, 307-55. Cambridge, UK: Cambridge University Press.

Levy, J.T. 2007. "Federalism, Liberalism, and the Separation of Loyalties." *American Political Science Review* 101 (3): 459-77.

Lewis, J. 2010. "The Council of the European Union." In *European Union Politics*, edited by M. Cini and N.P. Borragan, 141-61. Oxford: Oxford University Press.

Linder, W., and A. Vatter. 2001. "Institutions and Outcomes of Swiss Federalism: The Role of Cantons in Swiss Politics." *West European Politics* 24 (2): 95-122.

Livingston, W.S. 1952. "A Note on the Nature of Federalism." *Political Science Quarterly* 67: 81-95.

McMenemy, J. 1995. *The Language of Canadian Politics*. Waterloo: Wilfrid Laurier University Press.

Rodden, J.A. 2006. *Hamilton's Paradox: The Promise and Peril of Fiscal Federalism*. Cambridge, UK: Cambridge University Press.

Saunders, C. 2012. "Cooperative Arrangements in Comparative Perspective." In *The Future of Australian Federalism*, edited by G. Appleby, N. Aroney, and T. John, 414-31. Cambridge, UK: Cambridge University Press.

Scharpf, F.W. 2009. *Foderalismusreform*. Frankfurt: Campus.

Simeon, R. 1977. *Must Canada Fail?* Montreal and Kingston: McGill-Queen's Unversity Press.

—. 2006. *Federal-Provincial Diplomacy*. Toronto: University of Toronto Press.

Smiley, D.V. 1979. "An Outsider's Observation of Federal-Provincial Relations among Consenting Adults." In *Confrontation and Collaboration: Intergovernmental Relations in Canada Today*, edited by R. Simeon, 105-13. Toronto: Institute of Public Administration of Canada.

Smiley, D.V., and R.L. Watts. 1985. *Intrastate Federalism in Canada*. Toronto: University of Toronto Press.

Supreme Court of Canada. 1998. *Reference re Secession of Quebec*. S.C.R. 217

—. 2001. *Canada Ltée (Spraytech, Société d'arosage) v. Hudson (Town)*. SCC 40.

—. 2007. *Canadian Western Bank v. Alberta*. SCC 22.

—. 2011. *Reference re Securities Act*. SCC 66.

Ward, A., and L. Ward. 2009. *The Ashgate Research Companion to Federalism*. Farnham, UK: Ashgate.

Wheare, K.C. 1964. *Federal Government*. New York: Galaxy.

Ziblatt, D. 2006. *Structuring the State: The Formation of Italy and Germany and the Puzzle of Federalism*. Princeton: Princeton University Press.

THE SIZE OF THE FEDERAL AND PROVINCIAL GOVERNMENTS IN CANADA: SOME QUANTITATIVE EVIDENCE

François Vaillancourt

This chapter's purpose is to present evidence on the evolution of the relative size of Canada's federal and provincial governments. The evidence presented is for the 1989–2009 period (reflecting the availability of data) on five indicators: expenditures, revenues, debt, public employment and private output regulated by each level of governments. The conclusion examines how the provinces have evolved relative to each other for the same period.

EXPENDITURES

Figures 1 and 2 present the importance of federal and non-federal public expenditures in Canada by major type with respect to GDP.

Figure 1: Federal Public Expenditures by Sector as a Percentage of Total GDP, Canada, 1989–2009

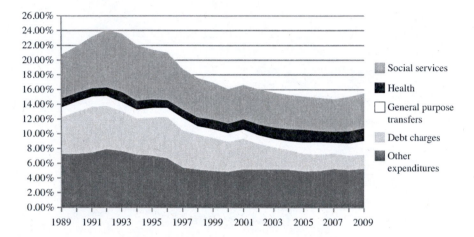

Source: Federal, provincial, and territorial general government revenue and expenditures, Table 385-0002, Statistics Canada; Expenditure-based gross domestic product, Table 380-0017, Statistics Canada. Territories are excluded.

"Other expenditures" include general government services, protection of persons and property, transportation and communication, education, resource conservation and industrial development, environment, recreation and culture, labour, employment and immigration, housing, foreign affairs and international assistance, regional planning and development, research establishments.

A Methodological Point

Note that prior to 1997 the government accounts compiled health and social service transfers to provincial governments under the Canada Assistance Plan and the Established Program Financing as specific transfers of the health and social service functions. In 1997, both accounts were joined to become the Canada Health and Social Transfer and subsequently were treated as a general purpose transfer. In 2004 this transfer was then split into the Canada Health Transfer and the Canada Social Transfer, the former being treated as a specific purpose transfer of the health function while the latter remained a general purpose transfer. Social Services expenditures in Figure 1 corrects for this change.

Due to the unavailability of data concerning the amount of federal transfers used by provinces to finance their health expenditures between 1997 and 2004, a smoothing technique has been applied in this paper to reflect the mean growth of those transfers during those years. In 1996, federal specific transfers of the health function amounted to approximately $9 billion. In 2005, when health transfers were reinstated as specific transfers, official data show a federal health expenditure of a little under $24 billion. Values for the years in between those two data points were obtained following the formula

Mean growth rate 1996–2005: $9024(1 + g)^{2005-1996} = 23774$
g solves for 0.1136, which we round to an 11 percent mean growth rate.

Figure 2: Non-Federal Public Expenditures by Sector as a Percentage of Total GDP, Canada, 1989–2009

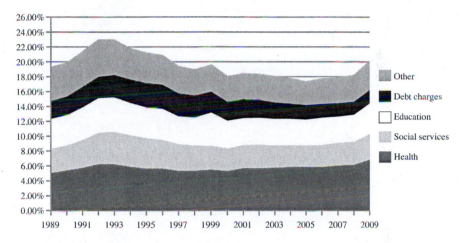

Source: Federal, provincial, and territorial general government revenue and expenditures, Table 385-0002, Statistics Canada; Expenditure-based gross domestic product, Table 380-0017, Statistics Canada. Territories are excluded.

"Other" includes: general government services, protection of persons and property, transportation and communication, education, resource conservation and industrial development, environment, recreation and culture, labour, employment and immigration, housing, regional planning and development, research establishments, and general purpose transfers to other government subsectors.

The first finding that comes out of Figures 1 and 2 is that while federal and non-federal (provincial+local) expenditures were of the same order with respect to GDP (20–25 percent) in the early 1990s, those of the federal government fell substantially to about 15 percent of GDP in the late 2000s while they remained almost unchanged for the provinces. As a consequence, the size of the federal government dropped in relative terms, as shown in Figure 3. Federal expenditures on debt charges as a percentage of GDP fell significantly during the period. This drop can be explained by the growth of GDP, the reduction in the outstanding amount of the federal debt following a decade's worth of budget surpluses, and the diminishing yields on Canadian government bonds and treasury bills. The average yield of a selected group of government debt instruments in 1989 was around 10 percent. The same value was observed to fall to around 5.5 percent in 1999 and further to 2.5 percent in 2009.[1]

The fall in the value relative to the GDP at the federal level of the category "Other expenditures" is not attributable to one specific expenditure source but rather to a

---

[1] Financial market statistics distributed by E-Stat.

generalized fall in the relative value of each program's expenses. Out of the 14 items registered under this heading, only four, namely "environment," "regional planning and development," "research establishments," and "other" (as defined by Statistics Canada) experienced a rise in their value relative to the GDP over the period, with only "research establishments" of some importance relative to the size of the economy. The deficit reduction policies of the mid-1990s are largely responsible for the important decrease in federal expenditures during the 1989–99 period. The smallest decrease was in the health function. Its level in 1998 relative to 1995 had fallen by less than 5 percent, compared to decreases as high as 60 percent in some other sectors.

Figure 3: Non-Federal Public Expenditures as a Percentage of Total Public Expenditures,* Canada, 1989–2009

Source: Federal, provincial, and territorial general government revenue and expenditures, Table 385-0002, Statistics Canada. Territories are excluded.

*This measure includes federal transfers to the provinces. The measurement is therefore of spending power rather than available resources.

REVENUES

How is the above spending funded? Figures 4 and 5 present the importance of various revenue sources for both federal and non-federal governments with respect to GDP. The figures show a drop in the relative size of federal revenues from 1989 to 2009 both with respect to GDP and, since there is no such drop for non-federal revenues with respect to GDP, relative to non-federal revenues. This finding is shown in Figure 6. Personal income taxes are a more important source of revenue at the federal level and consumption taxes at the non-federal one; corporate income taxes can vary in importance over time.

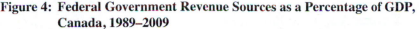

Figure 4: Federal Government Revenue Sources as a Percentage of GDP, Canada, 1989–2009

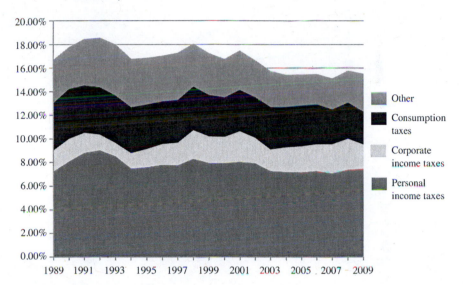

Source: Federal, provincial, and territorial general government revenue and expenditures, Table 385-0002, Statistics Canada; Expenditure-based gross domestic product, Table 380-001, Statistics Canada.

Figure 5: Non-Federal Government Revenue Sources as a Percentage of GDP, Canada, 1989–2009

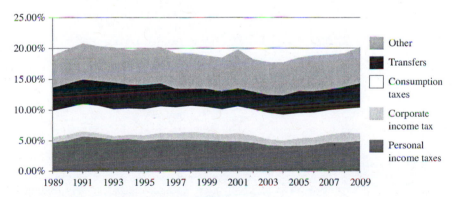

Source: Federal, provincial, and territorial general government revenue and expenditures, Table 385-0002, Statistics Canada; Expenditure-based gross domestic product, Table 380-0017, Statistics Canada. Transfers are federal transfers.

**Figure 6: Non-Federal Public Revenue* as a Percentage of Total Public
Revenue,* Canada, 1989–2009**

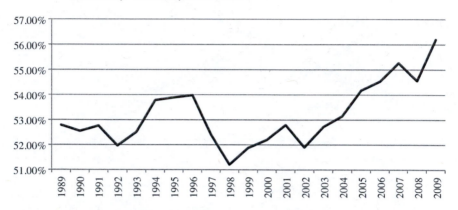

Source: Federal, provincial, and territorial general government revenues and expenditures, Table 385-0002, Statistics Canada.

*Both of these measures include federal transfers to the provinces. The measurement is
therefore of spending power rather than own-source revenues.

One point that does not come out clearly from Figures 4 to 6 (because of the
way they are drawn for their main purpose) is the relative importance of federal
transfers with respect to provincial revenues. This aspect is examined in index form
in Figure 7. The sharp decline in transfers observed around 1994–95 is attributable
to the federal government deficit reduction policies.

DEBT

While governments finance themselves mainly through taxation, they also incur
debt. Figure 8 shows the evolution of the net public debt in Canada. The peak in
1995 reflects major spending cuts announced in that year's federal budget.

The evolution of the Canadian public debt is influenced by the size of annual
deficits/surpluses. Federal and provincial deficits are presented in Figure 9.

Notwithstanding the improvement in the deficit position of the federal government, it still owes the largest share of the debt, as shown in Figure 10.

Figure 7: Federal Transfers to Provincial and Local Governments and Total Non-Federal Revenue, Canada, 1989–2009, Index (1989 = 1)

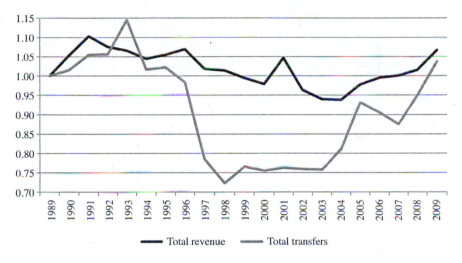

Source: Federal, provincial, and territorial general government revenue and expenditures, Table 385-0002, Statistics Canada; Expenditure-based gross domestic product, Table 380-0017, Statistics Canada.

Figure 8: Total Public Debt as a Percentage of GDP, Canada, 1988–2008

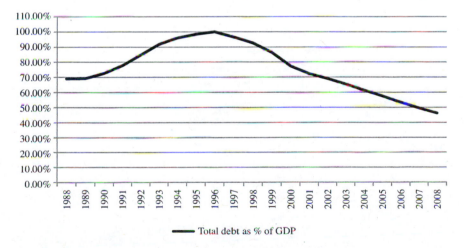

Source: Balance sheet of federal, provincial, and territorial general and local governments, Table 285-0014, Statistics Canada. The measure of debt in this figure refers to the net financial debt.

Figure 9: Federal and Provincial Budget Deficits as a Percentage of GDP, Canada, 1989–2009

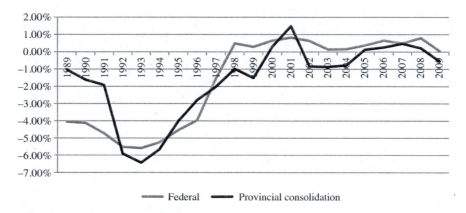

Source: Federal, provincial, and territorial general government revenue and expenditures, Table 385-0002, Statistics Canada; Expenditure-based gross domestic product, Table 380-0017, Statistics Canada.

Figure 10: Federal Debt as a Percentage of Total Public Debt, Canada, 1988–2008

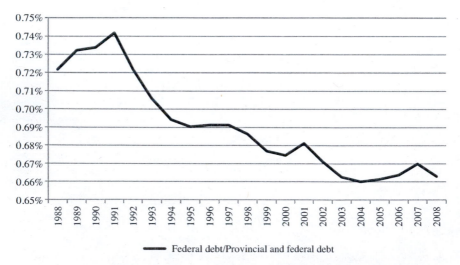

Source: Balance sheet of federal, provincial, and territorial general and local governments, Table 285-0014, Statistics Canada. The measure of debt here refers to the net financial debt.

EMPLOYMENT

One of the tools by which the federal government can assert its presence is through its employment of Canadians.

Figure 11 presents the evolution of non-federal public employment as a share of total public employment. It has increased over the 1989–2009 period by about 3 percentage points. Figures 12 and 13 present the importance of federal and non-federal public employment for Canada and the ten provinces in terms of total employment for three years: 1989, 1999, and 2009. The results show the significant differences between provinces in the importance of both types of public employer.

An examination of Figures 12 and 13 shows that federal employment is no more than 20 percent of non-federal employment for the three years considered. The importance of federal employment drops, while non-federal employment remains roughly unchanged. One also observes important differences between provinces; by 2009, federal employment is still above 4 percent of total employment in the Maritime provinces while less than 2 percent in Alberta. Differences in the import-ance of non-federal employment between provinces are less important.

Figure 11: Non-Federal Public Employment as a Percentage of Total Public Employment, Canada, 1989–2009

Source: Public sector employment, Table 183-0002, Statistics Canada. The data used do not distinguish between full-time and part-time positions.

Figure 12: Federal Public Employment as a Percentage of Total Employment by Province, Canada, 1989, 1999, and 2009

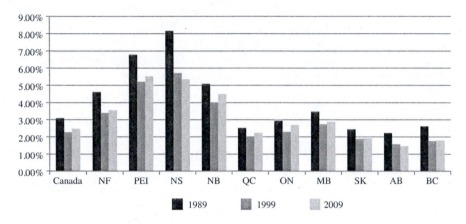

Source: Public sector employment, Table 183-0002, Statistics Canada; Labour force survey estimates, Table 282-0015, Statistics Canada. The datat used, i.e., people employed, do not distinguish between full-time and part-time positions.

Figure 13: Non-Federal Public Employment as a Percentage of Total Employment by Province, Canada, 1989, 1999, and 2009

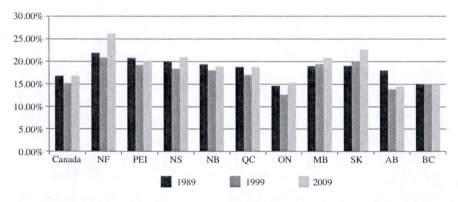

Source: Public sector employment, Table 183-0002, Statistics Canada; Labour force survey estimates, Table 282-0015, Statistics Canada. The data used, i.e., people employed, do not distinguish between full-time and part-time positions.

PRIVATE EMPLOYMENT REGULATION

The analysis above neglects the indirect role that governments play through regulations.

Figure 14 presents the share of output under federal regulation in Canada; the remainder is under provincial regulation. Figure 15 presents the provincial dimension using employment data; it shows variations across provinces.

Statistics regarding the output of the broadcasting and telecommunications industry and the publishing service industries were not released for the years 2007 and 2008. Figure 14 therefore shows estimated output values for these two industries during both years. Values were estimated by using the average growth rate of those industries' outputs between 2000 and 2006 (5.81 percent and 6.56 percent, respectively).

Figure 14: Output of Federally Regulated Industries as a Percentage of GDP, Canada, 1987–2008

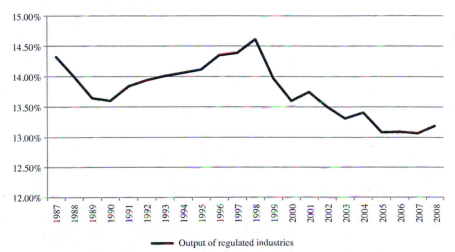

■■■ Output of regulated industries

Source: Gross domestic product by North American Industry Classification System, System of National Accounts benchmark values, Table 379-0023, Statistics Canada; Expenditure-based gross domestic product, Table 380-0017, Statistics Canada.

Federally regulated industries were selected, at the author's discretion, with reference to the definition offered by the Government of Canada and Statistics Canada's "Canadian Productivity Review." They include some transportation, broadcasting, and telecommunications firms, banks, and insurance carriers.

**Figure 15: Employment in Federally Regulated Industries as a Percentage
of Total Employment, Canada, 1991, 2000, and 2009**

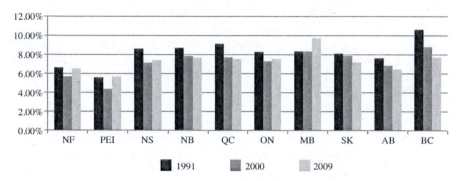

Source: Employment for selected industries, Table 281-0024, Statistics Canada; Labour
force survey estimates, Table 282-0015, Statistics Canada.

PROVINCES

Until now the discussion has differentiated between the federal and the non-federal
aggregates. But where changes are occurring also matters. The last four figures
examine this aspect.

Figure 16 shows that the share of GDP of the three most western provinces has
increased from 1999 to 2009 while that of Ontario and Quebec has decreased. Not
visible is the growth in Newfoundland

Thus, not surprisingly, Figures 17 and 18 show a growth in own revenues and
expenditures in these three provinces. Of interest is the difference in the behaviour
of own revenues in Quebec and Ontario. However, employment does not shift as
much. In particular, as shown in Figure 19, there is no drop in the share of public
employment in Ontario.

CONCLUSION

The evidence is consistent throughout the various figures and for the various indicators: the importance of the federal government declined in Canada from 1989 to
2009 while the importance of Western Canada increased. The growth of Western
Canada—fuelled by oil sands mined in an incorrectly priced environment and with
a total lack of a savings regime appropriate to exhaustible resource revenues—can
be seen as a Western Canada firestorm. Central Canada is being weakened through

Figure 16: Provincial Gross Domestic Product as a Percentage of National GDP, Canada, 1989 and 2009

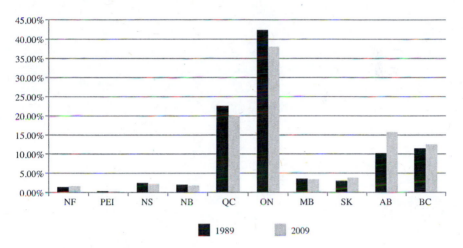

Source: Expenditure-based gross domestic product, Table 380-0017, Statistics Canada; Expenditure-based gross domestic product expenditure-based, provincial economic accounts, Table 384-0002, Statistics Canada.

Figure 17: Non-Federal Own Source Revenue by Province as a Percentage of Total Non-Federal Own Source Revenues, Canada, 1989 and 2009

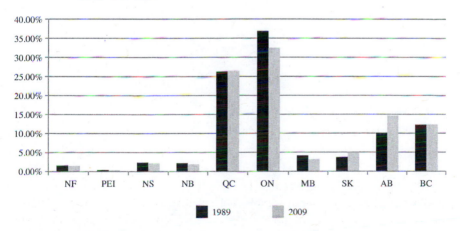

Source: Federal, provincial, and territorial general government revenue and expenditures, Table 385-0002, Statistics Canada.

Figure 18: Non-Federal Public Expenditures by Province as a Percentage of Total Non-Federal Public Expenditures, Canada, 1989 and 2009

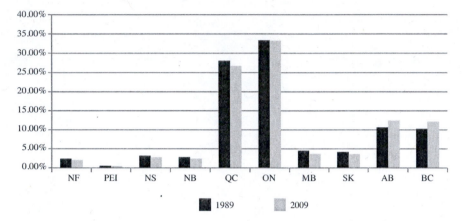

Source: Federal, provincial, and territorial general government revenue and expenditures, Table 385-0002, Statistics Canada.

Figure 19: Non-Federal Public Employment by Province as a Percentage of Total Non-Federal Public Employment, Canada, 1989 and 2009

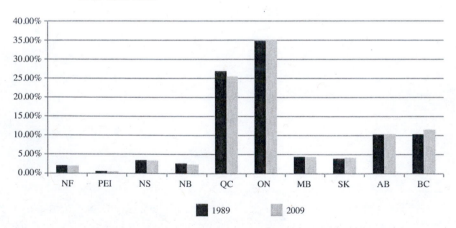

Source: Public sector employment, Table 183-0002, Statistics Canada.

"Dutch disease,"[2] turning Canada back into a staples economy. This is the challenge that must be addressed in the next ten years. One possibility is for the Alberta and Saskatchewan governments to act responsibly by pricing carbon properly, by setting aside a substantial part of oil and gas (uranium and potash, in the case of Saskatchewan) revenues into a savings fund holding assets outside Canada and by contributing to a new horizontal equalizations scheme. Another possibility is for the federal government to intervene by federalizing through Article 92 (10) the extraction of the oil sands and by using both the corporate income tax system (deductibility of royalties) and the transfer system to make the overall federal-provincial financing system more responsive to the long-term interest of Canada. For example, royalties saved could be fully deductible while those flowing to general revenues could be partially or not at all deductible.

---

[2] For a discussion of this concept, see Shakeri, Gray, and Leonard 2012, http://www.irpp. org/en/research/competitiveness/dutch-disease-or-failure-to-compete-a-diagnosis-of-canadas-manufacturing-woes/.

II

THE IMPLICATIONS OF THE 2011 FEDERAL ELECTION

THE WEST IN CANADA: ASSESSING THE WEST'S ROLE IN THE POST-2011 FEDERAL SYSTEM

Loleen Berdahl

"Thank you, people of the New West! Thank you, Canada! The West is In!" (Manning 2011b, 7). So proclaimed former Reform Party leader Preston Manning in September 2011, four short months after the federal election that resulted in Canada's first majority Conservative Party of Canada government. The 2011 election results suggested a reconfigured political party system in Canada. The separatist Bloc Québécois was all but obliterated, and the Liberal Party of Canada, the so-called "natural governing party of Canada" that governed with limited western representation, was reduced to third-party status. Both the governing Conservatives and the official opposition party, the New Democrats, had their political roots in Western Canada, and the lion's share of western MPs were part of the new Conservative majority government.

It has been suggested that the Conservative majority marks the political ascendancy of Western Canada: "Not just a majority government, but a shift of the geo-political centre of gravity of the country from the old Laurentian region of Quebec and Ontario to a new political base rooted in Ontario and the West" (Manning 2011b, 6-7), a change that "lags, but now mirrors, the westward shift of the Canadian economy, as resource-sector workhorses play an ever-increasing role in pulling Canada's economic wagon" (Manning 2011a).

But did the 2011 election result really mean a change for the West's role in the federation? The discussion that follows considers the implications of the 2011 election for government and public policy, political institutions (specifically, the House of Commons and the Senate), intergovernmental relations, and western regionalism. In doing so, it argues that while the 2011 election result marks a new *chapter* for the West, the result does not substantially alter the West's *role* in the federation.

While the focus here is on "Western Canada," defined as encompassing the four provinces of British Columbia, Alberta, Saskatchewan, and Manitoba, it must be noted at the outset that the very idea of "the West" as a region in Canada is not without dispute. The four provinces lack any true institutional home: all four participate in the Western Premiers' Conference, but so too do the three territories; in addition, the Western Premiers' Conference itself has only weak institutional ties (Bolleyer 2009, 79) and arguably limited political influence within the Canadian federation (Berdahl 2011, but see also Meekison 2004). The "affiliation" of individual provinces to "the West" can be fluid and situational, as Resnick notes: "For certain purposes, BC's inhabitants and politicians feel themselves part of western Canada or the West, yet for others they feel themselves apart from the other western provinces, including Alberta" (2000, 19). This varying definition of "the West" is seen in the 2010 New West Partnership agreement, whose signatories include only three of the four "western" provinces (Manitoba is not a signatory).

Further, the four provinces are not united by a single political culture. Wiseman argues that BC has a "discordant, bipolar political culture" (2007, 253), while Wesley (2011, 17-18, 23) maintains that Alberta political culture is defined by "populism, individualism and provincial autonomy," that Saskatchewan political culture places greater emphasis on security and collectivism, and that Manitoba political culture is defined by "modesty and temperance." Digging deeper still, it can be argued that the individual provinces themselves lack distinctive political cultures, with important divisions to be found between urban, rural, and northern areas (Henderson 2004), between Aboriginal and non-Aboriginal populations (Wiseman 2007, 105-6), between BC's interior and exterior (Resnick 2000, 18-19), and even between urban and suburban areas (Walks 2005). (Similar critiques have been levelled against the idea of Ontario as a single region; see, for example, White 2000.)

Despite these conceptual challenges with treating the West as a single region within the Canadian federation, the idea of "the West" endures, and the idea remains particularly relevant when considering the relationship between the four (diverse, unique) western provinces and the federal government. Yet these internal differences among and within the four provinces are not without consequence when considering the role of Western Canadian provinces within the federation.

GOVERNMENT REPRESENTATION

Until recently, Western Canadian provinces have typically found their MPs sitting on the opposition benches; indeed, between 1965 and 2000, less than one-third of Western Canadian MPs were in the governing party (Roach 2003, 4). The western provinces were strongly represented in Progressive Conservative governing caucuses, with three-quarters of western seats in 1979 and 1984 and one-half of western seats in 1988 being on the government side of the House. However, Progressive

Conservative governments were the exception during this period, and the Liberal Party, Canada's "natural governing party," had far less robust western representation; in seven of the nine Liberal governments between 1965 and 2004, less than 20 percent of Western Canadian seats were in government (1965–2000 data from Roach 2003, 4; 2004 data derived by author).

The limited Western Canadian representation in the Liberal governments was argued to have muted the expression of Western Canadian interests in federal policymaking. The oft-cited example of this is the National Energy Program (NEP), introduced by the Trudeau government in 1980, which had only two MPs from Western Canada, both from Manitoba. The NEP was widely perceived by many Western Canadians as being detrimental to their economic interests; further, as Wetherell, Payne, and Cavanaugh write, it was seen as being regionally unfair:

> Perhaps what seemed most offensive was that although the NEP and the federal government repeatedly emphasized fairness and sharing, not all natural resources were being treated equally. Gold, nickel and other resources were not treated the same way as oil and gas. In addition, exports of hydroelectric power were not taxed, nor was the federal government trying to "share" electricity revenues from producing provinces such as Quebec, Ontario, B.C., and Manitoba ... Since the government had few representatives from the West and none from Alberta, and since most of its support came from Ontario and Quebec, Liberal planners saw little benefit in alienating their electoral base for the sake of making the NEP more palatable to the offended provinces. (2006, 691)

While the effects of the NEP on the Western Canadian economy can be debated, in part due to the fact that the NEP coincided with "a deep North America-wide recession in 1982" (Emery and Kneebone 2011, 12), the program's *political* legacy was a profound sense among many in Western Canada that the federal government would not protect Western Canadian economic interests.

However, it is important to note that even stronger western representation within the federal government was seen to be insufficient to protect Western Canadian interests: in 1986, Brian Mulroney's Progressive Conservative government awarded a contract to service Canada's CF-18 fighter jets to Quebec-based Bombardier, despite the submission of a "technically superior" bid from Winnipeg-based Bristol Aerospace. As Gunther (2011) recalls, "Westerners were confident the government they had worked so long to elect would give the work to the Winnipeg company. When Mr. Mulroney and his ministers awarded it to Bombardier anyway, many Westerners decided the fix was in." By contributing to perceptions of federal unfairness, such policy decisions inevitably contributed to feelings of regional discontent (or "western alienation"), a topic discussed later in this chapter.

The election of the Harper Conservative minority government in 2006 meant that the majority of Western Canadian seats were again on the government side of the House. Echoing the pattern found under the Clark and Mulroney Progressive Conservative governments, the change in government from Liberal to Conservative resulted in a dramatic increase in the proportion of Western Canadian MPs in the governing caucus: over seven in ten Western Canadian MPs in 2006 and over three in four in both 2008 and 2011 were on the government benches.

The 2011 election result difference, then, lies not with increased representation within government but the fact that this representation is within a *majority* government. And unlike the Mulroney Progressive Conservative governments, which were elected on the support of Western Canada and Quebec, the Harper Conservative majority is a coalition of Western Canadian and Ontario support. After the 2011 election, Western Canada and Ontario have near-equal representation in the Conservative majority caucus, with 72 (43 percent) and 73 (44 percent) seats respectively. Conservatives from Atlantic Canada hold 14 seats (9 percent of the governing caucus), Quebec five seats (3 percent), and the northern territories two (1 percent).

Will strong Western Canadian representation within a majority government result in "better" public policy outcomes for the region? After the 2011 election, Prime Minister Harper stated that the Conservative majority meant that "Western Canada can breathe a lot easier ... Some specific policies seemed to be almost targeted to do damage in Western Canada. It's a great thing those policies won't be coming to fruition" (Fekete 2011a). While Harper did not specify the policies in question, climate change policy probably provides an illustrative example of the type of policy Western Canadians might expect to avoid under a Conservative majority: according to TD Economics, federal climate change initiatives would have rendered Alberta, Saskatchewan, and BC "the most adversely affected" due to their "greater concentration of heavy carbon emitting industries," while other provinces would be less affected (Drummond and Alexander 2009, 5). Harper's post-election statement suggested that public policies, such as climate change policy, would be considered in part according to their potential impact upon Western Canada.

In addition to protecting Western Canada from policy that may negatively and disproportionately impact upon the region, majority government status allows the Conservatives to move beyond so-called "western" policy issues, such as the elimination of both the long-gun registry and the Canadian Wheat Board's monopoly. (It must be noted that although these policies are often portrayed as enjoying broad-based support in Western Canada, a 2010 Ipsos Reid survey found that roughly six in ten BC, Saskatchewan, and Manitoba residents and almost one-half of Alberta residents supported the long-gun registry (Kennedy 2010), and in a 2011 Canadian Wheat Board plebiscite, "61 per cent of wheat farmers and 51 per cent of barley farmers voted in support of keeping the monopoly" (CBC 2011).) Moving public debate beyond these issues is arguably in the interest of the region; according to Roger Gibbins, "We've been cluttered up with a lot of very specific, a lot of small issues. And if they just clear the deck of these things, we can get down to the larger economic management issues that are more important for the country. It's a welcome opportunity, from my perspective, to move on" (quoted in Fekete 2011b).

Further, given both its political base in the West and the lessons of the NEP and the CF-18 decision, it seems reasonable to presume that the Harper majority government will take pains to avoid policies that are or appear to be unfair to Western Canada. An example of this was the October 2011 federal government decision regarding shipbuilding contracts: shipyards in Halifax and Vancouver were awarded contracts of $25 billion and $8 billion respectively, while the Quebec-based shipyard was not chosen. To avoid allegations of regional bias or unfairness, the decision was made through a non-political process; the *Globe and Mail*'s Jane Taber wrote, "Memories are still fresh, even though it happened back in the 1980s, of the repercussions that resulted from Brian Mulroney and his Progressive Conservative government awarding the CF-18 maintenance contract to Quebec instead of Winnipeg. Stephen Harper's Tories don't need a repeat of that" (2011c). (For a critical discussion about the independence of the delegated shipyard decision-making, see Howard 2011).

Thus, the strong western representation within a Conservative majority government headed by a Western Canadian prime minister can be expected to result in better protection of Western Canadian economic interests, resolution of so-called western policy issues, and either a non-political process (as in the shipbuilding case) or due consideration of Western Canada in the awarding of federal contracts. At the same time, while western influence over government policy-making is certainly higher than in the past, it still faces constraints. To again quote Gibbins, "It's not a western Canadian party that has come to power. It really is now a national party, but one with a lot of sensitivity to the particular features of Western Canada. The West has a very secure place at the table, but not the ability to sit down and write up the results" (quoted in Fekete 2011a). With 57 percent of its caucus being from outside the West, the Harper majority government will need to consider the political and policy interests of other regions. The Conservatives owe their majority status to Ontario as much as Western Canada, and given that the Ontario support may be seen as "softer" and more vulnerable in future elections, non-Western Canadian interests should be expected to trump at times.

This conjecture is particularly likely to be true if the Conservatives wish to expand their support in other regions. Crowley (2011) notes that "when the Conservatives finally won their parliamentary majority, expectations were high that many policies that had seemed to confer unearned advantages on Quebec would be swept aside. But Harper is no revanchist. He aspires to win more seats in Quebec in the future." While the Harper government is not reliant upon Quebec for its majority— a profound change from majority governments of the past—both future electoral aspirations and longstanding national unity concerns necessitate due consideration of Quebec interests. The challenge for the Harper government, then, is to balance its longstanding Western Canadian support with its current Ontario support and its desired future Quebec support—a balance that has stumped many previous federal governments.

Further complicating the West's influence within the federal government is the fact that there is no single "Western Canadian" interest, and by extension there is no single "Western Canadian" position on any given policy issue. For example, British Columbia and Manitoba are both hydro-power producing provinces, while Alberta and Saskatchewan are carbon producing provinces. These different economic interests lead to differing policy positions between the provinces on climate change, as was seen at the August 2010 Council of the Federation (COF) meeting, when Alberta and Saskatchewan stated their preference for carbon capture and storage initiatives and BC stated its support for cap-and-trade initiatives.

Overall, Western Canada enjoys strong representation within the new majority government caucus, and this fact, combined with Prime Minister Harper's strong awareness of the politics of western regionalism, means that federal policy-makers will give fair hearing to Western Canadian interests, when such interests exist. While majority governments of the past may have focused on balancing Ontario and Quebec interests, the new political landscape means that the federal majority government must now balance Western Canadian, Ontario, and Quebec interests. (How Atlantic and Northern interests will factor into this balance is uncertain.) The inclusion of Western Canada in this "national balance" is an important development but does not mean that the West has a dominant role in the federation.

INSTITUTIONAL REFORM: THE HOUSE OF COMMONS AND SENATE

The most recent census figures demonstrate the growing population relevance of Western Canada: as of 2011, more Canadians lived in Western Canada than in Quebec and Atlantic Canada combined. Western Canadian provincial governments make frequent mention of how Canada's population is shifting westward over time; indeed, in their official communications—for example, news releases pertaining to regional cooperation agreements such as the New West Partnership Agreement—Western Canadian provincial governments often stress the growing population weight of the western provinces within Canada (Berdahl 2011).

One might think that regional population growth would result in growing political weight. However, this growing population has been slow to translate into increased representation in the House of Commons, as the redistribution of House of Commons seats is legislatively set to occur only once every decade, after the decennial census. Further, for a number of reasons (see Sancton 2010; Mendelsohn and Choudhry 2011), Canada's House of Commons seat allocations deviate from the principle of representation by population. At the time of the 2011 federal election, Ontario, Canada's most populous province, suffered the greatest underrepresentation, while the deviations from "rep by pop" affected Western Canadian provinces in very different ways. Alberta and BC were each underrepresented relative to their populations, while Manitoba and Saskatchewan were each overrepresented; according to Mendelsohn and Choudhry, Alberta and BC were underrepresented by two seats and four seats respectively, while Saskatchewan and Manitoba were overrepresented by four seats and two seats respectively (2011, 8; based on 2001 census population figures; "rep-by-pop" seats rounded by author). In total, the four western provinces had a total of 92 of the House's 308 seats, or 29.9 percent, and the western provinces accounted for 30.7 percent of the national population in 2011. Thus, while BC and Alberta were underrepresented relative to their populations, the West's House underrepresentation is less than 1 percentage point.

The Harper government began its efforts to address the underrepresentation of provinces in 2007. The initial proposal would have benefited Alberta and BC more than Ontario and was opposed by the Ontario government (Mendelsohn and Choudhry 2011, 9). A second proposal would have left Quebec underrepresented and was also dropped. In October 2011, the Harper government introduced its third (and successful) proposal, the Fair Representation Act, which increases the size of the House of Commons to 338 seats, with 15 new seats to Ontario, six new seats to each of BC and Alberta, and three new seats to Quebec. As a result, in the 2015 federal election, 104 of the House's 338 seats, or 30.8 percent, will be allotted to Western Canada. (BC will have 42 seats, Alberta 34, Saskatchewan 14, and Manitoba 14).

What will this change mean for Western Canada? The new seats mean that BC will have increased weight within the House of Commons (moving from 11.8 percent to 12.54 percent of House seats), Alberta will maintain its current level of House representation (10.15 percent of House seats), while Saskatchewan and Manitoba (each dropping from 4.59 percent to 4.18 percent of House seats) will account for a slightly smaller proportion of the House seats. The proportionate weight of "the West" within the House of Commons will be largely unchanged.

Interestingly, the Fair Representation Act was not been without Western Canadian criticism. The act drew fire from *Vancouver Sun* columnist Yaffe (2011), who argued that "B.C. has had a strong record of electing Harper government MPs and surely deserves better, all the more because Harper pledged that he'd look out for B.C.'s interests." The *Calgary Herald* (2011) also called foul: "In a case of classic Quebec appeasement, the new proposal would enhance Quebec's representation well over what its population would dictate ... the new proposed seat distribution is a ludicrous pandering to Quebec when one considers the inequities faced by Ontario, Alberta and B.C. ... Alberta may finally get equitable treatment, but not so for B.C. and Ontario. The problem in addressing a clearly complicated dilemma is that Quebec always wins." (It must be noted that the *Calgary Herald*'s position was based on a factual error: the Fair Representation Act does not, in fact, allocate Quebec more seats than warranted by its population.) However, the Alberta intergovernmental affairs minister and the Alberta spokesman for the Canadian Taxpayers Federation, among others, welcomed the proposal (Thomas 2011).

Looking beyond House of Commons seat reapportionment, what might be expected with the Harper government's Senate reform agenda? Western Canadian interests have long supported the idea of Senate reform, and in particular the proposal for a "Triple E" Senate – "equal, elected and effective." This reformed Senate, it was suggested, would help to protect Western Canadian interests; writes Smith, "when the National Energy Program assumed iconic standing for the over-weening centralism of the federal government, the move to make the Senate elected, equal and effective followed" (2003, 63). The *Alberta Report* and the Canada West Foundation endorsed the Triple E idea (Smith 2003, 56), as did the Government of Alberta. The Reform Party of Canada adopted the reform proposal, and the idea carried forward into the Canadian Alliance and then Conservative Party of Canada. While the idea that Senate reform is either necessary or sufficient to ad-dress Western Canadian concerns has its critics (see, for example, Lawson 2005), Senate reform in principle enjoys popularity among the Western Canadian—and indeed, the broader Canadian—public (see, for example, Switzer 2011).

However, it must be stressed that the Senate reform proposals put forward by Harper are not identical to those promoted by the Western Canadian political elites of the 1990s. Harper's Senate Reform Act, introduced in June 2011, establishes guidelines for voluntary provincial Senate elections and imposes nine-year term limits on new senators.[1] Of the three "Es," it addresses only "elected," as changes to the distribution of Senate seats ("equal") and Senate powers ("effective") would require constitutional amendment.

In 2013, the Harper government submitted a number of reference questions to the Supreme Court to clarify the federal government's ability to reform the Chamber. In the event that the Supreme Court allows changes such as proposed in the Senate Reform Act, might Harper's Senate reform efforts change western influence within Canadian federalism? Critics argue that the reform proposals would actually *reduce* Western Canada's influence, as "elections would suddenly give the Senate, which has considerable powers that it rarely uses, the democratic legitimacy to flex its muscles" (O'Neil 2011b). This legitimacy may be seen as problematic by western provincial governments for two reasons. First, elected senators may be emboldened in articulating provincial interests, thus competing with and potentially undermin-ing premiers and provincial governments as the defenders of provinces. Comments made by Saskatchewan Premier Brad Wall illustrate this threat: in reference to the Saskatchewan government's role in successfully pressing the federal government to oppose the BHP takeover of PotashCorp in 2010, Wall stated, "We had our say in that. Is what we have today inferior? Would it even have been made at all bet-ter by a hybrid, elected, appointed, still whipped Senate? I don't think it would

---

[1] It is interesting to note how the Senate reform and House of Commons reapportion-ment proposals intersect: as representation by population is strengthened within the House of Commons, smaller provinces may see increased value in the representation of regional interests in the Senate. Indeed, New Brunswick Premier David Alward has argued that, due to Atlantic Canada's decreased influence in an expanded House of Commons, Senate reform is increasingly important to the region (Huras 2011).

be." Indeed, in his view, decentralization over the 1990s and 2000s has resulted in provinces that are now "the de facto triple-E Senate. The provinces are on the front line. This is where the action is" (Taber 2011b).

Second, in failing to address the distribution of Senate seats, Harper's Senate reform approach is unlikely to appease those who see Western Canadian under-representation in the Senate as one of its chief failings. BC Premier Christy Clark raised this concern, stating, "Twenty-four Senators for the entire Western Canada? The economic engine for our country? The economy of this nation is moving to the west; slowly but surely it is moving to Western Canada. To entrench an institution where we will forever be vastly under-represented just doesn't make any sense" (Taber 2011a). A similar critique was articulated by former Alberta premier Don Getty, who stated the current Senate reform proposal "locks in the problems of the Senate. If it's not equal, you just make the power base of Ontario and Quebec, with their huge Senate side as well as their House of Commons side, too much" (O'Neil 2011a). Even interim Liberal Party leader Bob Rae pressed this point, arguing that the Harper Conservatives "are freezing Alberta and British Columbia at six seats (in the Senate) for all time. I mean, if they have an elected Senate that's elected on the basis that Mr. Harper is proposing, he is screwing his own province and the same to British Columbia" (Raj 2011).

Overall, the western provinces have provided lukewarm support at best for Harper's reform plans. While Saskatchewan already had Senate election legislation in place, the province opted not to hold Senate elections in conjunction with the November 2011 provincial election, as the premier felt the costs of Senate elections should be borne by the federal government (McGregor 2011). In November 2013, in response to the Senate expense scandals, the Saskatchewan legislature repealed its Senate election legislation and passed a motion calling for Senate abolition. Also in November 2013, the Manitoba Attorney General introduced a motion requesting that the federal government initiate provincial consultations regarding Senate abolition (CBC 2013). BC Premier Christy Clark has stated that her support for Senate elections is tied to the more difficult and contentious provision that BC has increased Senate representation (Taber 2011a).

These provincial reservations are unlikely to deter the Harper government, but dismissing provincial concerns does present a risk of resurrecting a deep-seated belief that the federal government ignores the West's interests. As Verrelli (2008) argues, Harper's non-constitutional Senate reform agenda circumvents provincial involvement, and in this way represents a "closed" federalism approach reminiscent of Trudeau's failed 1978 Senate reform efforts. Senate reform has been a long-standing issue for many Western Canadians, and the symbolic recognition of this through Harper's Senate reform proposals will undoubtedly appeal to some in the short term. However, Harper's approach to achieving his ends may be ill-received by Western Canadian provincial governments and/or residents in the long run.

Taken together, the Harper government's institutional reforms are unlikely to increase the West's influence within the Canadian federation. The increased representation of BC and Alberta within the House of Commons does not significantly increase the proportionate weight of "the West" in the House, and electing senators without addressing issues of Senate seat distribution could reduce the political influence of premiers while perpetuating the regional imbalance in the Upper Chamber. The true value of these reforms lies in their symbolic recognition of the growing Western Canadian population and the long-standing western aspiration for a renewed Senate.

INTERGOVERNMENTAL RELATIONS

The election of the Harper minority government in 2006 raised questions about the future of federal-provincial relations, as Harper's vision of "open federalism," which "seek[s] to re-establish a strong central government that focuses on genuine national priorities like national defence and the economic union, while fully respecting the exclusive jurisdiction of the provinces" (Harper 2004), appeared to point toward a more classical approach to federalism. However, open federalism resulted in little change in practice (Bickerton 2010, 68): as Prime Minister Chrétien before him, Prime Minister Harper has favoured bilateral intergovernmental agreements over pan-Canadian agreements, and has tended to avoid consensus-based intergovernmental policy-making, "not wishing to tie the hands of [the federal] government by subjecting its decisions to a bargaining process in which a successful outcome depends on reaching a consensus with the provincial and territorial first ministers" (Bakvis, Baier, and Brown 2009, 133).

With its newfound majority status, the Harper government might renew its commitment to open federalism, first through increased decentralization and "respect for provincial jurisdiction," and second through its pursuit of a stronger national economic union. Should the Harper Conservatives anticipate support from the western provinces on such an agenda? Does the 2011 election result in any way alter intergovernmental relations between the four western provinces and the federal government?

Open federalism has been argued to be "consistent with the broader neoliberal approach to federalism, which, among other aims, seeks to use institutional reforms to lock in more market-oriented public policies" (Harmes 2007, 418). If this assertion is accurate, one might expect Western Canada provincial governments to support Harper's open federalism model: at the end of 2011, three of the four western provinces had governments that appeared to share ideological ground with the federal Conservatives (under, from west to east, the party labels of Liberal, Progressive Conservative, and Saskatchewan Party; the Manitoba electorate returned the NDP to power in October 2011). However, the Harper government may well lack true "conservative" or "neoliberal" partners in Western Canada. Both BC premier Christy Clark and Alberta premier Alison Redford are arguably more centrist than their predecessors, suggesting that the "mainstream rightwing parties in Western

Canada have shifted to a more centrist, small-l liberal position" (according to the University of Victoria's James Lawson, as reported by Ward 2011), and Brad Wall's Saskatchewan Party moves easily between centrist and centre-right positions. While there is no reason to assume that there will be an ideological schism between the western provinces and the Harper Conservatives, there is also no reason to expect that the western provinces will naturally support Harper's open federalism model on ideological grounds.

Rather than supporting open federalism as a general principle, the western premiers should be expected to adopt whatever position is seen as advancing their own province's interests. Lecours and Béland argue that "provincial governments in Canada know they are very likely to get support from their constituents in a public dispute with the federal government. In this context, provinces have an incentive to be aggressive when they deal with the federal government on issues they can frame as affecting their interests and/or identities" (2010, 582). *All* provincial premiers, regardless of region or political stripe, have incentives to advance provincial interests over federal. Western Canadian premiers have already demonstrated a willingness to oppose the Harper government when it suits their political purposes. Notably, and as previously mentioned, in 2010 Saskatchewan Premier Brad Wall placed significant pressure on the minority Harper Conservatives to block a foreign ownership bid for PotashCorp, a move that "clearly cut against the economic grain of [Harper's] ostensibly pro-foreign-investment Conservative government" (Geddes 2011). Similarly, in 2011, BC Premier Christy Clark broke with her predecessor Gordon Campbell's more peaceful approach to federal-provincial relations when she waged a public dispute over RCMP contracts (Smyth 2011).

Such province-specific interests are likely to be seen if the federal government continues in its efforts to strengthen the national economic union. Prior to the 2011 election, the Harper government pursued a stronger economic union on two fronts: internal trade reform and the establishment of a national securities regulator. Although the Harper government threatened to assert its powers to address persistent internal trade barriers (Canada 2007; Harper 2008), this threat has yet to be acted on, as the federal, provincial, and territorial governments have successfully negotiated a number of Agreement on Internal Trade (AIT) amendments, including the inclusion of new labour mobility (Ninth Amendment, approved in 2009) and agriculture chapters (Eleventh Amendment, approved in 2010), and strengthened government-to-government dispute mechanisms (Tenth Amendment, approved in 2009). Given that three of the four western provinces are signatories to the New West Partnership Trade Agreement, a sub-national trade enhancement agreement that goes beyond the AIT in scope, one might expect the western provinces to be supportive of future internal trade policy efforts. However, differing provincial interests regarding outstanding AIT issues, such as the lack of an energy chapter and the scope of the procurement chapter, will likely cause internal trade reform to hit a standstill again. The West was also unsupportive of Harper's pursuit of a national securities regulator: Alberta, Saskatchewan, and Manitoba, along with

Quebec, opposed the idea, while "B.C. fear[ed] a court ruling might give Ottawa broad economic power, not just narrow approval for the securities regulator" (Geddes 2011). The Supreme Court rejected the federal government's national securities regulator policy in December 2011; in January 2012, Finance Minister Jim Flaherty stated that the federal government plans to continue to pursue this issue, this time in cooperation with the provinces (CBC 2012). However, the West should not be expected to be a strong supporter of Harper's economic union agenda.

Similarly, the federal Conservatives can expect Western Canadian provinces to protect their own interests with respect to federal transfer programs and any attempts to reform federal transfers to individuals. Indeed, the western provinces can be expected to add to the complexity of such issues; three of the Canada's four "have" provinces are located in Western Canada and can be expected to have particular concerns about the structure of federal equalization; and Western Canadian and Ontario provincial governments can be expected to have differences on issues such as Employment Insurance (EI) reform (Geddes 2011). To this point, in January 2012, Premier Brad Wall argued that the structure of equalization and EI works against Saskatchewan's economic interests (Taber 2012), and in February 2012, Alberta Finance Minister Ron Liepert argued that the equalization formula should be changed to require "accountability" from recipient provinces: "If you qualify for equalization, you should have to show some results-based perform-ance" (Walton 2012).

In sum, there is little reason to presume that the western provinces will support (or, for that matter, oppose) Harper's open federalism model. While the majority status of the Conservatives undoubtedly changes the government's effectiveness in federal policy-making, it does not necessarily alter federal-provincial dynamics.

WESTERN DISCONTENT

Discussions of Western Canada often make reference to the sentiment of regional discontent with the federal government, more commonly referred to as "western alienation."[2] Over time, surveys have found that many Western Canadians feel that their provinces are treated poorly in the Canadian federal system. This regional sense of grievance shifts over time: in the 1970s and early 1980s, regional discontent was high, fuelled by policy disputes (notably with respect to energy policy) and limited western electoral representation in the governing Liberal caucus. Regional discontent subsided in the mid-1980s when Western Canada had strong electoral representation in the Mulroney Progressive Conservative government—only to re-emerge in the late 1980s and early 1990s.

---

[2] Parts of this section, previously presented in Berdahl 2010, are reproduced here with the permission of the Canada West Foundation.

What might the 2011 election result mean for western discontent? There is reason to suspect that it will decline, as analysis of the Canadian Election Studies of 2004, 2006, 2008, and 2011 suggest that regional discontent was already subsiding in Western Canada.[3] Conducted during and immediately after federal elections, the Canadian Election Studies often repeat survey questions to allow for the tracking of changes over time. One survey question repeated across the four election studies taps into feelings of discontent. Respondents were asked, "In general, does the federal government treat your province better, worse, or about the same as other provinces?"[4] Respondents who report that their province is treated worse than other provinces can be seen as expressing discontent with Canadian federalism.

The data suggest that Western Canadian discontent was already declining prior to the 2011 election. In 2004, a majority of BC, Alberta, and Saskatchewan respondents and four in ten Manitoba respondents stated that that federal government treated their province worse than other provinces. Discontent dropped in BC and Alberta in 2006, and then in all four western provinces in 2008. Overall, in all four western provinces, discontent was lower in 2011 than in 2004. By 2011, it was actually Quebecers and Atlantic Canadians and not Western Canadians who reported the highest levels of regional discontent.

Declining western discontent means that the West can assume a more positive, less aggrieved tone within the federation. Indeed, former Reform Party leader

---

[3] Data from the 2004 and the 2006 Canadian Election Surveys were provided by the Institute for Social Research, York University. The surveys were funded by Elections Canada and the Social Sciences and Humanities Research Council of Canada (SSHRC), and were completed for the Canadian Election Team of André Blais, Joanna Everitt, Patrick Fournier, Elisabeth Gidengil, and Neil Nevitte. The fieldwork of the 2008 Canadian Election Surveys was conducted by the Institute for Social Research (ISR) at York University and the study was financed by Elections Canada. The principal co-investigators were Elisabeth Gidengil, Joanna Everitt, Patrick Fournier, and Neil Nevitte. The survey fieldwork for the Canadian Election Study was conducted by the Institute for Social Research (ISR) at York University. The principal co-investigators for the 2011 CES were Patrick Fournier, Fred Cutler, Stuart Soroka, and Dietlind Stolle. Neither the Institute for Social Research, Elections Canada, nor the Canadian Election Survey Teams are responsible for the analyses and interpretations presented here.

[4] This question was asked in the 2004 and 2006 campaign period surveys, in the 2008 post-election survey, and in the 2011 survey. It should be noted that the question asks about how the federal government treats one's *province*, and not how the larger Western Canadian region is treated. It should also be noted that other possible dimensions of regional discontent, such as the perception that one's province does not receive its fair share of federal revenue transfers, are outside the scope of this analysis.

Preston Manning argues that the West has a responsibility to quell regionalism in other parts of Canada: "The West should never forget what it feels like to be 'out' and should use our increased influence to ensure that no Canadian—east or west, north or south, new or old, ever feels that way again" (Manning 2011b, 6). Manning reiterates, "Westerners especially, know what it is like to be 'out' of the federal power block, and should make special efforts to ensure that Eastern aliena- tion (in Quebec and parts of Atlantic Canada) does not become a permanent and debilitating national affliction" (Manning 2011a). Whether Western Canadians (or their MPs and/or premiers) feel this responsibility has yet to be determined, but, in the short term at least, Western Canadians might be expected to opt out of the ongoing politics of regionalism.

Is western regionalism likely to return in the long run? The real tests will occur when the Conservatives lose power and/or when the western provinces experi- ence a significant economic downturn. With respect to the latter condition, Mike Percy, former dean of business at the University of Alberta, argues that the 2011 election result does not mark the end of western alienation "because the structure of the Canadian economy is quite regionally specialized. If you look at the broad stereotypes, we have financial services in Toronto, manufacturing in the East, while it's resource-based in the West. And inevitably you have changes in terms of trade—the price of energy rises, for example—which create internal forces that cause real disparities in growth paths. That provokes responses in regions and the federal government is always stuck in the middle. Given the structure of the country, there will inevitably be regional tensions over the whole economic cycle" (quoted in Pitts 2011).

Yet the changing face of the West may well mute future western discontent. To again quote Percy, "Given the large interprovincial migration East to West, many Westerners are former Easterners. Alienation may still rear its head, but it is much less of a force" (Pitts 2011). Similarly, Bilodeau, White, and Nevitte find that "im- migrants from non-traditional source countries in Alberta and British Columbia supply significantly more favorable evaluations of the role played by the federal government than do Canadian-born respondents" (2010, 526). (Immigrants from traditional source countries hold views more similar to the Canadian-born respond- ents.) But this muting of regionalism by immigration, these authors note, does not mean its extinction: "The fact that immigrants develop somewhat stronger federal loyalties than the Canadian-born population in their respective provinces does not imply that they are completely impervious to local dynamics … in spite of the difference between immigrants and their corresponding Canadian-born provincial population, there is clear evidence of a strong reproduction of regional cleavages" (Bilodeau, White, and Nevitte 2010, 533).

Overall, while Western Canadian discontent is lower than in the past, the changes in that discontent between 2004 and 2011 simply demonstrate that attitudes shift over time. Here, the perceptions of former Prime Minister Paul Martin are likely correct: writing about an interview with Martin in 2007, the *Globe and Mail*'s Roy

MacGregor reported that "[Martin] has come to feel that Western alienation is something that ebbs and flows. It's not entirely without merit, but it may also be a permanent part of the Canadian condition." In short, while it is (in Percy's words) "very hard to be alienated when the prime minister is from Calgary and there are a number of very strong ministers from the West" (quoted in Pitts 2011), it is reasonable to assume that these sentiments may resurface at some point in the future.

CONCLUSION

In October 2011, *Globe and Mail* columnist John Ibbitson proclaimed that "the power shift from Central Canada to the West that everyone speculated about is no longer speculation. It's here ... The West isn't just in. It's in charge." While Ibbitson's words likely gladdened the hearts of some and caused consternation in others, they overstate the influence of Western Canada. To be certain, the 2011 election results mark a new chapter for "the West" within Canadian federalism. The Harper government will push through many of the so-called "western policy issues," consider the West's economic interests when constructing federal policy, and attempt to address (albeit not necessarily to western satisfaction) a number of "western" institutional reforms. Further, "as long as Mr. Harper's in charge, the Conservatives will continue to be animated by the alienated spirit of the West, ever suspicious of the potential excesses of federal power, long after the wheat board and gun registry are gone" (Libin 2011). Finally, the 2011 election result furthers the ongoing shift in western political culture, with the past tone of regionalism and grievance being replaced by a renewed sense of leadership and national engagement.

However, this new chapter does not mean a substantially altered role for the West in the federation. In the short term, the federal Conservative government will continue to need to balance western interests with those of other regions, and will need to watch its step as it does so. Prime Minister Mulroney found balancing Quebec and Western Canadian interests difficult, and Prime Minister Harper might well face a similar challenge in balancing Western Canadian and Ontario interests. Such a balancing act is further complicated by the fact that there is not one single "western" interest, and what satisfies Saskatchewan (or BC, or Manitoba) may be strongly opposed by BC (or Alberta, or Manitoba ...). Additionally, the Harper Conservatives may seek to gain Quebec seats in the next election, and to do so will require proper consideration of and appeal to Quebec interests. Stated simply, while the previous Ontario-Quebec balancing act has expanded to become a West-Ontario-Quebec balancing act, it remains a balancing act all the same.

A similar picture is seen in the longer term. As the structural changes (in terms of House seats and the proposed Senate elections) do not dramatically increase the West's political influence, the enhanced political power of the West is dependent upon the continuation of a government and a leader predisposed to be sensitive to western interests. Just as the West's increased economic "clout" may be temporary, subject to the vagaries of international natural resource prices, so too is the West's increased political "clout" subject to the vagaries of federal leadership. As it seeks to become Canada's new "natural governing party," the Conservative Party will likely be required to become a brokerage party (like the Liberal Party of Canada in decades past), and while the West can be expected to have substantial influence within this party, it will be one interest among many.

The 2011 election result is the capstone for many changes for Western Canada. The western provinces enjoyed, to varying degrees, considerable economic prosperity in the past decade, prosperity that was dampened but not demolished by the 2008 global economic downturn. The western provinces—including Saskatchewan and Manitoba—are enjoying population growth. Western regionalism and grievance are in decline, and three of the four western provinces have the distinction of "have" status within the Canadian equalization system. On top of this larger context of transformative change in Western Canada, the party preferred by the majority of Western Canadian voters now forms the federal majority government. All of these changes—economic clout, population weight, regionalism, equalization status, political clout—may well prove temporary. But there can be little doubt that the 2011 election result marked the start of a new chapter for Western Canada.

REFERENCES

Bakvis, H., G. Baier, and D. Brown. 2009. *Contested Federalism: Certainty and Ambiguity in the Canadian Federation*. Don Mills, ON: Oxford University Press.

Berdahl, L. 2010. *Whither Western Alienation? Shifting Patterns of Discontent with the Federal Government*. Calgary: Canada West Foundation.

—. 2011. "The New West? Western Canadian Region-Building in the 2000s." *Journal of Canadian Studies* 45 (3): 1-24.

Bickerton, J. 2010. "Deconstructing the New Federalism." *Canadian Political Science Review* 4 (2-3): 56-72.

Bilodeau, A., S. White, and N. Nevitte. 2010. "The Development of Dual Loyalties: Immigrants' Integration to Canadian Regional Dynamics." *Canadian Journal of Political Science* 43 (3): 515-44.

Bolleyer, N. 2009. *Intergovernmental Cooperation: Rational Choices in Federal Systems and Beyond*. New York: Oxford University Press.

Calgary Herald. 2011. "Appeasing Quebec: In Rebalancing Commons Seats, Quebec Always Wins." *Calgary Herald*, 22 October.

Canada. 2007. "Speech from the Throne by Michaelle Jean to Open the Second Session Thirty-Ninth Parliament of Canada." Ottawa, 16 October.

CBC. 2011. "Wheat Board Head Vows to Fight Federal Changes." *CBC News*, 17 October.

—. 2012. "Ottawa Bids for Scaled Back National Securities Regulator." *CBC News*, 26 January.

—. 2013. "Manitoba May Push Ottawa to Abolish Senate." *CBC News,* 26 November.

Crowley, B.L. 2011. "Even with Majority, Quebec a Key Challenge for Harper." *Ottawa Citizen*, 24 October.

Drummond, D., and C. Alexander. 2009. *Special Report: Answers to Some Key Questions about the Costs of Combating Climate Change: A Summary of the Pembina/David Suzuki Foundation Paper.* Toronto: TD Economics.

Emery, H., and R. Kneebone. 2011. "Alberta's Problems of Plenty." *Policy Options* (May): 10-16.

Fekete, J. 2011a. "Western Canada Can 'Breathe a Lot Easier'; Harper Maps Out Tory Majority." *Calgary Herald*, 4 May.

—. 2011b "Throne Speech to Have Western Slant." *National Post*, 2 June.

Geddes, J. 2011. "Girding for Battle with the Provinces." *Maclean's*, 14 February.

Gibbins, R. 2011. "Distance Between the West and Ontario Just Got Smaller." *Canada West Foundation Commentaries,* 5 May.

Gunther, L. 2011. "Shipbuilding Contract Is an Iceberg Waiting to Be Hit." *National Post*, 19 October.

Harmes, A. 2007. "The Political Economy of Open Federalism." *Canadian Journal of Political Science* 40: 417-38.

Harper, S. 2004. "My Plan for 'Open Federalism." *National Post,* 27 October.

—. 2008. "Strong Leadership to Protect Canada's Future." Address by the Prime Minister in Reply to the Speech from the Throne, Ottawa, 20 November.

Henderson, A. 2004. "Regional Political Cultures in Canada." *Canadian Journal of Political Science* 37 (3): 595-615.

Howard, C. 2011. "Under Harper, It's Tight Lips That Build Ships." *Globe and Mail*, 25 October.

Huras, A. 2011. "Senate Reform Now More Important: Alward." *Moncton Times & Transcript*, 28 October.

Ibbitson, J. 2011. "The Common Thread in Ottawa's Move This Week? They All Point West." *Globe and Mail*, 21 October.

Kennedy, M. 2010. "Two-Thirds of Canadians Back Long-Gun Registry: Poll." *National Post*, 5 October.

Lawson, R.J. "Understanding Alienation in Western Canada: Is "Western Alienation" the Problem? Is Senate Reform the Cure?" *Journal of Canadian Studies* 39 (2): 127-55.

Lecours, A., and D. Béland. 2010. "Federalism and Fiscal Policy: The Politics of Equalization in Canada." *Publius: The Journal of Federalism* 40 (4): 569-96.

Libin, K. 2011. "What the West Wants Next." *National Post*, 28 October.

MacGregor, R. 2007. "Paul Martin's New Mission." *Globe and Mail*, 28 July.

Manning, P. 2011a. "Political Shifts Mustn't Threaten Canada's Unity, Vision." *Globe and Mail*, 20 May.

—. 2011b. "How the West Got In." Remarks by Preston Manning to the Alberta Report 25th Anniversary Gala, 15 September 2011, Edmonton.

McGregor, J. 2011. "Senate Reform a Bumpy Ride – or Road to Nowhere?" *CBC News*, 15 June.

Meekison, J.P. 2004. "The Western Premiers' Conference: Intergovernmental Co-operation at the Regional Level." In *Canada: The State of the Federation 2002: Reconsidering the Institutions of Canadian Federalism*, edited by J.P. Meekison, H. Telford, and H. Lazar, 183-209. Montreal and Kingston: McGill Queen's University Press.

Mendelsohn, M., and S. Choudhry. 2011. *Voter Equality and Other Canadian Values: Finding the Balance*. Toronto: Mowat Centre for Policy Innovation.

O'Neil, P. 2011a. "Democratic Reform Minister Ready to Stand Firm." *Edmonton Journal*, 26 September.

— 2011b. "Harper Senate Reforms Would Hurt Alberta, B.C." *Vancouver Sun*, 6 October.

Pitts, G. 2011. "An Educated Eye on Alberta's Future." *Globe and Mail*, 20 June.

Raj, A. 2011. "Harper's Senate Reform Undercuts West, Rae Charges." *Postmedia News*, 8 June.

Resnick, P. 2000. *The Politics of Resentment: British Columbia Regionalism and Canadian Unity*. Vancouver: UBC Press.

Roach, R. 2003. *An (In)Auspicious Gathering: The Western Economic Opportunities Conference of 1973*. Calgary: Canada West Foundation.

Sancton, A. 2010. *The Principle of Representation by Population in Canadian Federal Politics*. Toronto: Mowat Centre for Policy Innovation.

Smith, D. 2003. *The Canadian Senate in Bicameral Perspective*. Toronto: University of Toronto Press.

Smyth, M. 2011. "Premier Ticking Off Harper and His Tories." *Vancouver Province*, 2 October.

Switzer, J. 2011. "Canadians Support Harper's Plans for Senate Reform, Poll Shows." *National Post*, 12 June.

Taber, J. 2011a. "Christy Clark Presses Harper to Reform – and Expand – the Senate." *Globe and Mail*, 23 June.

— 2011b. "Brad Wall's Senate Wish: 'Reform It, Abolish It, Paint It Pink." *Globe and Mail*, 24 June.

— 2011c. "Harper's Team Keeps Hands off $35-Billion Shipbuilding Hot Potato." *Globe and Mail*, 17 October.

— 2012. "Equalization and EI Hurt Saskatchewan, Premier Says." *Globe and Mail*, 10 January.

Thomas, N. 2011. "Alberta to Receive Six More Commons Seats under New Plan." *Edmonton Journal*, 28 October.

Verrelli, N. 2008. "Harper's Senate Reform: An Example of Open Federalism?" Special Series: Working Papers on Senate Reform, Working Paper 2008-16. Institute of Intergovernmental Relations, School of Policy Studies, Queen's University.

Walks, R.A. 2005. "The City-Suburban Cleavage in Canadian Federal Politics." *Canadian Journal of Political Science* 38 (2): 383-413.

Walton, D. 2012. "Alberta Should Have Proof Provinces Spending Equalization Wisely: Finance Minister." *Globe and Mail*, 10 February.

Ward, D. 2011. "The Changing Face of Provincial Politics: Rise of Redford in Alberta and Clark in B.C. Illustrates Shift to a More Centrist, Small-L Liberal Culture, UVic Prof Says." *Vancouver Sun*, 8 October.

Wesley, J. 2011. *Code Politics: Campaigns and Political Cultures on the Canadian Prairies*. Vancouver: UBC Press.

Wetherell, D.G., M. Payne, and C.A. Cavanaugh. 2006. *Alberta Formed, Alberta Transformed*. Edmonton: University of Alberta.

White, G. 2000. "This Region-State Is Also a Regionalized State." *Policy Options* (January/February): 90-1.

Wiseman, N. 2007. *In Search of Canadian Political Culture*. Vancouver: UBC Press.

Yaffe, B. 2011. "B.C. Gets Short End of Stick in New House of Commons Plan." *Vancouver Sun*, 28 October.

5

THE ORANGE WAVE:
A (RE)CANADIANIZATION OF
THE QUEBEC ELECTORATE?

François Rocher

To many observers, the 2011 federal election results—in particular, the sharp decline in support for the Bloc Québécois (BQ) and the exceptional support for the New Democratic Party (NDP) among Quebec voters—have been interpreted as a new commitment in Quebec to Canada and the federal government. This new reality could have an impact on federal-provincial relations. To address these issues, this chapter analyzes what the 2011 federal election means for Canadian federalism.

In a federal system where the executive's prerogatives are decisive, the governing party controls the issues and negotiating processes between the national, provincial, and territorial governments. Opposition parties are marginal players in the decision-making process. However, they can play a major role in the public debate on the decisions made by those in power. Consequently, they can offer an alternative view of federalism, bring about disaffection, and seek to represent political preferences that are ignored by the governing party. In this respect, the election of 59 New Democrats in Quebec is significant. Likewise, Quebec's very weak presence within the governing party may also have an impact on its ability to represent Quebec voters. Since the end of World War II, with the exception of Joe Clark's short-lived minority government in 1979 with only two MPs from Quebec, Quebec has never been so ill-represented in government. Only five Conservative members were elected to government in 2011, representing 3 percent of all Conservative MPs.

This chapter does not aim to provide the definitive answer to the question of whether the NDP's impressive performance in Quebec is a sign of Quebecers' recommitment to Canadian federalism. In the current context, the most honest answer is "We don't know yet." I prefer to highlight a number of factors that must be taken into account in looking at the 2011 election. In doing so, it would be equally as premature and risky to establish a direct correlation between the BQ's poor performance (which should be put in perspective) and the decline of the sovereignist option. These considerations lead us to raise a number of challenges now facing federal parties.

This chapter consists of four sections. The first discusses how, during and after the federal election, the English-speaking press analyzed and presented the BQ. This scenario serves as a backdrop to the second section, which offers an alternative meaning behind the 2011 elections. The third section analyzes Quebec's recent attitudes and preferences regarding Canadian federalism. From this basis we are able to take a critical look at the idea of a renewed interest in the increased political participation of the federalist parties and, moreover, the NDP. The final section identifies a number of general issues currently facing federal parties.

SHAME ON THE BLOC QUÉBÉCOIS ... AND "GOOD RIDDANCE"

It would be no exaggeration to say that the presence of the BQ in Ottawa has been perceived as a source of frustration and annoyance, a threat not only to the other federal parties but also to a great number of voters outside of Quebec. Political comments concerning the BQ were almost always negative. A systematic review of articles published in newspapers between 25 March (the day before the election was called) and 21 May (19 days after it) identified 148 articles discussing the BQ's presence in Ottawa and interpreting the campaign's development and the 2 May 2011 results in relation to the Bloc. Factual news stories were excluded from the database. My intention is not to discuss the campaign's key moments (for such an account, see Bélanger and Nadeau 2011) but rather to show how the BQ's presence was interpreted in the press.

Three moments stand out. The first phase of the campaign was characterized by a sense that the results would reproduce a parliamentary structure almost identical to the one just dissolved. Commentators thus expected the number of (re)elected Bloc members to be more or less the same. Then, after the French-language leaders' debate on 14 April, polls showed an impressive surge of support for the NDP. The opportunity to witness the weakening of the BQ changed the English press's perception of Quebec voters. Finally, the NDP's unexpected performance and the defeat of all but four Bloc members, including Gilles Duceppe in his own riding, led to differing interpretations of the meaning behind these results.

The election followed the Liberal Party's non-confidence motion declaring the government in contempt of Parliament, caused by the Conservative government's refusal to disclose the cost of previous justice legislation. While opposition parties claimed to be centred on transparency and parliamentary democracy, the Conservative leader began his campaign by asking voters to be wary of a possible coalition involving the BQ. Two themes stand out here. The first relates to the consequences of the Bloc taking part in a coalition government. Commentators urged the Liberals and NDP to reject this idea, which would open the door to irresponsible and unreasonable demands from Quebec:

> If a coalition that included the BQ actually did take power, the blackmail from the Bloc would be relentless. Every community of any size in Quebec would sense its chance to get a new, NHL-sized hockey rink; every crumbling highway bridge in the province might be rehabbed courtesy of taxpayers in the rest of the country. Every sugaring-off festival might become the proud recipient of a federal sponsorship grant. Contracts to build new navy ships, agreements to service new fighter jets, subsidies for inefficient farms and businesses also would be on the table (*National Post*, 25 March 2011, A14).

The second recurring theme is the inability to form a majority government and make important (and controversial) decisions while the BQ holds approximately 50 of Quebec's 75 seats (Daly 2011, A17). Therefore, the BQ was primarily responsible for the increase in minority governments since the 2004 elections: "Important but contentious legislation languished for lack of support from opposition parties," wrote John Ibbitson in the *Globe and Mail* (2011a, F1). Worse still, Andrew Potter, national news editor of the *Ottawa Citizen*, stated that support for the BQ illustrated behaviour troubling for democracy and toxic to politics: "The Bloc Québécois is now supported by what is essentially an ethnic voting block. Ethnic voting blocks are bad enough in any democracy—when people vote according to their race, language, or tribe, rational public policy becomes extremely difficult. But when that block has also decided to abstain from any role in the national government, the effect is absolutely toxic" (A11).

Others suggested rather that the presence of the BQ in Ottawa demonstrated Quebecers' withdrawal from federal issues as well as their desire to always demand more without actually wanting to participate in Canadian politics (Simpson 2011a, A19; *Montreal Gazette*, 30 March 2011, A20). Given the extreme difficulty, if not impossibility, of making political gains in Quebec (Ibbitson 2011b), the Conservative Party should simply turn its back on this province:

> The Tories may be finally resorting to the strategy advocated by political scientist Peter Brimelow in 2005: "While Quebec is at the centre of every major government decision ... the natural conservative tendencies of [English Canada] will continue to be frustrated. For the Canadian Right, the road to power lies not through Quebec, but around it." Former Harper advisor John Weissenberger advised the same course in 2004: "An Ontario-West electoral strategy is no longer laughable. With 201 of 308 seats ... it's entirely rational and ... a potential winner" (Kheiriddin 2011a, A16).

Up until mid-campaign, the feelings expressed towards the BQ in print media were negative and defeatist: the party would win just as many seats; this illustrated the disengagement of many Quebec voters vis-à-vis Canadian politics; they behaved like spoiled children, demanding everything without giving anything in return;

the BQ prevented the forming of a Conservative majority government; perhaps it would simply be better to stop trying to woo this ungrateful electorate. The tone changed when polls began to show an unexpected rise in NDP support following the French-language leaders' debate. Even more surprising was a survey conducted by the polling firm Angus-Reid during the debate showing that voters enjoyed the performances of Gilles Duceppe and Jack Layton equally (Angus-Reid 2011a). This increase in support for the NDP was accompanied by a sharp decline in support for the BQ (see Figure 1).

The perception of Quebec voters changed dramatically in the anglophone press. Some themes were recurring. The first was the hope that a federalist party would win the majority of seats in Quebec for the first time since the BQ emerged in 1993. In a burst of enthusiasm, the *Ottawa Citizen*'s Kelly Egan wrote, "The NDP are on the verge of doing something magical in Quebec. Giving us our country back." Adding that the BQ was on the verge of being marginalized, she exploded with joy: "Hallelujah! Good riddance to dem bums. One can only hope this pesky genie is back in the bottle for a very long time. In fact, throw the bottle out to sea" (2011, C1). The strong support for the NDP was seen as reflecting Quebecers'

Figure 1: Evolution of Voting Intentions in Quebec, 2011

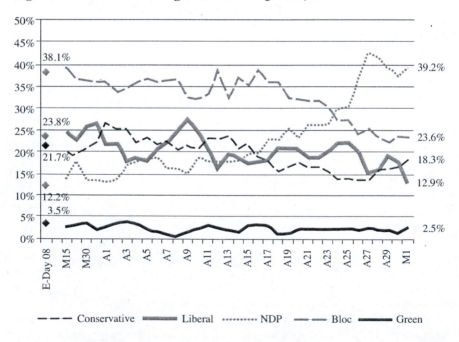

Source: Nanos (2011).

desire to enter into a genuine dialogue with the national community. Quebec would once again demonstrate both a sound and credible presence in the Canadian arena (Kennedy 2011, A16; Anderson 2011).

The second type of perception concerns possible reasons for this change, pointing to Duceppe's participation in the 17 April convention of the Parti Québécois (PQ). Duceppe delivered a speech reiterating the issues at the heart of the BQ electoral platform: sovereignty and the likelihood of holding another referendum in the event that the PQ won the provincial election. The *Toronto Star*'s Chantal Hébert wrote: "It is no coincidence that the New Democrats took their biggest leap in the polls on the heels of last weekend's Parti québécois convention and Duceppe's fiery call to arms to his fellow sovereignists" (2011, A6; see also Radwanski 2011, A14). The NDP had managed to convince the "soft nationalists" to support it, for the most part addressing the progressive social concerns of Bloc voters (Kheiriddin 2011b, A4; Simpson 2011b, A21). Voters' disaffection thus marked a return to the traditional left/right axis at the expense of the divide on constitutional issues (Watson 2011, A13). The perspective linked the two main arguments: increasing participation in federal politics because the NDP adopted positions close to the concerns of Quebec voters.

This way of thinking was well illustrated by William Johnson in the *Ottawa Citizen*: "Layton's pitch, fundamentally, is that Quebeckers are wasting their vote on the Bloc when they can get exactly the same policies from a Canada-wide party that can hope someday to form the government or be part of a governing coalition" (2011, A15). In short, during the last two weeks of the campaign, the press celebrated the BQ's fall in support. For commentators, that fall reflected Quebec voters' fatigue vis-à-vis Duceppe's uncreative campaign, decreased sovereignist fervour, and renewed interest in being part of the Canadian political system.

Unsurprisingly, then, many commentators cheered the election results—the BQ's representation reduced to four seats, 45 fewer seats than it held in the October 2008 election. The evidence was clear: it was possible to win a majority government without Quebec: "With the Bloc sweeping up votes in Quebec, English Canada elected only minority governments in the last three elections. Now, the rest of Canada won't be party to the whims of Quebec voters, where issues like Quebec separatism and multiculturalism have long fragmented the electorate" (*National Post*, 4 May 2011, A3). The *Globe and Mail*'s 3 May editorial set a tone that would be shared almost unanimously by the anglophone press: "The Bloc Québécois is effectively extinct, its leader defeated, its approach to federal politics rebuked. Three in four Quebeckers cast a vote for federalist parties. It may be a protest vote, a vote for the charisma and the nationalist-friendly promises of Jack Layton. But still, after years of Bloc obstructionism, Quebeckers are expressing a desire to participate in the affairs of their nation – of Canada" (2011)

Other commentators used equally celebratory terms to declare the BQ dead (Harper 2011, A4), destroyed (*Victoria Times Colonist* 2011, A16; Ibbitson 2011, A17), annihilated (Elliott 2011, A10), close to extinction (*Saskatoon Star Phoenix*

2011, A8), and having suffered a mortal blow (*Winnipeg Free Press* 2011). Layton was seen as deserving Canadians' gratitude for bringing stability to Parliament and strengthening national unity (Mandryk 2011, B10). Some looked forward to the support of an overwhelming majority of Quebec voters for federalist parties, showing that the BQ could not be considered the only legitimate voice for Quebec in Ottawa: "It does mean that Quebeckers, weary of the tired sovereignist games, are once again prepared to explore a federalist route to Ottawa. This is very good news for Canada and for Quebec" (Stevens 2011, A12). Some considered the strong vote for the NDP an expression of the will of Quebecers to work with other Canadians (Sallot 2011, A15), starting a new national conversation ensuring that Quebec once again had influence in Canadian politics (Panetta 2011, A4); others pointed out that Quebecers had overwhelmingly chosen to find themselves outside government (Braid 2011, A5).

The BQ's poor performance was considered good news because it not only eliminated an embarrassing political player from federal politics but also represented "a setback for the PQ" (Hamilton 2011, A8). However, the *Toronto Star's* Andrew Chung believed it would be a mistake to think that Quebec voters had become infatuated with the NDP. The shift should rather be interpreted as a protest vote (Chung 2011, A12) and a refusal to participate. Don Macpherson shared this perception of Quebec voters: "In switching from the Bloc to the New Democrats, it has exchanged representation in one opposition party for another, from one that demands everything to another that promises everything" (Macpherson 2011, A23). In short, the celebration was tempered by scepticism of optimistic interpretations.

Yet even in Quebec, it was tempting to see in the election results a reinvestment by Quebecers in Canadian politics. For example, a few days before the election, Denis Saint-Martin, a former adviser to Paul Martin and a political scientist at the Université de Montréal, interpreted the rise in support for the NDP in the polls as Quebecers' renewed interest in federalism. He wrote in *Le Devoir*: "One hypothesis is that current support for the NDP is a sign of a possible thawing in Quebec for Canadian federalism. Quebec federalists are not necessarily disappointed with federalism per se. Rather, they are disappointed with the Liberals and Conservatives having nothing to say on the identity issues that concern citizens" (Saint-Martin 2011, my translation). Saint-Martin also predicted that a strong NDP deputation could affect the dynamics of party politics in Ottawa and, inevitably, the federal-provincial relations dependent on them. Michel Seymour, a philosopher at the University of Montreal and former chair of the BQ's citizenship committee, also played with the idea of "winning back" Canada. Indeed, two days after the election, he wrote that by "supporting the NDP, Quebecers are saying that they would once again like to reach an agreement within Canada" (Seymour 2011, my translation). Finally, in a public statement, Quebec Premier Jean Charest maintained that the change represented Quebecers' desire to reinvest in the country's affairs (Gouvernement du Québec 2011).

A MOST PECULIAR CAMPAIGN

What's it all about? We should be cautious in concluding that in the 2011 election an overwhelmingly large number of Quebecers decided overnight to fully participate in the Canadian federation. Here it seems appropriate to recall five elements that contextualize the particular dynamic of the "orange wave."

First, nothing justified the general election apart from strategic considerations. The campaign did not focus on any major societal issue such as foreign policy, economic policies, health, or culture. It was primarily a way to end the constant conflicts that arose in the House of Commons between the minority Conservative government and the other parties who constantly threatened to defeat the government. The election's goal was to form a majority government—an appealing prospect for Conservatives because of the danger of a possible coalition of opposition parties—or to re-elect a minority government. In early 2011, the BQ's performance found favour with francophone voters, who showed more confidence in Gilles Duceppe (37 percent) than in Jack Layton (27 percent) (Léger Marketing 2011a). There was no reason to believe the election would show any difference.

Second, the federal government and the Conservative Party made no attempt to feed Quebec voters' dissatisfaction. Unlike the 2004 election, and less so than in the 2006 election, there was no sponsorship scandal (the Quebec Liberal Party lost 10 percentage points in votes cast in 2004), no cuts to spending on culture, no central issues like health care financing (as in 2008) (Gidengil et al. 2011, 161-4). In short, there was nothing to fuel resentment vis-à-vis the Canadian federal government.

Third, the BQ was unable to come up with any new material. Instead, the party seemed content to simply repeat the same arguments used since its creation: it exclusively defended Quebec's interests, and it promoted sovereignty. However, one cannot blame the BQ for not taking specific and comprehensive positions on the major political, social, cultural, and economic challenges facing Quebec (and Canada). The BQ platform, a 195-page document in 23 chapters, covered the party's vision across the board, on official languages, economic development, public finance, Indigenous nations, environmental policies, Canadian foreign policy, globalization, and international trade. The document attacked the policies of the Harper government: the Conservative Party is mentioned 180 times and the prime minister's name appears 36 times. The BQ sought to distinguish itself from Michael Ignatieff whose name appears 12 times, the Liberal Party three times and Liberal actions approximately 30 times. Surprisingly, the NDP and its leader aren't mentioned once (Bloc Québécois 2011).

One theme that emerged during the campaign was the need to prevent the formation of a Conservative majority government. As support for the PQ declined during the campaign, Gilles Duceppe sympathized with the PQ's cause, saying that the election of a strong contingent of Bloc members would be followed by the election of a PQ government with wind in its sails—thus destroying the idea that the Bloc formed an umbrella coalition of federalist and sovereignist nationalists dissatisfied with other parties. Thus, in this election, the BQ campaign brought little that was new to the partisan landscape.

Fourth, one must rely on the strong sense of disillusionment that accompanies politics. Indeed, the vast majority of Quebecers (87 percent according to a survey conducted in late May 2010) expressed their disappointment, weariness, and impatience with all political leaders (Gagnon 2010), a feeling significantly more pronounced in Quebec than in the rest of Canada. Although only one-third of Canadians truly connected with the federal parties, while large proportions of respondents held feelings of mistrust, scepticism, and even cynicism towards politics, "only" a third of voters belonged to the group of disillusioned or cynical citizens. Another third were rather sceptical, while being satisfied with the political options offered (Angus Reid 2011b). Since the survey included Quebec respondents, we can reasonably assume that the level of disappointment and cynicism was lower in the rest of Canada than in Quebec. Such negative feelings towards politics provided fertile ground for a protest vote. This disaffection helped in the rediscovery of Jack Layton, who led a less aggressive and more positive campaign than his opponents.

Fifth, we must not forget that a vast number of voters had grown weary of the BQ. A week before the elections, even though 52 percent of Quebecers said that they felt the BQ was useful to Ottawa, one-third considered it useless (Turbide 2011). A post-election survey conducted by Léger Marketing for *Le Devoir* showed that although there were several reasons voters chose the NDP, the three main ones were the desire for change (45 percent), the desire to prevent the formation of a majority Conservative government (34 percent), and the desire to end the BQ's power (33 percent). The same reasons were identified among former Bloc voters who supported the NDP, 50 percent of them saying they primarily wanted to prevent a Conservative majority, 41 percent saying they were tired of the other parties and wanted a change, and 33 percent saying it was time to support a party other than the BQ (Léger Marketing 2011b, 7-8).

In short, it seems unwise to argue that Quebecers have chosen to participate in Canadian governance by opting for a pan-Canadian party. Instead, they jumped on the bandwagon of another political party that had no chance of forming a government. Moreover, 83.5 percent of voters supported a party other than the Conservative Party, thus voluntarily and knowingly endeavouring to exclude them from majority power. Indeed, nobody ever doubted the re-election of a Conservative government. The question was, until the very end, if the government would win a majority of seats in the House of Commons. Quebec voters wanted to prevent the election of a majority government, and a good portion of them chose to transfer their support to the NDP to achieve this end. The result was that the NDP managed to elect more members even than during the historic breakthrough of the Bloc in 1993. However, the NDP's influence on federal-provincial dynamics is almost non-existent. Quebec's vote, for the most part, represented a protest: disenchantment with existing parties, dissatisfaction with Quebec's exclusion from federal policies, a desire for change.

A CANADIAN CHOICE?

Quebec was not at the heart of the political debates of the 2011 election. It would be premature to conclude that the BQ's quasi-extinction reflected that Quebec nationalism is running out of steam, replaced by a greater commitment to Canada. Instead, Quebec nationalism, for those who do not deny their participation in Canada, manifests itself differently, in particular through specific expectations regarding Canadian federalism, a certain notion of the role that Quebec should play, an opposition that is perceived only as centralist, and sensitivities surrounding Quebec's distinctive character. Nationalism, which should not be confused with the ups and downs of the sovereignist movement, has been present throughout Quebec's history and is characterized by stronger identification with Quebec than with Canada and stronger support for the Quebec government's role than for that of the Canadian state. As for the sovereignists, a good number of them continued to support the BQ. Moreover, a post-election survey showed that 55 percent of BQ voters believed that it was the best party to defend the interest of Quebec, while 36 percent did so because the party was in favour of the independence of Quebec (Léger Marketing 2011b, 10).

The BQ remained the second choice of voters, significantly ahead of the Conservatives and Liberals, and won nearly a quarter of the vote. The BQ used its presence in Ottawa not only to prepare the way for sovereignty and facilitate negotiations after winning a referendum: it also sought to provide a showcase for Quebec's national aspirations. Under the recurring term "the will to defend Quebec's interests," it served as a bulwark against the federal government's centralized interests, real or imagined. One must not underestimate the symbolic and structural consequences for the Quebec electorate of 20 years of the Bloc being in Ottawa. One could make the assumption that it helped reinforce two ideas that have now become mantras of Quebec politics and performance measurement indicators for other political parties.

The first idea suggests that there is a rift between the aspirations, values, and interests of Quebec and those of the rest of Canada, presented as an undifferentiated whole. Thus, all federal policies are analyzed through an oversimplified and distorted lens, focused on Quebec's interests. However, federal principles refer to two complementary dimensions: the recognition of and respect for the autonomy of the federated entities, but also the need for federal solidarity in respect to common political objectives (Rocher 2009). The BQ, like all provincial political actors (not to mention much of the intelligentsia), paid particular attention to the first factor and ignored the second. While these views have traditionally been shared by provincial political parties—in fact, they have been consistently shared in Quebec politics since the end of World War II—they were transferred to Ottawa two decades ago.

The second idea, a corollary of the first, is that Pan-Canadian federal parties enter potentially in conflict of legitimacy vis-à-vis the wishes expressed by the provincial political forces and, emblematically, by the Quebec National Assembly. During the patriation of the Constitution in 1981–82, 74 of the 75 Quebec Liberal MPs supported Pierre Elliott Trudeau's project, even though all the parties represented at the National Assembly voted unanimously against the exclusion of Quebec from the constitutional agreement. This opposition between the will of federalist MPs and autonomist MPs in Quebec led to the assertion that the legitimately elected federal representatives of Quebec approved the initiative and, at the same time, that Quebec was not and never had been excluded. With the arrival of the BQ, this equation was no longer possible. The "Quebec voice" could be coherent—by imposing a single view and valuing a single school of thought. In addition, the Bloc's presence has ensured that the province's political agenda has been echoed in the House of Commons, be it federalist (Quebec Liberal Party) or sovereignist (PQ). The "sounding-board" effect is now anchored in the imagination of Quebecers and expected from Quebec representatives in all political parties.

It is too early to conclude that a "re-Canadianization" of the Quebec electorate has now occurred, at least as an important variable that could explain the NDP victory, or to predict with certainty the complete disappearance of the Bloc. We have known for a long time that francophone Quebecers are less committed to Canada than other Canadians, including anglophone Quebecers and allophones. A 2009 survey conducted by the Association for Canadian Studies showed that Quebec residents relate the most to their province (at 44 percent) and the least to Canada (20 percent). As Table 1 shows, the ability of Quebecers to identify with the rest of Canada is only slightly higher than their ability to relate to the rest of the world (17 percent) (Association for Canadian Studies 2009).

In addition, the ability to identify with Canada is two to three times stronger in other regions of Canada than in Quebec. This is why it is not surprising that the Quebec identity is most pronounced within Quebec. Table 2 illustrates this reality.

A survey conducted in 2010 indicated that 60 percent of Quebecers have a predominantly Quebec identity (25.7 percent define themselves as "Québécois only" and 34.4 percent as "Québécois first"). This identity is even more pronounced among francophones (70 percent), while it is much less pronounced among anglophones (14 percent) and allophones (25 percent) (Association for Canadian Studies 2010). This result reflects a deepening trend that shows no sign of disappearing. Indeed, a compilation of surveys conducted since 1998, which asked Quebecers how they define themselves, witnessed a growing paramountcy of the Quebec identity while the Canadian identity lost 10 percentage points and "equally Canadian and Québécois" lost 5 points (see Figure 2) (Lisée 2011).

Table 1: Idenfication – Percentages according to Region

Q: With which of these groups do you identify the most?

	The World (%)	Canada (%)	Your Province (%)	Your City (%)	Your Linguistic Community (%)	Your Ethnic Group or Visible Minority (%)	None (%)	I Don't Know (%)
Atlantic	7.0	64.0	13.0	2.0	2.0	1.0	7.0	5.0
QC	16.9	20.0	43.9	8.9	3.9		4.7	1.7
ON	13.7	61.1	6.7	9.1	1.2	1.0	3.9	3.3
MB/SK	9.0	64.0	19.0	1.0	–	1.0	2.0	4.0
AB	16.0	53.8	17.3	5.1	0.6	0.6	5.8	0.6
BC	16.8	44.1	15.3	5.0	0.0	1.0	10.4	7.4
Total	14.3	48.6	19.1	7.0	1.6	0.7	5.4	3.2

Source: Association for Canadian Studies (2009).

Table 2: Identity Identification/Quebec

Q: There are different ways to describe yourself. Are you ...

	Francophones (%)	Anglophones (%)	Other (%)	Total (%)
Québécois only?	31.3	2.0	5.9	25.7
Québécois first, but also Canadian?	39.2	12.0	19.1	34.4
Both Québécois and Canadian?	19.5	21.0	25.7	20.4
Canadian first, but also Québécois?	7.2	45.0	20.4	12.1
Canadian only?	1.3	18.0	12.5	4.1
None of the above?	1.1	2.0	15.1	2.9
I prefer to not respond.	0.3	0.0	1.3	0.4

Source: Association for Canadian Studies (2010).

Figure 2: Quebec Identity, 1998–2010

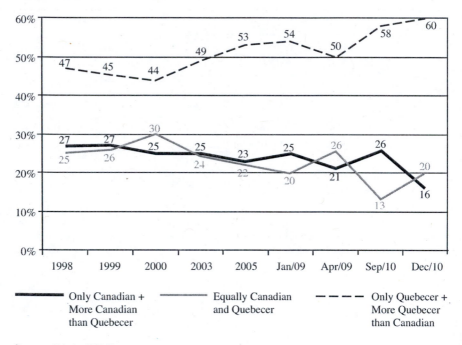

Source: Lisée (2011).

Within this context, one may wonder how it is possible to interpret the May 2011 election results as a dramatic reversal of such a strong trend.

Quebecers' relative disconnect with Canada is also reflected by their strong loyalty to their provincial government. Thus, in times of conflict between the federal government and the provinces, Quebecers differ from other Canadians in the sense that they are twice as likely as those in other provinces (62 percent to 32 percent) to support their provincial government (see Table 3).

Quebecers expect their voice to be strong and meaningful in Ottawa, and previously the BQ took on that role. Now it is up to the NDP to continue to do so. On top of their unwillingness to participate in governing, their participation is through an opposition party—a position that reflects Quebecers' weary cynicism and disillusionment with Canada, if not their self-exclusion from power.

Table 3: Loyalty over Federal-Provincial Conflict, by Regions

Q: When there is a conflict of interests between the federal government and the provinces, would you support your province, Canada or neither?

	Canada (%)	My Province (%)	I Can't Decide (%)	I Prefer to Not Respond (%)
Atlantic	40.0	32.0	25.0	3.0
QC	22.5	61.9	13.1	2.5
ON	51.1	20.6	25.4	2.9
MB/SK	40.0	26.0	23.0	11.0
AB	43.9	29.0	26.5	0.6
BC	44.6	19.3	31.7	4.5
Total	41.1	32.4	23.1	3.4

Source: Association for Canadian Studies (2009).

CHALLENGES FACED BY THE CONSERVATIVES AND THE NDP

On 2 May 2011, many Quebecers did not vote for the BQ, but they rejected the Liberals even more strongly and did not support the Conservatives. However, the Conservatives still managed to get their majority, showing that they no longer need to rely on the Quebec vote to govern Canada. As Margaret Wente noted in the *Globe and Mail* shortly after the election, "Mr. Harper has forged a historic new alliance between the West and Ontario, and he didn't need Quebec to win. Quebeckers' mass infatuation with the NDP may not last longer than snow in April, but their ability to hold federal governments to ransom may be gone for good" (Wente 2011, A21). The addition of seats to the House of Commons in the next election (fifteen to Ontario, six each to Alberta and British Columbia, and only three more to Quebec) will only help to strengthen this reality. Only the Liberals and the NDP, given the distribution of their supporters across Canada, need significant parliamentary representation from Quebec to be in a position to form a government.

If they want to preserve national unity, all federal parties will now have to take on the perilous profession of a tightrope walker and learn how to walk the rope.

Across Canada, the Conservatives increased their support by only 2 percent from the 2008 elections. They stayed afloat in British Columbia and the Prairies, made some progress in the Atlantic Provinces; but most importantly, they won 22 additional seats in Ontario (an increase of 5 percent of support) and lost five ridings in Quebec (a 5 percent loss). It may be tempting for the party to guarantee another majority by governing so as to strengthen its base, particularly in Ontario, while excluding Quebec. In so doing, the Conservatives would reinforce the disconnect between Quebec voters and Canada and deepen the traditional divide between Quebec and the federal government. Presently, however, instead of demonstrating an openness to including Quebec, they seem to be moving in the opposite direction. Although some federal decisions have been well received in Quebec, such as the decision to settle the dispute with the province involving compensation for the sales tax harmonization, or the project to build a new Champlain Bridge, other decisions have raised strong opposition, among them the abolition of the long-gun registry; Bill C-10 on crime; the appointment of a unilingual auditor; the stop and go surrounding the fight against greenhouse gas emissions; and the rebuilding Canada's identity around monarchial and military symbols. The growing number of policies opposed by Quebec political actors can only alienate a significant portion of Quebec voters from this party. More importantly, the decisions must strengthen the feeling of many that there is little to expect from Canadian federalism and that the Quebec government is the only credible representative of Quebec's interests. The federal-provincial tensions, though normal in any federation, can only become more pronounced. Prime Minister Harper would be well advised instead to avoid crises, restrict confrontations with Quebec, and at least give the impression of governing on behalf of all Canadians.

The challenges facing the NDP seem even more daunting. In the 2011 election, in terms of percentage, they were able to make gains in all regions except in Newfoundland and Labrador. Those gains were made, for the most part, at the expense of the Liberals. In Quebec, the NDP may fall victim to its own success. The party must overcome three obstacles while working towards one goal.

The first obstacle involves Jack Layton's successor: Thomas Mulcair needs to demonstrate the talent necessary to win the support of Quebecers. He also needs to bridge the gap between those New Democrats who historically built the party and those who have only just converted.

The second obstacle, equally as significant, will be translating in Parliament the commitments made during the 2006 NDP Convention. The "Sherbrooke Declaration" recognized Quebec's national character, endorsed the principle of asymmetrical federalism, and insisted on respecting the jurisdiction recognized by the Constitution. To maintain its newly acquired support, the NDP will need to show greater sensitivity to the needs of Quebec without alienating its traditional electorate that tends to value a more assertive federal party. In other words, the NDP will have to find the philosopher's stone that turns lead into gold.

The third obstacle will be for the party to unite the left and centre-left and to stand as a credible alternative to the Liberal Party and eventually become an alternative to the Conservative Party. As the official opposition, the NDP is uniquely positioned to face the Conservative Party, which monopolizes the centre-right. The NDP's positions, which are more in line with Quebec's many progressive policies, can help solidify the support obtained in the last election.

Finally, the federal election that resulted in the unprecedented "orange wave" could provide a unique opportunity to reconcile, if possible, the two axes of Canadian politics—the one that separates the left and the right, and the other that often opposes nation-building projects between Canada and Quebec. In order to maintain the support of its newly acquired electorate, in a context where the official opposition can only marginally influence the Conservative government, the NDP will have to find a creative way to square the circle.

CONCLUSION

New Democrats were able to channel the protest vote towards Stephen Harper's Conservative government by focusing on Quebec voters' weariness with the BQ. We cannot conclude, then, that the 43 percent vote for the NDP illustrates support for the party's more "progressive" positions. Rather, a post-election survey shows that Quebec support for the party came from all ideological backgrounds: 35 percent of NDP voters considered themselves as centre, centre-right, or right—a significantly higher proportion than Bloc voters (23 percent). Bloc voters perceived themselves as being more centre-left or left (48 percent) than those who supported the NDP (29 percent) (see Table 4).

Table 4: Left-Right Ideological Spectrum/Percentage by Political Party

Q: From an ideological standpoint, do you consider yourself to be ...?

	Total (%)	LPC (%)	PC (%)	NDP (%)	Bloc (%)
Right	5	5	14	3	2
Centre-right	14	12	33	11	4
Centre	22	37	18	21	17
Centre-left	20	22	2	21	31
Left	8	2	0	8	17
I don't know	26	14	27	29	25
I prefer to not respond	6	9	6	6	5

Source: Léger Marketing (2011c, 10).

The same survey showed that 60 percent of Quebecers (and 67 percent of Quebec francophones) did not believe that the election results had helped Quebecers to connect with other Canadians (Léger Marketing 2011c, 12). In short, the NDP's electoral base is, for the moment, fragile.

The May 2011 election illustrates the large divide that exists between Quebec voters and Conservative policies: Quebec was the province that most clearly rejected the Harper government, with Conservatives receiving only 16.5 percent of the vote, far short of the 39.6 percent achieved across Canada. Once the Conservative government meets the expectations of its voters, establishes the policies announced in its election platform, and consolidates its support in the areas where its presence is strong or is likely to become strong (e.g., Ontario), the divide between Quebec voters and the federal government is likely to widen. And with it, the sense of powerlessness and marginalization felt in Quebec will further increase. The question is whether Canada isolates Quebec, or whether the latter, not feeling at home in Stephen Harper's "new Canada," further distinguishes itself.

Federal issues such as intergovernmental agreements, joint-program funding, and fiscal transfers involve the federal government and the provinces more than the opposition parties who sit in the House of Commons. However, when these issues are discussed in Ottawa, a significant number of Quebec voters will expect the NDP to play the role filled by the BQ between 1993 and 2011. Quebecers' strong loyalty to their provincial government, combined with their weak identification with Canada, cannot help but pose a challenge to the NDP, which must also represent the preferences and interests of its supporters outside Quebec. The party's failure to reflect Quebec's priorities would have serious consequences with many Quebecers, while doing so could generate distrust in the NDP in the rest of Canada. The NDP's election wins in Quebec could turn into a Pyrrhic victory not only for the party but also for political stability in Canada. It is too early yet to sing a eulogy for the Bloc Québécois.

REFERENCES

Anderson, B. 2011. "How This 'Unnecessary Election' Has Changed Canada for the Better." *Globe and Mail*, 1 May.

Angus Reid. 2011a. *Élections fédérales canadiennes 2011. Les Québécois accordent une bonne note à Duceppe et Layton pour le débat en français*. http://www.angus-reid.com/wp-content/uploads/2011/04/2011.04.16_Debate_FRA.pdf.

—2011b. *Élections fédérales canadiennes 2011. La plupart des Canadiens voient les élections avec méfiance, scepticisme et cynisme*. http://www.angus-reid.com/wp-content/uploads/2011/04/2011.04.25_Segment_FR.pdf.

Association for Canadian Studies (Association d'études canadiennes). 2009. *L'état de l'union canadienne : Est-ce que les attitudes à l'égard du fédéralisme sont en train de changer?* www.acs-aec.ca/pdf/polls/12487948486642-FR.doc.

—. 2010. *L'identité du Québec en 2011 : les attachements, l'identité et la diversité*. http://www.acs-aec.ca/pdf/polls/Quebec%20Identity%202011-FR.doc.

Bélanger, É., and R. Nadeau. 2011. "The Bloc Québécois : Capsized by the Orange Wave." In *The Canadian Federal Election of 2011*, edited by J.H. Pammett and C. Dornan, 111-37. Toronto: Dundurn.

Bloc Québécois. 2011. *Parlons QC. Plateforme électorale – élections 2011*. Montréal, Bloc québécois.

Braid, D. 2011. "Harper Earns Majority His Way." *Calgary Herald*, 3 May, A5.

Chung, A. 2011. "Why Quebecers Switched Parties en bloc." *Toronto Star*, 4 May, A12.

Daly, J. 2011. "Wasteful Election." *Vancouver Province*, 30 March, A17.

Egan, K. 2011. "A Chance to Get Our Country Back." *Ottawa Citizen*, 27 April, C1.

Elliott, H. 2011. "Democracy Doing Its Job." *Hamilton* Spectator, 3 May, A10.

Gagnon, K. 2010. "Les électeurs du Québec sont découragés, rebutés, désabusés." *La Presse*, 7 May. http://www.lapresse.ca/actualites/quebec-canada/politique-quebecoise/201005/06/01-4277983-les-electeurs-du-quebec-sont-decourages-rebutes-desabuses.php.

Gidengil, E., N. Nevitte, A. Blais, J. Everitt, and P. Fournier 2011. *Dominance and Decline: Making Sense of Recent Canadian Elections*. Toronto: University of Toronto Press.

Globe and Mail. 2011. "Stephen Harper's Double Victory," 3 May, A26.

Gouvernement du Québec. 2011. Déclaration du premier ministre du Québec en réaction aux résultats des élections fédérales du 2 mai 2011, publié le 4 mai. http://www.noodls.com/viewNoodl/9905033/plq---parti-lib233ral-du-qu233bec/r233action-de-jean-charest-aux-233lections-f233d2.

Hamilton, G. 2011. "'Dirty' to Be in Power in Ottawa : That's Why Quebecers Voted for Teens and Absent Anglos." *National Post*, 4 May, A8.

Harper, T. 2011. "Harper Owes a Debt to Layton; New Democrat Wave Helps Split Anti-Tory Vote in Ontario." *Toronto Star*, 3 May, A4.

Hébert, Cl. 2011. "Why Quebec Voters Love Jack, Not Gilles." *Toronto Star*, 23 April, A6.

Ibbitson, J. 2011a. "Five Reasons Ottawa Is Turning You Off and Why You Should Get Over Them (and Vote)." *Globe and Mail*, 26 March, F1.

—. 2011b. "Bloc's Grip on Quebec Puts Province on the Outside Looking In: Ontario and B.C. Will Decide Who Governs Canada, not La Belle Province." *Globe and Mail*, 11 April. http://www.theglobeandmail.com/news/politics/ottawa-notebook/blocs-grip-on-quebec-puts-province-on-the-outside-looking-in/article613338/.

—. 2011c. "Centrist Compromise Spurs Tory Win; Voters Give High Marks to Harper for His Stewardship of the Economy." *Globe and Mail*, 3 May, A17.

Johnson, W. 2011. "How Jack Layton Courted Bloc Voters." *Ottawa Citizen*, 28 April, A15.

Kennedy, J. 2011. "An Election about Democracy." *Ottawa Citizen*, 30 April, A16.

Kheiriddin, T. 2011a. "Who Needs Quebec?" *National Post*, 29 March, A16.

—. 2011b. "Better Socialists than Separatists." *National Post*, 26 April A4.

Léger Marketing. 2011a. "La politiques provinciale et fédérale au Québec. Février 2011." 14 February. http://www.ledevoir.com/documents/pdf/sondage_federal13fev.pdf.

—. 2011b. "Sondage postélectoral." 7 May. http://www.ledevoir.com/documents/pdf/sondage_post_electoral.pdf.

—. 2011c. "Sondage post-électoral. Les lendemains des élections fédérales : perceptions et attentes." 10 May. http://www.acs-aec.ca/pdf/polls/Sondage%20post%20%C3%A9lectoral%2010%20mai%202011. pdf.

Lisée, J.-F. 2011. "La décanadianisation du Québec s'accélère." http://www2.lactualite.com/jean-francois-lisee/la-decanadianisation-du-quebec-saccelere/7024/.

Macpherson, D. 2011. "Quebec Opts into Canada, but We Do So Grudgingly and Maybe Temporarily – Exchanging One Opposition Party for Another." *Montreal Gazette*, 3 May, A23.

Mandryk, M. 2011. "Waking up Refreshed." *Regina Leader Post*, 3 May, B10.

Montreal Gazette. 2011. "Quebecers Want In? Don't Vote for the Bloc." 30 March, A20.

Nanos. 2011. *The Political Mood of Canadians*, FMC Annual Conference, 3 June. http://www.fcm.ca/Documents/presentations/2011/workshops/The_Political_Mood_of_Canadians_EN.pdf.

National Post. 2011. "Keep Separatists out of the Coalition." 25 March, A14.

—. 2011. "From Canada's Election." 4 May, A3.

Panetta, A. 2011. "Vote Could Mean Long-Term Change in Ottawa; NDP's Emerging Role in Quebec Will Alter the National Dynamic." *Waterloo Region Record*, 3 May, A4.

Potter, A. 2011. "Blame the Bloc: The Country Has Been Ungovernable Thanks to the Large Group of Parliamentarians Who Have Opted out of Canada." *Ottawa Citizen*, 31 March, A11.

Radwanski, A. 2011. "Why This Campaign Is Good for Democracy." *Globe and Mail*, 30 April, A14.

Rocher, F. 2009. "The Quebec-Canada Dynamic or the Negation of the Ideal of Federalism." In *Contemporary Canadian Federalism. Foundations, Traditions, Institutions*, edited by A.-G. Gagnon, 81-131. Toronto: University of Toronto Press.

Saint-Martin, D. 2011. "Que signifie la montée du NPD au Québec?" *Le Devoir*, 30 April.

Sallot, J. 2011. "The NDP Has Come a Long Way in Quebec." *Ottawa Citizen*, 3 May, A15.

Seymour, M. 2011. "Élections fédérales – Que s'est-il donc passé?" *Le Devoir*, 4 May.

Simpson, J. 2011a. "Quebec Separatism: Guess What'll Rear Its Ugly Head One More Time." *Globe and Mail*, 30 March, A19.

—. 2011b. "We Never Saw It Coming: The Old Face of Jack Layton Suddenly Seems New." *Globe and Mail*, 29 April, A21.

Star Phoenix. 2011. "Majority Gov't Needs to Serve All Canadians." 3 May, A8.

Stevens, G. 2011. "Canadians Realign the Political Landscape." *Canadian Charger*, 3 May, A12.

Turbide, M. 2011. "Le Bloc toujours utile à Ottawa." *La Presse*, 22 avril.

Victoria Times Colonist. 2011. "A Massive Shift in Parliament." 3 May, A16.

Watson, W. 2011. "A Ho-Hum Election Could Bring Big Changes." *Ottawa Citizen*, 26 April, A13.

Wente, M. 2011. "Here's Why Stephen Harper Really Won." *Globe and Mail*, 5 May, A21.

Winnipeg Free Press. 2011. "Brilliant Outcome." 3 May. http://www.winnipegfreepress.com/opinion/editorials/brilliant-outcome-canada-121142334.html.

6

INSTITUTIONAL REFORM

David E. Smith

The Crown may not immediately rush to mind in the context of the subject of institutional reform. Presumably this reticence is why Canada is still a monarchy — although Canadians do not like to think of themselves as subjects — and why there has never been a republican movement of any significance since the Rebellions of 1837. But with the 2012 celebrations marking the 60th anniversary of the queen's accession, Canadians were reminded of the monarchy. Elizabeth II now surpasses George III (who became king the year after the battle of the Plains of Abraham); she trails Victoria by only two years as the longest-reigning monarch in British history. Together, the three — George III, Victoria, and Elizabeth II — have ruled for 185 of Canada's 254-year history. Whatever one's constitutional sympathy, it is hard to ignore such persistence, an inclination the current government of Canada appears committed to promoting, as evident in the reinstitution of the designation "royal" for the Canadian navy, and in the edict from Ottawa that the sovereign's photograph be prominently displayed in chancelleries abroad and in government offices at home.

This comment hardly seems of sufficient interest, let alone importance, to mention in a volume exploring "the 'new' Canadian federal environment." Nonetheless, I see it as symbolic of a substantive change in the country's politics. "Symbolic" is the appropriate word because this perception of the Crown — its symbolism — is invariably invoked when the subject is raised. The reason why is easily explained: symbolism requires no interpretation; it is about ceremony and is largely visual. But there is another dimension to the Crown — the power or rule aspect — that civics courses say disappeared with the arrival of constitutional monarchy and responsible government but is in fact part of modern parliamentary government. I refer to the prerogative power of the Crown, normally exercised on advice of the first minister. Prerogative power remains significant in two areas of public policy: foreign relations (as in the 2010 Khadr decision, when the Supreme Court of Canada found Omar Khadr's rights violated but left the government to rectify the injury because of its prerogative in foreign relations), and what might be called the condition of Parliament. It is the latter I address here, and within that area I mention only the summoning, dissolution, and prorogation of Parliament. This last matter, prorogation, and in particular the events of 2008, are well known, and I do not intend to dissect the events or actions of the individuals involved—except to say this: the contrast between what occurred four years ago in Canada and decades-long practice in the United Kingdom (confirmed, I would add, when the present coalition government in London was formed) is eminently set down by a late colleague of mine in a letter (dealing with dissolution) written to *The Times* a quarter of a century ago:

> It is often argued in Britain that because there are no precedents for a royal refusal of a request to dissolve Parliament, the power to refuse is moribund. Surely ... the fact that acute controversy concerning the role of the Crown has been consistently avoided in the United Kingdom for more than a century is evidence, not that the Sovereign has been bound by convention invariably to follow advice of a government to dissolve Parliament, instead of seeking an alternative ministry, but that ... all ministers have been particularly scrupulous to shield the Sovereign from the necessity of making any debatable use of the royal discretion. (Heasman 1985)

If ever there was such constitutional sensitivity in Canada, that is no longer the case. The greater frequency of minority governments here than in the United Kingdom may be one explanation, since the pressure of governing increases when legislative majorities disappear. Yet discussions among party leaders in the United Kingdom following the general election in May 2010 did not involve the queen, until the prospective prime minister was invited to Buckingham Palace. The aura, experience, and independence of the sovereign from government in London contrasts with the absence of these characteristics for the governor general in Ottawa. The visibility of the sovereign is one of her strengths—just being there is enough. Arguably, the more visible Canada's governor general is, the more vulnerable he or she appears. Governors general must do something—charity, sports, arts, the North, the disadvantaged—to anchor themselves in the public's mind and in public life.

Events of the past several years have placed the governor general much in the public eye. It is one thing to recite Bagehot's trinity of rights due the sovereign: to be consulted, to encourage, and to warn; it is another for a governor general, enveloped by constitutional controversy and the focus of media attention, to make a decision that he or she knows will inevitably lead to public criticism. The most significant feature of the controversy in 2008 was that the governor general seemed relevant to the situation. The media and the public paid close attention to the issue as it developed, and at no time did the question of constitutional monarchy as Canada's form of government enter the debate. Tom Flanagan, who at the time advanced the argument (in the *Globe and Mail*) that "only voters have the right to decide on the [proposed Liberal-NDP] coalition," also acknowledged that it was "the Governor General, as protector of Canada's constitutional democracy, [who] should ensure the voters get [that] chance" (Flanagan 2009). Significantly too, no governor general's "party" emerged, although Michael Ignatieff's decision two years later—unprecedented in Canadian history—to press publicly for an extension to Michaëlle Jean's term as governor general hinted at what such advocacy might look like. Whether or not the prime minister's initiative to seek prorogation so early in a session, at the same time the opposition parties talked of forming a coalition to replace the government, constituted a parliamentary "crisis" remains an open question, although there is no doubt it was an uncommon occurrence. Of central importance, however, is that in controversial circumstances the governor general of the day acceded twice to requests of the first minister to prorogue Parliament. Constitutional choices are not just events from the past; their influence continues at all levels and all times. Recent precedents are no less compelling as guides to future decisions than precedents that arise out of actions of prime ministers a century ago.

One consequence of the election of 2011, which produced a majority government, is that the subject of the prerogative has disappeared from the daily news, but by no means for good. The episodic nature of the debate that accompanies the subject is part of its continuing importance. Canada is not a European country where political practice takes the form of multi-party or coalition government. If it were, then the matter of the Crown's powers would be less contentious than it is, because its exercise would not be perceived to benefit one party over another.

When Stephen Harper sought a candidate to replace Michaëlle Jean as governor general, he was reported to have established a "secret committee to search for candidates" who would possess constitutional knowledge and be non-partisan. Ned Franks, a constitutional authority, praised the "new" process and "recommended that it be made permanent in law" (Curry 2010). How that might be accomplished, he did not specify. Still, there was the sense that a precedent was being established and that henceforth the nomination of individuals with close partisan attachments to the government of the day would not in future be tolerated. From this perspective, the relationship between formal and political executives had to a degree altered, and in a manner quite different from countries where that relationship is in fact regulated by statute law. At the same time Canada's new governor general was being designated, Germany chose a new president through a "secret" election by a college of electors composed of members of the federal Parliament and of state representatives. Despite the institutional separation intended to discourage partisan influence, the presidential vote, according to the *New York Times*, was a "Test [for] Merkel's Ailing Coalition," one that the coalition survived: "Merkel's Pick Wins German Presidency" (Kullish 2010a, 2010b). No one in Germany appeared to find this manner of selecting the president problematic for the intrusion of partisan politics it permits, but then German presidents possess few of the prerogative powers that rest in the hands of Canada's governors general.

When the subject of the Crown arises as symbol, or in activities separate from Parliament, the current government demonstrates a regard and a heightened concern that some of its recent predecessors lacked. Think of Clarkson and Martin, or Schreyer and Trudeau. This is not true, however, when the subject is the Crown-in-Parliament. Think here, instead, of "the fixed election date fiasco, the questionable use of prorogation to avoid defeat, the misuse of the confidence convention by *both* the Martin and Harper governments ... the nonsensical debate over the legitimacy of coalitions and the disingenuous musings over whether a party must have the most seats to be called upon to form a government" (Benoit and Levy 2011). How is one to reconcile protestations of loyalty to the Crown, which under constitutional principles established as long ago as 1688 means the Crown-in-Parliament, with exhortations to Conservative supporters that the "party must fight ... against ... attacks on our *democratically elected government*" (emphasis added) or radio advertisements asserting that Stéphane Dion "thinks he can take power without asking you, the voter. This is Canada. Power must be earned, not taken" (Naumetz 2011).

Under the Canadian constitution there is no constituent power outside of Parliament. Nonetheless, politics today increasingly pits the people against Parliament, or more precisely, against the opposition in Parliament—to the opposition's disadvantage, it should be said, since the opposition is less "elected" than government and, by inference, less legitimate on that account. The extra-parliamentary dimension has always been an important part of Canadian politics, as a history of political parties makes clear. But it has never been as pervasive as now. Reasons external to Canadian developments may be cited for this change, the transformation in political communication an obvious example. That is a bigger topic than can be discussed here, but I do not want to ignore it and thereby suggest that what is happening in Canadian politics is solely the result of action by government.

Still, a homegrown reason that helps to explain the rise of the people is the extraordinary organizational activity that accompanied the creation of the Conservative Party of Canada (CPC). Its success at establishing a mass membership base and the financial security this has provided are familiar topics in the media, in part because of the edge they give the Conservatives over their competitors. Phrases like "permanent campaign" and "the arms race that never stops" convey the sense of an external force that propels politics from outside of Parliament. How many times in the new session have MPs been told that bills before them "were part of the Conservative election platform" and that the majority government has "a clear mandate"? Opposition parties cannot keep up. The parliamentary method, Lord (Gilbert) Campion, former clerk of the House of Commons at Westminster, 1937-48, once said, is "to control government by talk" (Campion 1952). Canadian opposition parties might be disposed to turn that maxim around and say the parliamentary method has become control of talk by government. Yet it would be a mistake to think that Parliament's problem today is the consequence of this or any other government alone. The fact is, no one seems interested in, or listens to, legislative debate anymore.

I am writing a book on opposition in Canadian politics, and I could, at some length, offer multiple reasons for this parlous condition. However, I will limit my analysis to one cause but remind you that there is more than one. The feature I single out for discussion here is officers of Parliament, particularly their growing numbers and extended reach. Paul Thomas has written that officers of Parliament are "independent, accountability agencies created first to assist Parliament in holding ministers and the bureaucracy accountable and, second, to protect various kinds of rights of individual Canadians" (Thomas 2003). While that description may sound helpful, the interposition of officers of Parliament in the operation of responsible government raises the question of whether their activities strengthen or undermine that foundational principle of the Constitution. To take a specific example: Does the work of the auditor general assist the Public Accounts Committee of the Commons, or does it supplant the committee? Independence and accountability are contradictory principles. Are ministerial responsibility and accountability any less contradictory? Do we have here the nub of a conflict of constitutional proportions? In Canada in the past decade, accountability has prevailed, with deleterious consequences for legislative opposition. Consider the response in 2011 of Information Commissioner Suzanne Legault to a court ruling on access to Cabinet records that found against openness: "Canadians should be concerned," she said. "As it stands, the access-to-information law is the only way Canadians can ensure they can hold the government to account and are able to participate in the democratic process in a meaningful way" (quoted in de Souza and Minsky [2011]). Whither, one might ask, the opposition in Parliament?

The creation of officers of Parliament has become a tactic in political conflict. The Federal Accountability Act, which provided for several new officers (parliamentary budget officer, lobbying and integrity commissioners), is a prime example. The relationship between ministers and officers, and between officers and Parliament — whose agents they are — is fraught with uncertainty. The essential feature that distinguishes the officers has broadened, in the view of some observers, from protection against political influence to separation from Parliament.[1] Controversy in 2010 and 2011 surrounding the integrity commissioner (Christine Ouimet) saw the auditor-general "castigate" her for "failing to do her job," followed by seven officers sending a joint letter to Commons committees in which they diplomatically observed that "it is timely to examine whether the issues reported by the Auditor-General could have been identified [by parliamentarians] sooner" (Ditchburn 2011). The interim auditor-general John Wiersema declared that "the public is waiting far too long to be warned about significant risks in the drugs they take" — an opinion opposition critics and the *Globe and Mail* pounced on, accusing the government of toying with patients' health and safety. Liberal health care critic Hedy Fry was

---

[1] It needs to be said, of course, that this is not solely a Canadian phenomenon; Bruce Ackerman of Yale Law School has written about what he calls "constrained parliamentarianism" to describe the postwar practice, in Westminster-style legislatures and elsewhere, of "insulating sensitive functions from political control" (Ackerman 1997).

quoted as saying, "It is taking the Harper government years to let … the public know of safety risks involving prescription drugs" (Scoffield 2011). A reversal of the principal-agent relationship appears to be occurring, one that in the opinion of legal scholar John Whyte has "constitutional weight":

> With respect to many of the functions of governments we have created every form of parliamentary watchdog office, parliamentary information office and parliamentary policy office. Implicit in this dramatic development is distrust of the good faith of government in implementing legislated policies, and in forthrightness of government in informing legislators what they are doing and what they are achieving, and in helping legislators meet their responsibility for, and their ability to grasp, details about the operations of the government. The growth of independent legislative officers from one perspective might be seen as the refinement of legislative oversight of government but, in reality, it represents a significant shift in how political accountability is achieved in our constitutional system. This system of specialist review represents a new element of separation of powers—one that has acquired constitutional weight, at least in the sense of constitutional practice. (Whyte 2011)[2]

Duff Conacher, of *Democracy Watch*, concurs: "We have these watchdogs over government accountability, but the laws that govern them mean that they cannot be held accountable" (Nitoslawski 2011). Indeed, the media have fallen into the habit of referring to officers of Parliament as czars, arguably peculiar nomenclature for protectors of rights. Even more curious is the Ipsos-Reid finding in 2004 that Sheila Fraser was 'immensely trusted by Canadians because "she ha[d] no vested interest and [was] viewed by Canadians as being above politics" (Chase 2004).

Rule by the non-elected expert, election as a disqualification for gaining trust: once again, the implication of this development for elected politicians, especially in opposition, is immense. Politicians are without influence because the political contest is no longer perceived as taking place across the aisle but (in Whyte's words) "between executive government and the more neutral, more specialist and more normatively driven agencies of accountability—the courts, regulatory agencies and the oversight officers and commissions… Political engagement [focuses on] … resort to the formal rules and processes by which government is held in check." There is a movement away from custom and convention as guides for parliamentary behaviour and in their place, the demand to codify rules and penalties, the last of which, Whyte concludes, "may be a more effective way of checking the misuse and abuse of power, but it likely weakens legislators' sense of their responsibility for prudent political judgment and invites less nuanced political engagement from them" (Whyte 2011).

In this context, a synonym for "less nuanced" might be "vituperative" as a description of debate in the House. Criticism of the "tone" of House proceedings, pleas

---

[2] See too Bell (2006, 13-21). For a contrary view, see Galloway (2010, A4).

for a return of (lost) civility, claims that the conduct of MPs from both sides of the chamber is reproachable—all of these are so common as not to require comment, except in a sense that goes beyond political etiquette. Australian scholar Judith Brett argues that "from the perspective of those experienced with the modern, informal meeting and its consensual means of reaching a decision, parliamentary procedure is no longer seen as enabling but as precluding cooperative action" (Brett 2011). In short, the public does not like the way parliamentarians behave and, contrary to the accepted societal norm of cheering for the underdog, they blame the opposition for what they dislike. While it may take two to argue, the public see the opposition as the more culpable, and for a reason that infuriates parliamentary purists: it is not elected. It gets in the way.

Does the House of Commons have a future? Perhaps that question might be deemed too purple, or yellow, or black; extravagant too. But one wonders. A couple of decades ago, Tom Courchene spoke about the "Tragedy of the Commons," and he was not talking about sheep. It is old hat to say that everyone wants to move onto the Commons' territory—the media, the provinces, the Senate are prime suspects. But the House and its members are themselves partly to blame for this trespassing: they get out of practice when they delegate their role as critics, watchmen, and auditors. There are two meanings to the word "auditor": to audit accounts, and to listen. The Commons increasingly seems to favour the second, responsive posture. While not the only reason, and perhaps not the most important reason, this is indisputably one reason why the public seems so disillusioned with legislative politics and with the ritual of elections that is its necessary preliminary. The contest of accountability, which is one way of describing what once took place on the floor of the House of Commons, seems to have moved elsewhere.

In 2011, Bill C-20, generally known as the Fair Representation Act, amended existing electoral law so as to increase the size of the House of Commons (from 308 to 338) by the addition of 15 seats for Ontario, six each for Alberta and British Columbia, and three for Quebec. Given the topic of my remarks, it would be remiss not to say something about the terms of the bill. Principal among these terms are an enlarged House (by 10 percent); more representation where there is more population, namely, Ontario, British Columbia, Alberta; more representation where there is not more population, namely, Quebec; and the status quo ante elsewhere. On the matter of increasing the size of the House, there is some concern, particularly in the ranks of the Liberal Party, about seat inflation. Stéphane Dion has argued for "proportionate representation of the non-growth provinces without raising the total number of MPs." While he explains that some provinces (including his own) would then have fewer MPs than they do now, what is important is not the absolute number of seats but the number relative to the total. I suspect he has not made his case to the man on the Regina omnibus, or even more problematic, to the voter in Eastend, Saskatchewan, whose population (471 in 2006), like that of most non-urban centres in the province, grows smaller with each census count. Moreover, as my colleague John Courtney has argued, "To enhance their chances of having at least one member of the federal cabinet, the Atlantic provinces, Manitoba, and Saskatchewan can be counted on to oppose any attempt to reduce their seat allotments in the Commons" (Courtney 2004). Redistribution is an incendiary subject in Western Canada for reasons that go back to the census of 1911; reducing a western province's seats in the House of Commons is not in the cards, or it is not until there is some significant change in the allocation of senators among the provinces.

On the matter of additional seats for Ontario, British Columbia, and Alberta, no one opposes this overdue recognition of underrepresentation. I would say, however, that media (and some academic) commentary on the subject is overly optimistic about the results. Repeatedly, it is said that the new seats will promote increased demographic diversity and increased urban representation in the Commons. That is probably true, up to a point; but the drawing of the electoral boundaries is the task of commissions in each province, and the legislation governing this activity allows for deviations in population from the provincial quotient of plus or minus 25 percent (which means there can be a 50 percent spread). This deviation is necessary because people still live—often very far—away from the burgeoning metropolitan centres. Twenty years ago, the Lortie Commission on Electoral Reform and Party Financing recommended reducing the deviation from 25 to 15 percent, but that has not happened. Reporting in a pre-computer age, Lortie recommended expediting the process of redistribution, which appears to be happening now since the data being cited are not the preliminary census returns but populations projected as of 1 July 2011.

Additional seats for Quebec are not turning out to be the controversial issue that might have been expected, and perhaps *was expected* two years ago, when the first iteration (Bill C-12) of the redistribution legislation appeared, and then for all practical purposes disappeared. Two years ago the enthusiasm of the moment was rep-by-pop for the underrepresented. The admixture of population *and* territory, both of which had been essential elements of the Canadian formula under different guises since Confederation, appeared to have been abandoned. That has changed, and the only opposition to the change seems to be coming from the Liberals for reasons that appear scholastic in the current context of parliamentary life.

Finally, there are the majority of provinces for whom the grandfather clause and senatorial floor guarantee a perpetuation of the status quo. They accept the rep-by-pop argument on behalf of the growing provinces, and the non-rep-by-pop argument on behalf of Quebec. This surely is an achievement in a process of negotiation that has become a decennial event in parliamentary life in Canada, one whose resolution qualifies the process for inclusion under the rubric "constitutional practice."

REFERENCES

Ackerman, B. 1997. "Meritocracy v. Democracy: What to Do about the Lords." *London Review of Books,* 8 March. http://www.Irb.co.uk/v29/n05/bruce-ackerman/meritocracy-v-democracy/print.

Bell, J.G. 2006. "Agents of Parliament: A New Branch of Government?" *Canadian Parliamentary Review* 29 (1): 13-21.

Benoit, P., and G. Levy. 2011. "Viability of Our Political Institutions Being Questioned." *Hill Times*, 25 May, 15.

Brett, J. 2001. "Parliament, Meetings and Civil Society." *Department of the Senate Occasional Lecture Series at Parliament House*. Canberra, Australia. Accessed 7 May 2009. http://www.aph.gov.au/SENATE?pubs/pops/pop38/c08.pdf.

Campion, L. 1952. "Parliament and Democracy." In *Parliament: A Survey*, by L. Campion, L. Amery, D. Brogan, et al., 9-36. London: George Allen and Unwin.

Courtney, J.C. 2004. *Elections.* Vancouver: UBC Press.

Curry, B. 2010. "Secret Committee, Seeking Non-Partisans: How Harper Found the Next G-G." *Globe and Mail*, 12 July, A1.

De Souza, M., and A. Minsky. 2011. "Ruling Could Lead to Increased Secrecy." *Regina Leader Post*, 14 May, A10.

Ditchburn, J. 2011. "Better Scrutiny of Watchdogs Recommended." *Globe and Mail*, 4 March, A6.

Flanagan, T. 2009. "Only Voters Have the Right to Decide on the Coalition." *Globe and Mail*, 9 January, A13.

Galloway, G. 2010. "Watchdogs – or Lapdogs?" *Globe and Mail*, 28 December, A4.

Chase, S. 2004. "Straight-Talking Fraser Strikes Fear on the Hill." *Globe and Mail*, 12 February, A4.

Heasman, D.J. 1985. "Queen's Prerogative." *London Times*, 24 October.

Kullish, N. 2010a. "Presidential Vote Tests Merkel's Ailing Coalition in Germany." *New York Times*, 26 June, A5.

—. 2010b. "Merkel's Pick Wins German Presidency." *USA Today*, 1 July, 7A.

Naumetz, T. 2011. "Conservatives 'Lay Track' to Attack Media, Real Opposition Party in New Parliament." *Hill Times*, 13 June, 1.

Nitoslawski, J. 2011. "One-Man Ethics in Government Crusader Conacher to Leave Gig in Ottawa." *Hill Times*, 4 March, 4.

Scoffield, H. 2011. "Auditor Auditor-General Calls on Health Canada to Improve Drug Monitoring." *Globe and Mail*, 22 November, A8. http://www.theglobeandmail.com/news/politics/auditor-general-calls-on-health-canada-to-improve-drug-monitoring/article4171582/.

Thomas, P. 2003. "The Past, Present, and Future of Officers of Parliament." *Canadian Public Administration* 46 (3): 287-314.

Whyte, J.D. 2011. "Constitutional Change and Constitutional Durability." *Journal of Parliamentary and Political Law* 5 (3): 419-36.

III

HEALTH POLICY, ECONOMIC FEDERALISM: WHO IS IN CHARGE?

NEVER MORE THAN A STEP FROM PARADISE: CANADIAN PROVINCES AND THE PUBLIC FUNDING OF HEALTH CARE SERVICES

Pierre-Gerlier Forest[1]

> You were never
> More than a step from Paradise
> You had instant access, your analyst told you ...
>
> – Ted Hughes, *Birthday Letters* (1998)

The Canadian health care system is a collection of 14 public plans—ten provincial, three territorial, and one federal—offering coverage for most health care services provided in the country. These plans share a set of common principles embodied in the Canada Health Act (CHA) of 1984, a piece of federal legislation, and are funded through a mix of taxes, premiums, and (limited) user contributions. Provinces get financial support from the federal government to operate their health care systems, but the funding they receive comes with conditions and constraints. In particular, medically necessary hospital and physician services must be provided on the basis of need rather than a patient's ability to pay. Provinces and territories must offer "first-dollar" coverage for such services and accept responsibility for the public

---

[1] I want to thank Larry Brown, Owen Adams, Greg Marchildon, and Marcel Saulnier for their comments and help with data and sources. No need to add that these first-rate experts and excellent friends are not responsible for any way the paper misrepresents reality, or for its conclusions. The Pierre Elliott Trudeau Foundation supported me while I was conducting this particular piece of research.

oversight and management of the health care system. The Canadian public has repeatedly expressed its support for "Medicare," as it is familiarly called, and embraces the notion of equity that is central to its operation.

While the primary role of provinces in health care is indisputable, this doesn't mean that the Canadian health policy framework doesn't have a "national" character (Banting and Boadway 2004). Three fundamental dimensions of this framework were initially imposed—and thereafter, sustained—by the central government: public funding (who pays), public administration (who decides), and public coverage of hospital and medical services (what is insured). If provinces play a defining role, it is by determining the actual structure of the system (i.e., where care must be delivered) and, more importantly, who is to provide the service—two responsibilities that were never seriously contemplated by federal authorities. In addition to the federal government, a wide range of non-governmental organizations are a centralizing force in the Canadian health care system. These groups attempt to develop and promote common principles and national standards, from the training of providers to the accreditation of hospitals and health care programs. That being said, it can't be denied that the highly fragmented nature of the decision-making system and the fact that it is immersed in the politics of each province both contribute to hiding rather than revealing commonalities and shared characteristics.

The Canadian health care system was long presented as a model of cooperative federalism. It is true that the two major "national" programs at the core of the system—a universal hospital insurance plan established in 1957, and a medical insurance program adopted in 1966—were developed by the federal government with the collaboration of the provinces. The federal government promised at that time to fund half the cost of each program, without asking much from the provinces other than a commitment to principles like universal access to core services and the "portability" of benefits between provinces.

In the 1990s, however, confronted with huge deficits and threatened by a mounting public debt, the federal government decided unilaterally to revisit its participation in cost-shared programs, including health care. In 1995, a combination of new fiscal arrangements together with severe cuts in direct (cash) transfers to the provinces resulted in a drastic diminution of federal funding, which in 1997–98 came to represent less than 27 percent of total provincial health care expenses (Marchildon 2006, 45). Accordingly, at the end of the decade, what was originally conceived as a fiscal and policy compact based on equal participation from both levels of government started to look more and more as a mere federal "mandate," in which obligations were unilaterally imposed on the provincial partner without adequate financial compensation. Provinces like Alberta and Quebec openly toyed with the idea of denouncing the partnership and operating the system on their own terms, arguing that the current arrangement was unfair and unsustainable.

It is telling that the title chosen in 2002 for the final report of a (federal) commission of inquiry on the future of health care was *Based on Values* (Commission on the Future of Health Care in Canada 2002). The title underscores that the health care system is conceived by many citizens as the embodiment of Canadian values and, even, of Canadian identity. It is very difficult to modify a program with that sort of iconic status. Compounding this challenge, despite a wide consensus among experts that reform and adaptation are much in need, few results have been achieved—even with significant public refinancing. Canada, once a beacon of innovative health policy, is now cast as a laggard in many international comparisons (Conference Board of Canada 2011). Frustrated users and rogue health professionals have started looking for options *outside* the public system, with the tacit assent of conservative governments at federal and provincial levels.

Will this trend herald a long-sought makeover of Canada's health policy framework? It is difficult to say, if only because both experts and stakeholders are deeply divided on the course the country needs to follow. Voices on the right are calling for a relaxation of the CHA's principles, if not simply for an abrogation of the act, and for increased access to private health care (Emery 2010; Steinbrook 2006; Rovere and Skinner 2011). Voices on the left want more discipline in the system, in particular from physicians, and argue that public health care could die from an excess of misplaced "freedom" in the choice of providers or treatment, or from its willing compliance to the interests of the private sector (Evans and Vujicic 2005). In fact, neither camp is currently of much help for decision-makers, as most solutions they advance imply a major political fight. And there is not much appetite for "big bang" approaches among the public, given its 20 years experience with failed reforms and broken promises. In this environment, changes to the system are more likely to come about by stealth, without any clear sense of policy purpose and direction or assurance that the resulting changes will actually translate into lasting improvements.

IS REFORM AN OPTION?

Woes of the health care system are not that different in Canada than in other developed countries: costs escalating just a little too fast for comfort, by an average rate of 3.6 percent a year in the past decade; users as well as providers complaining about access and waiting lists, notwithstanding billions of dollars of public investment directly targeted at these issues; difficulties in adapting the system to address chronic disease and other conditions associated with the aging of the population; overarching questions of quality and safety, not to mention the failure to develop a robust and workable IT network, despite huge subsidies and sincere efforts on the part of governments (CIHI 2010; OECD 2010; Health Council of Canada 2011).

What makes Canada distinct from most other OECD countries, however, is not the list of challenges it must face but the limited number of answers that can be provided, given the structural and political constraints in which the health care system operates. Indeed, two characteristics of the system make reform, "real" reform, even more complex and difficult than it should be (Forest and Denis 2012).

First, the nature of public coverage varies in every province, with the result that universal solutions are often inapplicable. Although hospital and medical services are covered, if "necessary," as per the constraints imposed by the CHA, all the provinces have added to the core "basket of services." These services may vary quite significantly, depending on the fiscal capacity of the province and on the particular needs and pressures of the local public (Marchildon 2006). What one province decides to ration, cut, or integrate, another province still needs to supply. Citizens of New Brunswick can be denied access to essential medications unless they have already exhausted all their other resources. Home care and long-term care for the elderly are covered in every part of Canada, but the service and the costs vary considerably from one place to the other. Meanwhile, residents of Quebec enjoy the benefits of universal coverage for pharmaceuticals and free access to *in vitro* fertilization—publicly subsidized services not available to citizens in most other jurisdictions. All this, of course, is perfectly in line with what theories of federalism would have predicted: the trade-off between national standards and responsiveness to local circumstances has ultimately favoured the latter (Zhong 2010).

It was not by design that the coverage of one's health needs started to vary according to the province of residence. The public health system was supposed to take care of everything necessary, and it still does. The problem resides in the grey zone that exists between what is medically proven to be *necessary* and what is perceived by health providers or an exacting public as *essential*: not only the new drugs and high-end devices, as can be expected, but also services generated by the "medicalization" of social and natural conditions, such as aging or infertility.

The fact that there was initially no mechanism in place for information-sharing among provinces is telling as well; uniformity in coverage was postulated, and the view was that only fringe services with no real impact would make their way into individual provincial baskets. In reality, the play of democratic competition among political parties at the provincial level, and the constant pressure coming from professionals and other groups to catch up with other provinces, have stimulated the growth of public coverage above and beyond what was originally defined as core services.

The second element of complexity is the ambiguous and sometimes careless manner in which Canadians use the words "public" and "private" when discussing health care. For example, when an eminent and sensible health policy expert writes that Canada needs a "parallel private sector," it would be imprudent to conclude that she envisions competition between this new sector and a state bureaucracy (MacKinnon 2004). Most care in Canada is already provided in the private sector, by physicians expecting personal "profit" in return for the services they dispense. Moreover, most Canadian physicians are paid on a fee-for-service basis, and the largest majority are self-employed, fully autonomous professionals. Those same physicians, if they opt to do so, could even stop billing the public insurance plan and start charging patients directly. Some restrictions apply but, all in all, this looks pretty much like a healthy private sector.

In fact, our expert's proposal only means that insurance companies should be allowed to cover people for services already provided for "free" under the public plan, a practice that is either discouraged or forbidden in a majority of Canadian provinces. Presumably, the newly privately insured patients would then be able to buy their way to the head of any waiting list or to ignore evidence-based restrictions on costly or experimental treatments. This is a form of "privatization," no doubt, but it takes a good leap of faith to see it as health reform. Another scenario would see independent clinics bidding for contracts in competition with public institutions. This model has been tested already with some success, notably because it can fit easily into the existing economic and legal framework of the CHA: private delivery under public control and with public funding.

Conservative columnists like to compare the health care system of Canada to those of North Korea and Cuba (Mercer 2000) but, in reality, a large portion of the health sector is funded privately. In 2008, the public share of total health expenditures was close to 70.2 percent: ergo, nearly 30 percent of costs were paid out to the private sector (CIHI 2010, 65). This ranks Canada way above the United States (46.5 percent) or even Switzerland (59.1 percent) for public spending levels, but in a different league from countries such as Sweden (81.9 percent), New Zealand (80.4 percent), or France (77.8 percent). A number of services that would be deemed essential in most other countries, from dental care to pharmaceuticals to eye care, are not provided publicly in Canada. Once more, however, the Canadian national average hides important provincial and territorial variations, with a public share of only 67.4 percent in the relatively rich and highly urbanized province of Ontario, but 93.8 percent in the Arctic territory of Nunavut (CIHI 2010, 33).

The policy consequences of this reality are not well understood, but it is safe to say that any reform initiative that ignores this variation among provinces and territories will result in (mostly) unwanted outcomes. If Alan Williams (1997) was right in thinking that a policy threshold exists in health care systems, at which point they become either predominantly private or public, Canada is fast approaching the tipping point. Policy-makers cannot afford to be indifferent to this theory, given that the public system in some provinces already includes a sizable private component when new measures of privatization are considered. Likewise, the policy tools needed to integrate health organizations along the "continuum of care" cannot be identical within a "mixed" system and within a system where there is a dominant viewpoint—either decisively public or decisively private—as each commands different approaches to authority and reacts to different incentives.

PRIORITIES IN HEALTH CARE

Setting priorities in the context of a mixed or hybrid system is not easy (Tuohy, Flood, and Stabile 2004; Schmid et al. 2010). When resources are allocated according to the *needs* of the public, a vocal group of potential users will invariably protest, claiming that paying for the care they *want* is a fundamental human right. In 2005, a Montreal patient and his physician, arguing that the prohibition against private medical insurance was incompatible with Canadian human rights legislation, were vindicated in a landmark decision by the Supreme Court of Canada (Chaoulli v. Quebec), in which a slight majority of judges decided that Quebec's prohibition of private insurance restricted access to essential health care (Dickens 2005). Other cases are currently pending in other provinces. Reciprocally, if people with the "willingness and the ability to pay" are given an opportunity to determine the allocation of resources according to their wants, an even more important group of people will oppose a distribution of services that leaves many without care.

Rationing is never simple or pleasant, but in a hybrid system it becomes nearly impossible politically. To properly allocate "values" (to use the language of traditional political analysis), institutions depend upon a common culture—a set of goals, principles, and norms that are "taken for granted in the guidance of day-to-day policy without violating deep feelings of important segments of the community" (Easton 1979, 193). Under conditions of hybridization, this culture dissolves, and the system struggles to keep its balance unless there is a way to relax the constraints on resources, whether by some bending of the rules or by adding to the wealth that must be shared. Destitute patients in need of care can be served by private institutions or providers if the burden is widely shared and the service is highly subsidized. Inversely, doctors seeing "private" patients do not pose a problem for the public system if sufficient resources keep waiting times short for mainstream services. Abundant funding is bliss for politicians when they need to delay tough decisions in social contexts where public opinion is divided and diverging interests openly conflict—generally the norm in Canada.

Looking at the recent evolution of the Canadian health care system, what happened in the past decade appears to be a straight case of growth induced by dissent. Health care spending grew at a much faster rate than inflation and in excess of all "drivers" such as aging, pharmaceuticals, and medical advances (Ruggeri 2006; Di Matteo and Di Matteo 2009; Dodge and Dion 2011). In parallel, decision-makers avoided making a clear commitment either for or against the development of privately funded, "fast-track" access to services, confident that increased public budgets would offset the impacts of the private sector on the health care system (Rovere and Skinner 2011; OECD 2010). After the Supreme Court decision in Chaoulli opened the door to private funding of surgical procedures in 2005, Quebec was forced to revisit its statutory prohibition against private insurance for publicly insured services. Yet, at the same time, the government announced a bold reform of surgical pathways together with a substantial increment in funding, to make private care unpalatable for a majority of patients.

Strategies of this sort require substantial increases in public health-care budgets, which, in turn, demand new or more generous funding. These revenues might have come from raising provincial taxes, but more often than not, they have not. In many cases, provincial governments moved in the opposite direction, actually reducing the so-called "tax burden" on their citizens, at the same time as they complained about their rising responsibilities. Needless to say, tax reductions have benefited wealthier taxpayers most, a situation that has paved the way for even more demand for private care, at least in theory.

Another solution was to prioritize health care in budget allocations over other public expenditures, from education to infrastructure. Although this trend is becoming more evident, it has happened at a slower pace than expected. Despite warnings about inevitable trade-offs between health care spending and the public financing of other "primary" public goods, economists have determined that the so-called "crowding out" effect of health care on other provincial expenses is still relatively marginal. A careful study of this issue, albeit conducted at the beginning of the 2001–10 period, concluded that the growth rate of health care expenditures has had no discernible impact on the other big categories of provincial social spending, including education and social services—at least not yet (Landon et al. 2006).

That's primarily because there was a third way that enabled the provinces to avoid, or perhaps just delay, making these painful choices. This third way entailed capitalizing on the federal structure of the country, asking the central government to come up with the funds. And Ottawa obliged. Three major federal-provincial financial agreements in 2000, 2003, and 2004 guaranteed the provinces in excess of CAN$ 40 billion at the end of fiscal year 2013–2014—starting from CAN$ 15.5 billion in 2000. This money came, and still comes, with very few strings attached, in spite of vague commitments to transparency and accountability.

The political rhetoric used at the time of each accord is revealing. First, it repeatedly placed the preservation of accessibility at the forefront of all collective efforts to sustain public health care. Second, it clearly identified the areas in which massive investment was required if the public was to maintain trust in the system, given the pressure coming from the private sector. This particular focus explains, for instance, the dominant role of diagnostic services, which are explicitly mentioned in the three accords. The insistence on primary care (2000 and 2003) and wait times (2004) is also related. Third, and finally, the accords normalized a state of affairs in which the federal government is less and less the leading force in health policy and is seen instead as "first among equals" (Forest 2014). An analysis of the unfolding of the wait times strategy, in the years subsequent to the 2004 accord, would show a deep contrast in tone and in expectations with the federal government's bullish behaviour during the 1980s or 1990s.

THE COST OF INDECISION

Two related consequences could be attributed to the massive reinvestment of federal money into health care, post-2000. Both are counterintuitive, but this is not unusual in health policy. In this field, after all, the Golden Rule is that an increase in the supply of health care will not result in a diminution of the demand for health care but in an actual increase, sometimes at a faster rate than the growth in new services and resources.

Federal funding was intended to strengthen public health care. Yet, in reality, it encourages hybridization by delaying the moment of truth for provincial decision-makers. Instead of making a clear choice between a system where access is determined by need, "with things being held in balance by quantity rationing based on a socially approved system of rules," and a system where access is determined by willingness and ability to pay, "with things being held in balance by price adjustments in competitive markets," most provinces let both systems thrive and, up to a certain point, compete (Williams 1997, 55-8).

This outcome is not necessarily bad, since choosing would create winners and losers while indecision gives everyone a chance to get what they need or want. But it is costly. Competition without risk produces waste and a certain degree of carelessness, in private and public sectors alike. A recent report on the insurance industry in the drug sector in Canada signalled that employers (i.e., private) plans "have been managed very lightly, or have implemented limited measures to control costs" (Stevenson 2011, 3). Private sector operations in other sectors of health care are not very transparent, but there is no reason to believe they too do not experience "light management" and limited control. Expecting the public sector to provide comparable services, while at the same time caring for most people with high needs and high health risks, is a recipe for cost inflation at its worst.

Another outcome of increased federal funding for health care is that the provinces have been spared the pain of making any significant reform. Money that was supposed to "buy change," as the former health commissioner Roy Romanow insisted in his 2002 report (Commission on the Future of Health Care in Canada 2002, 17), was instead used to subsidize complacency—notably in dealings with providers—and to quiet those voices expressing concerns with the lack of progress in matters like integration or effectiveness. Rightly or wrongly, provincial politicians felt that access trumped everything else in the minds of the public, and they have invested most of their newly acquired resources to address this issue.

In the short term, relationships between Ottawa and the provinces have unquestionably benefited from the federal largesse, especially when it was associated with a more relaxed attitude on the part of the central government towards the affirmation of federal leadership. This approach is particularly true of the current Conservative government, which has repeatedly stated that it would attempt to respect the constitutional division of responsibilities and try not to interfere in provincial oversight of health policy. In any case, while everybody knows the current model is not sustainable, whether because it consumes an ever-growing proportion of public resources or because it leaves the health care system without a clear set of priorities and directions, it might prove very difficult to pull out from a situation that fuels dependency to such a degree and for all players.

The federal government is on (relatively) good terms with the provinces. The provinces are able to buy peace with physicians and other provider groups. The physicians don't have to limit their patients' access to care. Who would want this to change? The fact that all the four major political parties at the federal level were favourable to the renewal of the current health accord, without giving any serious indication relative to their policy views on health and health care issues, is a case in point.

BUDGETING FOR THE STATUS QUO

An intriguing aspect of the 2004 accord was the introduction of a 6 percent "escal-ator." It was agreed that annual cash transfers from the federal government should increase by 6 percent every year, effective in fiscal year 2006–07. (In effect, the transfer grew even faster, because special funds, like the $5.5 billion Wait Times Reduction Transfer, were folded into the main health transfer on an ongoing basis.) Inflation in Canada is way below 6 percent per year, with an average of 2.02 percent for 2001–10. The average growth rate of GDP for the same period was around 1.88 percent. By any measure, 6 percent is not mere "indexation." The Romanow Report, in an effort to acknowledge that health is what economists call a "superior good," recommended the introduction of an escalator based on GDP growth, corrected by a factor of 1.25 (Commission on the Future of Health Care in Canada 2002, 70). This modest proposal was received by fiscal "realists" of that time as a "most glaring weakness" of the report (MacKinnon 2004, 16). So, how did 6 percent become a national norm?

The answer has not much to do with health economics, even writ large, but it clearly rests with the politics of Canadian health care. When the provinces came to the table with the federal government in September 2004 to discuss health care funding, they were experiencing, on average, a 7 percent annual increase in their total health expenditures. Consequently, they expected the federal government to consent and commit to a corresponding increase of its cash transfer. The federal government reacted to this highly sophisticated request by a no less sophisticated counterproposal of 5 percent, based on an estimate of the annual growth of an "enriched" CHA basket of services. There is probably no need to explain how it ended in the middle.

This decision might have been made on the basis of shallow evidence, yet it has had a huge impact. Contrary to the language of "positive change for Canadians" that figured at that time in the federal-provincial backgrounders, the escalator en-sured that the status quo would prevail. To begin with, it meant minimal intrusion of federal policy into the provincial management of health affairs. In stark contrast to what was experienced in the 1990s, when cuts in federal transfers forced the provinces to revisit their health care and social commitments, the guarantee of sta-bility and predictability signalled that provincial policies and plans would develop without interference. The same reasoning holds for health system stakeholders, who were able to count thereafter on a constant flow of money to sustain their various arrangements with the provinces. Experiments were to take place, concessions would be made, a few incremental innovations might be implemented, but the fundamental compact would stand, with the power structure intact.

The problem is that there is no status quo in health care. Health systems change all the time, if in an uncertain and largely irrational manner, under the influence of a myriad of factors: technological innovations, new therapies, demographic transformation induced by immigration and aging, economic cycles, culture shifts, and so on. In the absence of a clear reform agenda, stable and predictable funding means that the health system is able to adapt itself to the pressures of change, but in a reactive manner only. Moreover, cost control is very unlikely to be effective.

TRADE-OFFS AND PRIORITIES

The inflationary impact on provincial budgets of a 6 percent annual increase in federal health transfer payments is not well understood. Most of the time, studies focus on endogenous cost pressures like increasing demand or aging and on the corresponding growth in health care expenditures. Inflation is acknowledged, of course, but it is cast primarily as a health policy issue rather than a fiscal or inter-governmental issue.

It is not that simple. In a perfect world, provinces would set a limit on their spending and keep the growth rate under 6 percent, content to see the federal share of health expenses grow quietly year after year. In reality, the spending increase since the 2004 accord averaged 6.7 percent (Health Council of Canada 2011, 3). Provinces with large populations, like Ontario or Quebec, were barely able to keep the growth in public health spending close to the mark, averaging 6.1 and 6.2 respectively. Smaller provinces generally fared worse, with scores averaging 8.0 for Nova Scotia or 9.6 for Alberta, among others (CIHI 2010, 148). In fact, pledges from provinces wishing to achieve a lower rate in the future have been met with scepticism, notably by parliamentary officers who should have rejoiced in this expression of fiscal responsibility (Ontario 2011, 21-8; Canada 2010, 15-20).

The situation is something of a paradox. Governments that avoid setting prior-ities in health care are still forced to make decisions at a higher level, when they allocate their limited fiscal resources among multiple budget categories. Health care is not the only public good for which provinces have a responsibility. Taxpayers look to governments to deliver everything from quality education to infrastructure and transport, and from public safety to culture. If health spending increases at a faster rate than a province's revenues—partly because of endogenous factors, but also partly because of the ripple effect of growing federal transfers—something else has to give.

In seven Canadian provinces out of ten, health represents 40 percent or more of all program spending, and it is growing. Reputed experts have predicted that provinces urgently need "to generate additional own-sources revenues or compress non-health care program spending by a substantial amount each year" (Dodge and Dion 2011, 19). Or in the words of Janice MacKinnon, in her time one of the most respected provincial ministers of finance, "Health care, health care, and only heath care?" (MacKinnon 2003, 228-56). The provinces like to pretend they have nearly all the attributes of fully sovereign states; the very real possibility that meeting their obligations in the health sector may limit their capacity to fulfill their other policy goals should be cause for concern for all Canadians.

Fortunately for those governments, most have been able thus far to avoid having to make the tough decisions. The discrepancy can be explained in part by the fact that health care was not the only sector in which federal transfer payments increased. Social transfers and equalization payments also rose over the same period. Clearly, health took its share, and a bit more, but provincial budgets grew at nearly the same pace, thanks to rising federal transfers. Indeed, provinces were incited to a kind of flight forward, accelerated in 2008 by the global financial crisis and the subsequent federal economic action (i.e., stimulus) plan. In the end, nearly every clientele of provincial bureaucracies must have benefited from the outpouring of federal funds, estimated to represent close to one-third of the real increase in provincial revenues in recent years. What will happen when the taps run dry remains to be seen.

Once more, it is important to recognize that this process is political in nature. To quote Aaron Wildavsky, "Budgets are conflicting commitments," and budget decisions are struggles for power among interest groups, inside and outside the bureaucracy (Widavsky 1988, 8). The political arbitrage of premiers and provincial ministers of finance applies not to abstract social goods, like health or universities, but to rival factions represented at cabinet level. For example, allocating close to half the province's budget to one particular minister, even if the portfolio is worthy of this level of support, must have a political cost. Although public support for a constant expansion of services can be taken for granted, especially if no tax increases follow, there is little tolerance for cuts and deficiencies in other public programs. Furthermore, it might be difficult to sustain the loyalty of political supporters and allies if they continually find themselves on the wrong side of every budgetary decision.

A STEP FROM PARADISE

Polls indicate that a growing proportion of Canadians believe that the problems of the health care system cannot be solved within the current policy framework. Access, including for basic "core" services like family medicine, along with integration of care and quality, is on everybody's agenda. The lesson of the past decade, if there is one, is that adding new resources is not a solution in and by itself, even if the investment is massive. It can bring some relief in domains where delays are excessive, as demonstrated by the "national" wait-times strategy included in the accords of 2003 and 2004. According to the Health Council of Canada, eight out of ten Canadian patients are now treated within the pan-Canadian benchmarks announced by governments in 2005—for hip and knee replacement, hip fracture repair, cataract surgery, radiation, and bypass surgery (Health Council of Canada 2011, 7). But money doesn't provide for integrated care or necessarily ensure that interventions are safe and appropriate. This is where the policy framework plays a role, either to facilitate or to hinder progress.

Canadian health care has been a hybrid system since its inception, and the notion that more hybridization will translate into a better functioning organization is doubtful. If the proportion of privately funded health care is a rough indicator of the degree of hybridization, there was an important leap back in the 1990s when, on average, private sector care went from 25 to 30 percent of total health expenditures (Marchildon 2006, 44-6). This shift happened largely because of cuts and restrictions in the public system, but it is also a fact that patients used more private care at the end of the decade than at its beginning. Did the change bring more flexibility and better integration? Not really. Actually, it didn't even bring better or faster access or improved productivity, as Romanow concluded at the end of his inquiry. More intense privatization of Canadian health care would bring a different allocation of resources, along with different principles than the principles that prevail right now, but it wouldn't necessarily solve problems of rigidity or malfunctioning, which are at the root of growing costs and poor outcomes.

The trouble is that an agreement on the problems affecting the health system never translates into an agreement on the solutions. Each analyst, every interested party, comes with its own remedy, arguing that we're "never more than a step from Paradise."

Bringing about meaningful change would require that all parties focus on the processes that set priorities to enable informed decision-making, rather than *fetishizing* over any single potential solution. However, the current incentives, including the flow of "stable and predictable" federal money, all work to promote fragmentation and incessant pressure for new resources. Moreover, it is nearly impossible for decision-makers to make any sort of hard choices when the only commonly agreed purpose is to facilitate access, independent of considerations of genuine medical necessity, usefulness, or effectiveness. Because the CHA, which has played an important role in guarding the system against numerous attempts to dismantle it, enshrines this commitment to accessibility, it may be the first thing that needs to go.

To be replaced by? This question is vitally important, because simple abrogation won't do any good. Without a national framework for health care, the whole Canadian system would quickly look like the patchwork of plans and regimes that already characterize the coverage for pharmaceuticals in the country. Uniformity may not be an important concern, but in the current situation it is still a proxy for equity, and equity counts. Then there is a need for a new consensus on principles to guide decision-making, because the generalized failure to institute changes has sustained a costly status quo (Drummond and Burleton 2010). Canada is one of the few countries in the OECD in which attempts to improve performance have been mostly cosmetic for more than a decade.

The CHA ensured that equity would be the touchstone of every policy. Yet there is room for equally important considerations such as accountability, efficiency, and innovation, the long-term keys to the system's sustainability. As just one example, the knowledge developed in Canada about the social determinants of health, and the need for a health system that aims to reduce fundamental inequities, should find a place in a new health care framework.

It remains an open question who can initiate this transformation. In the 1990s, when the fiscal situation forced provinces to consider real and painful trade-offs among all sorts of essential programs, their common agenda for "change and renewal" was more innovative than it is now, with its quasi-exclusive focus on sustainability. Not only were they able to agree on accessibility or on the notion that all Canadians must be served according to their needs but they were also insisting on the importance of social programs that were "affordable, effective, and accountable" (Ministerial Council 1996). Their willingness to make room for collective *and* individual responsibility, including presumably the responsibility of each citizen to contribute his or her just share of taxes, would still resonate with the public. The current insistence on decentralization, combined with a good dose of fiscal realism, should allow this conversation to resume.

On 19 December 2011, Jim Flaherty, the federal minister of finance, announced a new federal funding framework for health care. The dollar amounts are not unreasonable, especially in the first few years, but the underlying message is one of disentanglement. While the co-funding of health care services by the federal government will continue into the future, as Ottawa will pay its share, its active participation in the co-management of the national system is clearly over. In the blunt words of the federal minister of health, Leona Aglukkaq, "Decision-making about health care is best left to the provincial, territorial and local levels" (Aglukkaq 2012).

This new approach clearly could not satisfy those who have called for an "em-powered" federal government imposing conditions on the provinces to foster bold reforms, *à la* Romanow. It is a real blow to those who have lobbied for an expansion of the system, notably in fields like pharmaceuticals or home care. Provinces and territories also expressed reservations. Certainty of funding has always been part of their long-term objectives in past negotiations with Ottawa, but the framework is ambiguous about the limits that provinces should respect when "experimenting" with reforms. While the federal government did not insist on the conditionality of its future financial contribution, the prime minister nonetheless reaffirmed his government's support for the Canada Health Act and, supposedly, for the boundaries it imposes on privately funded health care and other market-oriented solutions.

The federal government is expecting that a wide range of actors, new and trad-itional, will contribute to the success of the new "policy." Ottawa is waiting for the provinces to take the lead in bending the cost curve and orienting the system towards quality and efficiency. However, it also encourages non-governmental actors from the voluntary and private sector to lead initiatives aiming at changing practices and improving standards of care. This approach is based on a leap of faith rather than on solid evidence. States and provinces are supposed to be laboratories for policy innovation, but in fact very little is known of their success in imagining, implementing, and disseminating innovations all by themselves (Inwood, Johns, and O'Reilly 2011). The gap in knowledge is even wider for the non-profit and the private sector, especially respecting policy development. Finally, the emergence of "hybrid" institutions and partnerships where the three sectors are supposed to collaborate is even more puzzling: will joint decision-making result in better solutions, or will the lowest common denominator prevail?

It is much too early to say if the new approach will bear the results expected by the government. It is highly improbable that the national health system will change radically in just a few years and just as unlikely that it will suddenly collapse. Like other large social systems, public health care is both resilient and resistant to change, and often for the same reasons.

REFERENCES

Aglukkaq, L. 2012. Speaking notes by the Honourable Leona Aglukkaq Minister of Health and the Canadian Northern Economic Development Agency: Opening Remarks. Canadian Medical Association (CMA) 145th Annual Meeting. http://www.hc-sc.gc.ca/ahc-asc/minist/speeches-discours/_2012/2012_08_13-eng.php.

Banting, K., and R. Boadway. 2004. "Defining the Sharing Community: The Federal Role in Health Care." In *Money, Politics and Health Care: Reconstructing the Federal Provincial Partnership*, edited by H. Lazar and F. St-Hilaire 1-77. Montreal: IRPP.

Canada. Office of the Parliamentary Budget Officer. 2010. *Fiscal Sustainability Report*. Ottawa: PBO.

Canadian Institute for Health Information. 2010. *National Health Expenditure Trends, 1975 to 2010*. Ottawa: CIHI.

Commission on the Future of Health Care in Canada. 2002. "Building on Values: the Future of Health Care in Canada, Final Report." Ottawa: The Commission.

Conference Board of Canada. 2011. "Concerned about Future Performance: How Canada Performs: Health." http://conferenceboard.ca/HCP/Details/Health.aspx.

Dickens, B.M. 2005. "The Chaoulli Decision: Less than Meets the Eye – or More." In *Access to Care, Access to Justice: The Legal Debate over Private Health Insurance in Canada,* edited by C.M. Flood, K. Roach, and L. Sossin, 19-31. Toronto: University of Toronto Press.

Di Matteo, L., and R. di Matteo. 2009. *The Fiscal Sustainability of Alberta's Public Health Care System*. School of Public Policy, University of Calgary.

Dodge, D., and R. Dion. 2011. "Chronic Healthcare Spending Disease: Background and Methodology." Toronto: CD Howe Institute.

Drumond, D., and D. Burleton. 2010. "Charting a Path to Sustainable Health Care in Ontario: 10 Proposals to Restrain Cost Growth without Compromising Quality of Care." Toronto: TD Bank Financial Group.

Easton, D. 1979. *A Systems Analysis of Political Life*. 2nd ed. Chicago: University of Chicago Press.

Emery, J.C.H. 2010. "Understanding the Political Economy of the Evolution and Future of Single-Payer Public Health Insurance in Canada." University of Calgary, School of Public Policy.

Evans, B., and M. Vujicic. 2005. "Political Wolves and Economic Sheep: The Sustainability of Public Health Insurance in Canada." In *The Public-Private Mix for Health Care*, edited by A. Maynard, 117-40. Oxford: Radcliffe Publishing.

Forest, P.-G. 2014. "Be Careful What You Wish For … Policy Development and Federal Funding of Canadian Health Care." In *Bending the Cost Curve*, edited by G.P. Marchildon and L. di Matteo. Toronto: University of Toronto Press.

Forest, P.-G., and J.-L. Denis. 2012. "Real Reforms in Health Systems: An Introduction." *Journal of Health Politics, Policy and Law* 37 (4): 575-86.

Health Council of Canada. 2011. *Progress Report 2011: Health Care Renewal in Canada*. Ottawa: HCC.

Inwood, G.J., C.M. Johns, and P.L. O'Reilly 2011. *Intergovernmental Policy Capacity in Canada: Inside the Worlds of Finance, Environment, Trade, and Health*. Montreal and Kingston: McGill-Queen's University Press.

Landon, S., M. McMillan, V. Muralidharan, and M. Persons. 2006. "Does Health-Care Spending Crowd Out Other Provincial Government Expenditures?" *Canadian Public Policy* 32 (2): 121-41.

MacKinnon, J. 2003. *Minding the Public Purse: The Fiscal Crisis, Political Trade-Offs, and Canada's Future*. Montreal and Kingston: McGill-Queen's University Press.

—. 2004. The Arithmetic of Health Care. Montreal: IRPP.

Marchildon, G.P. 2006. *Health Systems in Transition: Canada*. First North American edition. Toronto: University of Toronto Press.

Mercer, I. 2000. "Failure Defined as Success in Socialized Medicine." *Vancouver Sun*, 26 October.

Ministerial Council on Social Policy Reform and Renewal. 1996. *Report to Premiers*. St John's: Newfoundland Information Service.

OECD. 2010. "Overcoming Challenges in Health Reform." *OECD Economic Surveys: Canada*. Paris: OECD.

Ontario. Office of the Auditor General of Ontario. 2011. "The Auditor General's Review of the 2011 Pre-Election Report on Ontario's Finances." *Report Toronto*, AGO.

Rovere, M., and B.J. Skinner 2011. "Canada's Medicare Bubble: Is Government Health Spending Sustainable without User-Based Funding?" Vancouver: Fraser Institute.

Ruggeri, J. 2006. "Health Care Spending, Fiscal Sustainability, and Public Investment." *Public Policy Paper*. Regina: Saskatchewan Institute of Public Policy.

Schmid, A., M. Cacace, R. Götze, and H. Rothgang. 2010. "Explaining HealthCare System Change: Problem Pressure and the Emergence of "Hybrid" Health Care Systems." *Journal of Health Politics, Policy and Law* 35 (1): 455-86.

Steinbrook, R. 2006. "Private Health Care in Canada." *New England Journal of Medicine* 354: 1661-4.

Stevenson, H. 2011. *An End to Blank Cheques: Getting More Value out of Employer Drug Plans*. Toronto: Reformulary Group.

Tuohy, C.H., C.M. Flood, and M. Stabile. 2004. "How Does Private Finance Affect Public Health Care Systems? Marshalling the Evidence from OECD Nations." *Journal of Health Politics, Policy and Law* 29 (3): 359-96.

Wildavsky, A. 1988. *The New Politics of the Budgetary Process*. Glenview, IL: Scott, Foresman & Co.

Williams, A. 1997. "Priority Setting in Public and Private Health Care: A Guide through the Ideological Jungle." In *Being Reasonable about the Economics of Health: Selected Essays by Alan Williams,* 54-64. Edited by A.J. Culyer and A. Maynard. Cheltenham, UK: Edward Elgar.

Zhong, H. 2010. "The Impact of Decentralization of Health Care Administration on Equity in Health and Health Care in Canada." *International Journal of Health Care Finance and Economics* 10 (3): 219-37. DOI 10.1007/s10754-010-9078-y.

8

FEDERALISM AND SECURITIES REGULATION IN CANADA

Eric Spink[1]

The 2011 constitutional references dealing with the proposed federal securities legislation were "not only about securities regulation [but] also about the very essence of Canadian federalism" (Grammond 2011). The securities references were the latest battle between two radically different visions of federalism—centralist versus decentralist—that have been warring in Canada since Confederation. The next battle, in the form of another constitutional reference triggered by anticipated federal systemic-risk legislation, already looms on the horizon. Because the division of powers "remains 'the primary textual expression of the principle of federalism in our Constitution'" (*Reference SCC* 2011, para. 54), the courts' constitutional conclusions in the securities references also reflect their view on the competing visions of federalism.

This paper examines in detail the factual context of the securities references and the "legislative facts" underlying the courts' constitutional conclusions in order to illustrate the competing visions of federalism. Legislative facts "are those which establish the purpose and background of legislation, including its social, economic and cultural context" (*Danson* 1990, 1099). Legislative facts inform the "pith and substance" analysis which "looks at the *purpose* and *effects* of the law to identify its 'main thrust'" (*Reference SCC* 2011, para. 63). When 18 of 19 justices (including all nine at the Supreme Court) reach essentially the same conclusions on legislative facts, rejecting the federal government's core constitutional argument because it was not supported by the "legislative facts adduced by Canada" (*Reference SCC* 2011, para. 116), those facts are important.

Because the proposed federal securities legislation replicated existing provincial legislation, the legislative facts consisted mainly of descriptions of our existing securities regulatory system. Over 5,000 pages of evidence were filed in the

---

[1] This chapter is current as of 5 January 2014.

references, most of it narrative descriptions of a system itself composed of over 5,000 pages of legislation, regulations, rules, policies, and regulated contracts. This paper focuses on the enormous contradictions between the descriptions presented by the federal government and the provinces,[2] which illustrate the two competing visions of federalism in the securities references.

My perspective is that of a veteran observer of federalism from the front lines of securities regulation. I wrote four reports filed in evidence in the securities references, describing our regulatory system based on my experience as a former director of enforcement, member, and vice chair of the Alberta Securities Commission and as an official with Alberta Finance during the development and implementation of the so-called passport system of securities regulation. In this paper, I go further in describing my personal observations about the inner workings of our system and how it evolved to meet the functional policy objectives of securities regulation. It will be apparent that I agree with the courts' constitutional conclusions, although the focus of this paper is not so much on those conclusions as it is with how the rejection of the federal government's evidence reflects upon the corresponding vision of Canadian federalism.

The first substantive section of the paper outlines the decisions in the securities references and their treatment of the contradictory evidence. It explains the rejected federal evidence as "constitutional rhetoric"—inaccurate assertions, assumptions, descriptions, and criticisms of our existing regulatory system intended to support a federal constitutional claim of provincial incapacity. It describes how that rhetoric dominated the public debate for decades and became conventional wisdom in Canada, how the adoption of that rhetoric by the International Monetary Fund finally prompted the provinces to respond, and how the evidence in the securities references then unfolded as a contest between myths and facts. Ironically, the facts showed that our much-maligned decentralized system is probably the best in the world in terms of meeting the functional policy objectives of securities regulation.

The second section shifts the analysis to why our decentralized system seems to excel, describing the system as an example of successful federalism. It examines what constitutes good securities regulatory policy and the processes used to make good policy at a granular level, addressing several misconceptions about securities regulatory policy. It examines the failure of proposals for a federal securities regulator in the mid 1990s, how the policy-making process then evolved into our current passport system, and the political considerations underlying Ontario's refusal to join the passport system.

---

[2] For convenience, most references in this paper to "provinces" mean those provinces that argued against the proposed federal legislation at the Supreme Court: Quebec, Alberta, New Brunswick, Manitoba, British Columbia, and Saskatchewan. References to "provincial" arguments or evidence have a corresponding meaning and do not include arguments or evidence from Ontario (the only province to argue in favour of the federal legislation).

The final section examines the securities references as an example of "constitutional risk"—the risk that a constitutional agenda may generate incentives for retrograde policy that override functional policy considerations. I describe other examples of how this kind of constitutional turf war can be toxic from a policy perspective. I then examine the impact of the reference decisions on the federal government going forward, describing other federal legislation that now appears *ultra vires* and recent suggestions that the federal government may introduce legislation related to systemic risk, triggering a sequel to the securities references. I conclude with a call for a more transparent process to deal with proposed constitutional changes that will reduce constitutional risk in the future.

THE SECURITIES REFERENCES

At the end of 2011, in a landmark decision, the Supreme Court of Canada struck down proposed federal securities legislation as *ultra vires*. The decision was unanimous and consistent with the previous reference decisions of the Alberta and Quebec Courts of Appeal. These decisions revisit the most contested constitutional question in Canada's history—the scope of provincial jurisdiction over property and civil rights versus federal jurisdiction over trade and commerce—which has always reflected centralist versus decentralist views of Canadian federalism. The decisions essentially reaffirmed the constitutional status quo by characterizing existing securities legislation as property and civil rights, not trade and commerce.

Although the federal government consistently portrayed its securities legislation as a policy initiative, it was widely recognized to be, as Alberta's then-finance minister described it, an "unprecedented federal power grab" (Rabson 2010). The theme of the 2011 State of the Federation conference—"rebalancing"—scarcely describes the scale and aggressiveness of the federal constitutional claim. This point is crucial to any understanding of the securities references and their aftermath.

If valid, the federal government's arguments in the securities references would have produced a seismic shift of jurisdiction in other areas by effectively overturning the seminal decision in *Citizens Insurance Company v. Parsons*, 1881. The Alberta Court of Appeal compared the reference with the federal government's earlier campaign to assume the national regulation of the insurance industry and described the reference as "an attempt to overturn all those earlier cases [including *Parsons*], and to rewrite Canadian constitutional history" (*Reference ABCA* 2011, para. 42; Armstrong 1976). At the Supreme Court, British Columbia's counsel described the proposed act as a constitutional Trojan horse that would result in the complete evisceration of provincial power over securities regulation and other areas. MacIntosh (2012b, 232-8) lists over a hundred Ontario statutes that might be construed as falling within the trade and commerce power, if federal securities legislation had been valid.

FAILING ON THE FACTS: THE MYTH OF TRANSFORMATION AND OTHER CONTRADICTIONS

The Supreme Court rejected the federal government's core argument that "securities markets have undergone significant transformation in recent decades, evolving from local markets to markets that are increasingly national, indeed international [which] has given rise to systemic risks and other concerns that can only be dealt with on the national level" (*Reference SCC* 2011, para. 33). This argument, the Supreme Court said, "requires not mere conjecture, but evidentiary support. The legislative facts adduced by Canada in this reference do not establish the asserted transformation. On the contrary, the fact that the structure and terms of the proposed Act largely replicate the existing provincial schemes belies the suggestion that the securities market has been wholly transformed over the years" (*Reference SCC* 2011, para. 116).

Some commentators (collected in Anand 2012a) have severely criticized the Supreme Court's decision, particularly the court's rejection of the asserted transformation. For example, Puri (2012a) argues that the decision "fails to demonstrate an understanding of Canadian capital markets" and suggests that the court "ignored" or "turned a blind eye" to the federal evidence of transformation (Puri 2012b, 15, 18). Trebilcock (2012, 42) suggests that "the facts—along with their policy relevance—appeared not to matter." However, those criticisms do not address the contradictory evidence presented by the provinces, or even acknowledge its existence. As described below, a review of the contradictory evidence shows that the courts did not ignore the federal evidence but rather rejected it in favour of the provincial evidence, and were correct to do so.

The Supreme Court euphemistically described the federal government's failure to present "a factual matrix that supports its assertion of a constitutionally significant transformation" (*Reference SCC* 2011, para. 115). The majority decisions at the Courts of Appeal were also restrained, but pointed more specifically to facts contradicting fundamental elements of the claimed transformation:

- Securities markets were international before Confederation (*Reference ABCA* 2011, para. 20; *QCCA Reference* 2011, paras. 288, 413-4).
- While technology has speeded up modern trading, and markets are larger and more complex, these factors do not serve to transform the pith and substance of the matter from property and civil rights into the regulation of trade and commerce because the regime still regulates individual contractual and property rights, as sophisticated, complex, and fast as they may now be (*Reference ABCA* 2011, para. 20).
- No securities legislation regulates or manages capital flows *(Reference ABCA* 2011, para. 25)* and so does not regulate interprovincial or international trade (*QCCA Reference* 2011, para. 289).

- Systemic risk is not a constitutional head of power and the proposed act does nothing not already being done by the provinces with respect to the reduction of systemic risk which, in any event, is a matter of property and civil rights in the context of securities regulation (*Reference ABCA* 2011, paras. 23-4). The federal government failed to show that provincial legislation was unable to reasonably prevent systemic risks (*QCCA Reference* 2011, paras. 205-10).
- Our existing securities regulatory system is a world leader, including in the area of systemic risk prevention or management (*QCCA Reference* 2011, para. 368). The federal government's assertions "regarding the fragmentation of the system, the duplication and complexity of procedures, the high system costs and the general inability of the provinces to manage ... systemic risk are contradicted by this reality" (*QCCA Reference* 2011, para. 369).

Those findings were more than enough to sink the transformation claim, but they were only the tip of the iceberg of contradictory evidence. The courts properly avoided commenting on "the policy question of whether a single national securities scheme is preferable to multiple provincial regimes" (*Reference SCC* 2011, para. 10) because that question was not relevant to the constitutional issues as a matter of law. Of course, that policy question remains crucial to any federalism analysis, and it is especially interesting here because it highlights the biggest contradictions in the evidence:

- The most credible assessments available rank the performance of our decentralized system among the best in the world (if not the best) in terms of meeting the functional policy objectives of securities regulation (Spink 2010b, paras. 3-20).
- Canada's obsession with regulatory structure is unique. The rest of the world seems to recognize that structure is not necessarily relevant to functional performance, that there is no ideal structure, and that there need not be a single regulator (IOSCO 2003b, 9; IOSCO 2008, 9; IOSCO 2011b, 21; Corcoran 2010; Spink 2010b, paras. 3-10, 17-8).
- To the extent that structure may be relevant to functional performance, it appears that decentralization has been a strength, not a weakness, of our system (Courchene 1986, 2010a, 2010b; Spink 2010b, 2010c, 2010d; Rousseau 2010a; Suret and Carpentier 2010; Choi 2010; Macey 2010a). Centralization "effectively abandons the diversity and dynamic-efficiency features of [decentralization]," replacing them with "an entirely different approach, one with new players, new politics and no history" (Courchene 2010b, 10), so centralization would appear to be a retrograde step from a functional policy perspective.

That evidence radically contradicted conventional wisdom in Canada, which had been shaped by a series of reports from royal commissions and federally constituted panels in 1935, 1964, 1979, 2003, and 2009. Those reports portrayed our existing system as inefficient and dysfunctional due to its decentralized structure, which was described in pejorative terms like "fragmented," "balkanized," "patchwork," and "hodgepodge." What explains such extreme contradictions?

There is a rhetorical pattern evident in those reports and similar opinions: each is based on an underlying assumption that a single-regulator structure is inherently superior to a decentralized system as a matter of policy (Spink 2010b, paras. 11, 38-40). As soon as we question that assumption, it appears, like "transformation" and "fragmentation," to be unsupported by empirical evidence and, moreover, to be a rhetorical device constructed to support federal constitutional claims — constitutional rhetoric. The constitutional agenda therefore explains the strategic origins of the rhetoric and the contradictory evidence describing our existing system.

THE CONSTITUTIONAL AGENDA: PROVINCIAL INCAPACITY

One of the federal government's primary constitutional objectives in the securities references was meeting the "provincial incapacity" test stated in *General Motors* 1989, where the court found that "competition cannot be effectively regulated unless it is regulated nationally" (*General Motors* 1989, 680). A similar finding in the securities references was necessary in order for federal securities legislation to be valid under the "general" or "second branch" of the trade and commerce power.

The provincial incapacity test was immediately recognized as being crucial to the future of Canadian federalism generally, and particularly to the constitutionality of federal securities legislation (Swinton 1990, 1992). The test has also been criticized for its vagueness and the low evidentiary threshold applied in *General Motors* 1989 (Leclair 2003, 2010; Karazivan and Gaudreault-DesBiens 2010; Lee 2011). Leclair (2010, 570-2) believes that Chief Justice Dickson had both competition and securities regulation in mind when formulating the test and that it is "a purely rhetorical device" (590) that took "normative statements founded on the belief of the provinces' ontological incapacity to work for the economic good of Canada as a whole" and "morphed" them into "empirical truths" (595). He describes Chief Justice Dickson's approach as founded on the premises that "effectiveness can only be achieved by the federal polity and efficiency is reducible to uniformity, [which are] normative statements that do not appear to be validated by empirical reality" (591-2).

The federal government's evidence and arguments in the securities references were focused on the provincial incapacity test. The asserted transformation from local to global markets was needed to claim that securities markets had outgrown provincial jurisdiction, making federal legislation necessary to address what would otherwise be a "constitutional gap" (*Reference SCC* 2011, para. 83). The transformation theory suggested such a gap by pointing to the provinces' constitutional inability to regulate interprovincial and international trade and emphasizing the increasingly national and international dimensions of securities markets (Canada 2010, paras 109-10). Pejorative descriptions like "fragmented" and "balkanized" suggested provincial incapacity by asserting that structural and substantive uniformity are necessary for the system to be "effective" (Expert Panel 2009, 41; Anand 2005; Anand and Klein 2005; Puri 2010, 2012a).

Provincial incapacity is therefore more than just a constitutional test: it also reflects the two competing visions of Canadian federalism. The federal government's vision of federalism is evident in the constitutional rhetoric leading up to the securities references, as summarized below.

OVERVIEW OF CONSTITUTIONAL RHETORIC ABOUT SECURITIES REGULATION

The origins of the transformation and fragmentation rhetoric can be traced back to broader constitutional rhetoric about provincial incapacity in the 1930s. The 1935 Royal Commission on Price Spreads asserted that the provinces were incapable of performing a number of functions important to the national economy (including securities regulation) and that going forward a unitary approach was essential as a matter of policy—all in support of proposals to amend the constitution to give the federal government jurisdiction over those functions (Canada 1935, 39, 274, 286-7; Spink 2010b, paras 38-40; Wilbur 1969, 18). The leading constitutional scholars of the day shared that centralist view, urging, for example, the repeal of the British North America Act and a complete rewrite of the constitution (Kennedy 1937, 399) to give the federal government legislative authority over matters of national economic importance (Kennedy 1937; MacDonald 1937; Scott 1937).

The opposing—essentially decentralist—vision of federalism can be traced back to Oliver Mowat and Ontario's constitutional struggles with Sir John A. Macdonald over "provincial rights" in the late nineteenth century. The best-known illustration of that vision in the 1930s was the broad provincial opposition to federal "New Deal" legislation that resulted in the legislation being largely struck down by the Supreme Court of Canada in 1936 and the Privy Council in 1937. Less well-known are the constitutional battles fought alone by Alberta's Social Credit government, elected in 1935, against the federal government and the banks. Those battles were remarkably fierce: in 1936 Alberta became the only province in Canada ever to default on its sovereign debt obligations, the result of being the only province to resist a constitutional amendment to create a Loan Council that would control provincial borrowing (Ascah 1999, 62; Mallory 1954, 129-35); in the winter of 1936–37, the banks prepared a proposal to pay lower interest rates on Albertans' deposits and charge higher rates on Albertans' loans as retribution for Social Credit initiatives (Ascah 1999, 70-1); and Alberta refused to participate in the (Rowell-Sirois) Royal Commission on Dominion-Provincial Relations appointed in 1937, addressing *The Case for Alberta* 1938 to "the Sovereign People of Canada and their Governments." *The Case for Alberta* opposed any transfer of powers to the federal government and supported decentralization on the basis of what we would now refer to as subsidiarity, saying that provincial jurisdiction "conform[s] to the principle that the responsibility for any function should be left [to] that Government which can most readily perform that function" (Alberta 1938, 9).

Because the 1930s rhetoric was aimed at supporting constitutional amendments, it focused simply on asserting a policy need for uniformity—uniformity being synonymous with federal jurisdiction (Canada 1935, 39). The 1964 Porter Report (Canada 1964) took the provincial-incapacity rhetoric a step further by implying that the federal government already had the constitutional authority to enact securities legislation under the "first branch" of the trade and commerce power dealing with the regulation of interprovincial and international trade. It suggested "a national agency under federal legislation which would take over the major responsibility in this area from the provinces" and that the "federal regulatory agency ... might at first require only registration of issues being distributed interprovincially and internationally" (Canada 1964, 348). The rhetoric about the policy need for a unitary approach also escalated with references to the "hodgepodge of [provincial] legislation" and "fragmentation of administration," suggesting that "the job [will] be accomplished most effectively if a federal agency takes the lead in setting high and uniform national standards" (Canada 1964, 344-9).

The Proposals for a Securities Market Law for Canada (Canada 1979) were the first explicit assertions of federal constitutional jurisdiction over securities regulation. The proposals included a draft act that purported to apply to all but "intraprovincial transactions" (Anisman 1981, 365-7) and a constitutional opinion almost identical with the federal government's position in the securities references (Anisman and Hogg 1979).

The rhetoric intensified with the 2003 report of the Wise Persons' Committee (WPC 2003), which claimed the transformation from local to international markets "made it increasingly difficult for the provinces to regulate effectively" (WPC 2003, 12). It used "fragmented" as synonymous with "decentralized," claiming, "Policy development is slow and inflexible. The need for consensus often results in a lack of uniformity, overregulation or policy paralysis. The system is too costly, duplicative and inefficient. The regulatory burden impedes capital formation. Canada's international competitiveness is undermined by regulatory complexity" (WPC 2003, 25).

The 2009 report of the Expert Panel on Securities Regulation (EP 2009) said that markets were more international than ever before and described transformation in terms of systemic risk (EP 2009, 1, 11). The report said, "We do not believe that multiple securities regulators will be able to work effectively as part of a national systemic risk management team, as structural challenges will likely compromise its ability to be proactive, collaborative, and generally effective in helping to address larger capital market issues on a timely basis," and "we believe that the current structure fundamentally misallocates resources, causing securities regulation to be less efficient and effective" (EP 2009, 40). Our existing structure was described as "balkanized" or "fragmented," never as "decentralized." In what was perhaps the pinnacle of the constitutional rhetoric, only the proposed federal securities regulator was described as "decentralized" (EP 2009, 3, 47).

These assumptions about a single-regulator structure being inherently superior as a matter of policy were questioned by some (Schultz and Alexandroff 1985; Pidruchney 1985; Courchene 1986; Roy 1986; Swinton 1992; Daniels 1992; MacIntosh 1997; Fluker 2009; Lortie 2010, 2011; Jackman 2011; Lee 2011). However, most media reports and academic commentary repeated the assumptions (Banwell 1968; Hogg 1974; Anisman and Hogg 1979; Anisman 1981, 1986; Tse 1994; Doyle 1996; Leckey and Ward 1999; Lehman 1999), and the accompanying rhetoric intensified in the decade preceding the securities references. Uniformity became synonymous with effectiveness and efficiency; moving to a single-regulator structure became synonymous with "reform"; and the focus of discussion shifted to why any province would resist "reform" and why the move to a single regulator was taking so long (Harris 2002, 2003, 2005; Anand 2005; Anand and Green 2005; Anand and Klein 2005; Anand and Green 2010; Hjartarson 2010; Monahan 2010; Puri 2010; Anand and Green 2011).

The provinces did not challenge the constitutional rhetoric until shortly before the securities references, and by then it had been repeated for so long that it had become conventional wisdom. Most Canadians believed, and still believe, the constitutional rhetoric because it continues to be repeated, not just by the federal government and supportive academics, but also by international bodies such as the Financial Stability Board (FSB 2012) and the International Monetary Fund (IMF). The federal government's representatives have influence with these bodies: the federal Department of Finance, the Office of the Superintendent of Financial Institutions, and the Bank of Canada are members of the Financial Stability Board, and the current executive director of the IMF representing Canada is Thomas Hockin (former chair of the Expert Panel on Securities Regulation). As described in the next section, it was the repetition of constitutional rhetoric by the IMF that finally prompted the provinces to challenge the rhetoric, previewing the evidence and arguments in the securities references.

CHALLENGING CONVENTIONAL WISDOM: MYTHS VERSUS FACTS

In 2007, the IMF conducted a Financial Sector Assessment Program – Detailed Assessment of the Level of Implementation of the IOSCO Principles and Objectives of Securities Regulation in Canada (FSAP). Because it uses the assessment methodology developed by the International Organization of Securities Commissions (IOSCO 2003b), the most comprehensive and rigorous by far, the FSAP is the most credible available measurement of the functional performance of securities regulatory systems (Spink 2010b, para. 11).

The 2007 FSAP assessment of Canada was conducted in a highly charged atmosphere. The IMF examined two provincial regulators (Quebec and Ontario) with diametrically opposed perspectives on a single regulator. Ontario was allied on that issue with the federal government and was the only province refusing to join the passport system. Quebec essentially represented the "passport jurisdictions," which looked forward to the FSAP results because they expected a positive assessment but were concerned that the IMF would go beyond IOSCO's assessment methodology and repeat the constitutional rhetoric about a single regulator structure, which was particularly intense in Canada at the time. That prompted the Council of Ministers of Securities Regulation (representing all provinces except Ontario) to respond publicly to "intense negative rhetoric from those who advocate creating a single securities regulator," describing criticisms of the existing system as "myths" and "misinformation" and pointing to functional assessments by the OECD and World Bank ranking Canada's securities regulatory system as one of the best in the world (Selinger 2007). The rhetoric was also described as "fiction," "untrue" and "irresponsible" by the British Columbia Securities Commission, which said it "neither supports nor opposes creating a single regulator ... What we do oppose is advocating a single regulator, or any other type of reform, on the basis of mythology" (Hyndman 2007).

That was the first time the provinces challenged the constitutional rhetoric and, although the "myths versus facts" approach proved extremely effective in the securities references, it had no appreciable impact on public opinion or the IMF. When the IMF published Canada's (stellar) FSAP results early in 2008, it also published a Financial System Stability Assessment – Update (IMF FSSA 2008) recommending a single-regulator structure for Canada on the basis of those same myths. The IMF seems poised to do something similar early in 2014 when it will publish the results of Canada's most recent FSAP assessment conducted in 2013 (Spink 2013). Whatever the IMF does or says, it will be important to recognize the distinction between the IMF's functional and structural opinions on Canadian securities regulation.

FUNCTIONAL VERSUS STRUCTURAL OPINIONS: METHODOLOGY MATTERS

The contrast between the IMF FSAP 2008 and IMF FSSA 2008 illustrated the distinction between *functional* and *structural* opinions, which is crucial to understanding the contradictory evidence in the securities references (Spink 2010b). The FSAP was a *functional* opinion, measuring performance in terms of implementing functional policy objectives according to a stated methodology. The FSSA was a *structural* opinion, asserting that a single-regulator structure would be functionally superior to our existing system, without disclosing a methodology.

The following table compares the aggregate grading from the FSAP assessments of Canada (2008), the United States (2010), Australia (2006), UK (2011), France (2005), and Germany (2011).[3]

Table 1: Comparison of Aggregate Gradings from FSAP Assessments

Number of IOSCO Principles	*Canada**	*United States*	*Australia*	*UK*	*France*	*Germany*
Implemented/Fully implemented (FI)	24	16	21	19	18	21
Broadly implemented (BI)	4	8	5	10	7	4
Partly implemented (PI)	1	5	2	0	2	2
Not implemented (NI)	0	0	1	0	0	0
Not applicable (NA)	1	1	1	1	3	3
Total	30	30	30	30	30	30

Source: Author's compilation.

*These are the gradings resulting from the implementation in Canada of National Instrument 31-103 and National Instrument 41-104, which were pending in 2008; gradings prior to implementation were FI, 22; BI, 4; PI, 3; NI, 0; NA, 1. See IMF FSAP (2008 at 20-1, 35-6, and 49).

IOSCO's assessment methodologies were designed primarily as tools for identifying areas of potential improvement for each regulator being assessed (IOSCO 2003b, 5; IOSCO 2008, 5; IOSCO 2011b, 16), not to rank the relative performance of regulatory systems in different jurisdictions, but the FSAP results obviously invite comparison. Canada's high performance contradicted the rhetorical assumptions underlying the FSSA structural opinion, highlighting its lack of methodology and relative credibility. It was the first time that constitutional rhetoric (represented by the FSSA 2008 structural opinion) and a methodological assessment of functional performance (the FSAP 2008 functional opinion) were presented side by side, allowing comparison of myths and facts.

---

[3] The chart shows results of FSAP Detailed Assessments of the Level of Implementation of the IOSCO Principles and Objectives of Securities Regulation for each country, available at http://www.imf.org/external/np/fsap/fssa.aspx.

The evidence in the securities references included other functional opinions published by the World Bank, OECD, and Milken Institute, ranking Canada's securities regulatory system against others around the world. The World Bank's annual "Doing Business" reports' chapters on "Protecting Investors" ranked Canada fifth in the world from 2007 to 2011 and fourth from 2012 to 2014 (World Bank 2013). Two OECD publications ranked the Canadian securities regulatory system second among 21 countries in terms of "overall securities market regulation" (OECD 2006) The Milken Institute's "Capital Access Index" ranked Canada first in the world in 2009 and 2010 (Milken 2010). Together with the FSAP, these are the only functional opinions based on disclosed methodologies.

The methodology used by the World Bank and OECD has been criticized (Siems 2005), and the resulting rankings were described as a "flimsy foundation" for arguments that our system performed well, and "not particularly relevant to actual performance" (Anand 2010b). While I agree that every assessment methodology should be scrutinized because some are better than others, the much more crucial distinction is between functional opinions that use a methodology and structural opinions that do not use a methodology. Scrutinizing the methodology and empirical foundation enables us to consider what level of credibility to afford the resulting opinion, while no methodology means no measurable credibility. We may choose to attach less weight to the World Bank/OECD assessments opinions than to the Milken Institute and FSAP assessments. The fact remains that, of all the methodological assessments available, Canada's securities regulatory system ranks no worse than fourth in the world and, according to the better methodologies, Canada is first in terms of functional performance.

These methodological assessments allow us to see past the constitutional rhetoric in historic portrayals of our system and focus instead on what Canada has been doing right. The next section examines Canadian securities regulation as an example of successful federalism.

SECURITIES REGULATION AS AN EXAMPLE OF SUCCESSFUL FEDERALISM

Before examining why our existing system seems to excel, it is useful to put Canada's high performance rankings in perspective and clarify what is meant by good securities regulatory policy.

Keeping Rankings in Perspective

The high performance rankings of our existing system are consistent with my personal experiences in Canadian securities regulation since 1988. The rankings are a tribute to the many regulators and government officials who worked hard to develop better regulatory policy and better processes for developing that policy across Canada, and who were historically under-appreciated, over-criticized, and even impeded by constitutional rhetoric. However, we must heed IOSCO's caution that their assessment "is not an end in itself" (IOSCO 2003b, 5; IOSCO 2008, 5; IOSCO 2011b, 16) and resist any tendency to rely too much upon performance measurements or rankings, especially when they are favourable.

Canada's high rankings do not mean that our system cannot be improved. Rather, they mean that our existing system is at or near the front of the continuous-improvement process in which every securities regulatory system is engaged. Every system must continuously adapt and evolve in order to achieve its functional policy objectives in a dynamic environment. It is prudent to use the rankings to recognize that Canada produces good securities regulators and good securities regulatory policy, and has consistently done so for a long time. Recognizing that allows us to understand what we have been doing right from a functional policy perspective.

What Is Good Securities Regulatory Policy?

IOSCO's objectives and principles of securities regulation (IOSCO 2003a; IOSCO 2010) and assessment methodology (IOSCO 2003b; IOSCO 2008; IOSCO 2011b) describe the global consensus on good securities regulatory policy in consider-able detail, including examples of current practices. IOSCO recognizes, however, that best practices will and should change to keep up with market developments (Corcoran 2010) and that there is often no single correct approach to a regulatory issue, so making good regulatory policy is as much an art as a science.

To understand how Canada makes good policy, it is first necessary to debunk two myths about securities regulatory policy: 1) that faster policy-making is necessarily better, and 2) that uniformity is a necessity. These myths pervade the constitutional rhetoric and are evident in descriptions of our consensus-based policy-making process as "duplicative," "cumbersome," "protracted" (EP 2009, 2), and resulting in "a lack of uniformity" (WPC 2003, 25).

Faster Policy Is Not Necessarily Better

Faster policy-making is not necessarily better—indeed, the opposite is often true. The chair of the British Columbia Securities Commission recently observed that "investors and markets should be able to look to a regulator that is seasoned and keeps a steady hand on the tiller—a regulator that knows when to act quickly, and when to wait for better information" (Leong 2012, 9-10).

The first job of a regulator is to do no harm, and there is an unfortunate history of fast policy responses doing harm. Policy can be made quickly, but doing so increases the risk of error. Regulatory errors tend to have more significant impact than regulatory successes (which are typically incremental functional improvements) because errors divert the evolutionary process towards a dead end in terms of policy, which remains damaging until reversed. An error-avoidance mentality is therefore crucial in an environment where it is normal for stakeholders to exert pressure on regulators or elected officials to, in effect, err in favour of that stakeholder (the risk of regulatory capture). The greatest danger has been when political pressures force regulatory responses that, in hindsight at least, were ill-considered and damaging.

In the evidence in the securities references, the most prominent example of this error avoidance was that Canada's slower response to the issues addressed by the US Sarbanes-Oxley Act in 2002 was qualitatively superior to the faster US response (Rousseau 2010a, 117-21; Rice 2010, para. 172(a); Choi 2010, paras. 88-94; Macey 2010a, 28-30). In summary, the evidence regarding the Sarbanes-Oxley Act demonstrated the need to distinguish between speed and quality in policy-making; how quality is significantly more important than speed; how speed in policy-making is only good if it produces the right policy; and how very bad speed can be when it produces the wrong policy. The myth that faster is always better thus ignores the most significant factor determining the impact of any particular regulatory policy: quality (Spink 2010d, para. 3).

Once we recognize the predominant value of quality, it becomes apparent that focusing on the speed of policy development can be an artificial exercise (Rousseau 2010b). For example, some of the evidence criticized our policy-making process for taking too long to make new rules governing alternative trading systems (ATS), which have been a policy issue in Canada since 1990 (Russell 2010). I respectfully disagreed with those opinions (Spink 2010d) because, in my experience, the consensus-building process is precisely what produces quality regulation. Complaints about the speed or efficiency of the process obscure the functional mechanisms that determine quality, underestimating both the volume and value of the work involved (Spink 2010d, para. 9).

The ATS rules illustrate how consensus-based regulation should work in situations where there is strong consensus on the regulatory objectives and principles but uncertainty about how best to implement them in a particular context (Spink 2010d, para. 10). These situations are common, and bringing multiple, expert perspectives to bear on such policy issues is not duplicative—it is additive and often highly productive. Consensus therefore tends to produce better-quality regulation than a single perspective. So-called delays should be recognized as maximizing quality and preventing error—postponing decisions on changes because more time or information is required to make the right policy decision and the current situation is not urgent enough to warrant the risk of an immediate but regrettable decision (Spink 2010d, par. 8). There are often no clear starting or endpoints in regulatory policy that can be used to start and stop the clock, so regulation is more appropriately viewed as a dynamic and continuous process (Spink 2010d, para. 5). The most important thing is not the speed of the process but whether it is moving in the right direction.

Uniformity Is Not Necessary

The second myth is that uniformity is necessary to achieve efficiency and effectiveness. The purported need for uniformity has always been the primary argument for a federal regulator, so the provinces introduced a great deal of evidence intended to show that forced uniformity was unnecessary and undesirable.

The most prominent examples in evidence were the differences in exempt-market regulation—the rules governing sales of securities without a prospectus. In Alberta, the vast majority of new capital is raised in the exempt market (Spink 2010c, para. 32). Historically, exempt-market rules in Alberta and British Columbia have allowed investors to accept more risk than similar rules in Ontario.

Exempt-market regulation deals with local investors and, typically, local issuers and enterprises. Local market conditions differ significantly across Canada, so regulatory philosophies naturally differ based on those conditions (Rousseau 2010a, 115-17, 122-5; Suret and Carpentier 2010, 15-41). The history of resource exploration and development in Alberta and British Columbia explains their different regulatory philosophy regarding the capacity of investors to accept risk in the exempt market (Rice 2010, paras. 156-8, 175-6; Suret and Carpentier 2010, 23-41; MacIntosh 2012b, 257-8).

These philosophical differences are subtle—a slightly different view of the balance between regulatory costs and benefits in the local exempt market—but subtle differences in regulatory policy can make a significant difference. Alberta (among others) revised its exempt-market regulation in 2002 and subsequently observed a dramatic increase in activity (ASC 2004; Spink 2010c, para. 32; Robinson and Cottrell 2007).

While it is possible to criticize the policy decisions made by each provincial regulator, the different approaches reflect real competition among regulators to find the best form of exempt-market regulation for their particular market. It is therefore wrong to view these differences as a lack of consistency or efficiency: they instead demonstrate how policy differences among jurisdictions may (and apparently do) increase efficiency. Arguably, the different approaches to exempt-market regulation are the most sophisticated examples of regulatory policy development in Canada and are the jewels of our system.

The fact that regulators sometimes agree to harmonize their rules, and that harmonization sometimes extends to the point of complete uniformity, does not mean that uniformity is necessary or always desirable. The reality is that some things can't be harmonized, some shouldn't be harmonized, and regulatory competition is healthy even when rules are harmonized (Spink 2010c, para. 21). Healthy regulatory competition exists "when different regulators share the same overarching regulatory objectives, but, in implementing comparable regimes, compete with each other to develop the most effective and least costly ways to achieve these goals" (Tafara and Peterson 2007, 52).

Internationally, uniformity has always been practically impossible, so systems have evolved towards harmonization and the mutual recognition of other jurisdictions' regulatory standards. In 2007, the US Securities and Exchange Commission (SEC) signalled a change from its long-standing strategy of seeking "regulatory convergence" among jurisdictions toward a new framework founded on "bilateral substituted compliance" and mutual recognition, in part because it "has the benefit of not discouraging regulatory experimentation (a risk with a regulatory convergence approach), but without encouraging regulatory arbitrage" (Tafara and Peterson 2007, 55). Tafara and Peterson observe:

> Despite its undeniable theoretical advantages, *complete* regulatory convergence has proven difficult to achieve over any short-to-intermediate time frame. The reasons for this are many, but the magnitude of the task stands out: the entire complement of individual regulations and standards that need to be "converged" to allow for full market integration are quite numerous. Another reason, less frequently mentioned in the convergence dialogue but perhaps just as important, is that some jurisdictions simply have fundamentally different regulatory philosophies. When these differences are significant, complete convergence may not be possible and, indeed, may not even be desirable, if eliminating these philosophical differences results in less regulatory experimentation and a rigid one-size-fits-all approach to market oversight. (Tafara and Peterson 2007, 50)

The policy objective is "to build a framework that facilitates international access and rejects protectionist tendencies but, at the same time, protects investors and market integrity" (Jenah 2007, 83). Our current passport system is an example of such a process and framework. Before examining the passport system in more detail, it is useful to describe how our existing system evolved as an example of "federalism as process" (Courchene 2010b, 5-6).

FEDERALISM AS PROCESS

Securities regulation can be viewed as performing three basic functions: 1) making the rules (policy development and implementation); 2) enforcing the rules (encouraging compliance, investigating and prosecuting violators); and 3) adjudication (the quasi-judicial function). I focus here on the first function because it most clearly illustrates securities regulation as process, and how that process has evolved in Canada.

Delegated Legislation and the Expanding Rulebook

When I started working in securities regulation in 1988, the Alberta Securities Act, Regulation and Policies, totalled about 300 pages. Today the consolidated version is about 3,000 pages and would be more than twice that size if it included all the rules imposed by self-regulatory organizations and the approved contracts used by regulated entities such as exchanges and clearing agencies. The act and traditional regulations have actually shrunk in size, and the growth has been in the rules made by securities regulators (delegated legislation). What explains this phenomenal expansion of delegated legislation?

In my experience, the expansion of rules is primarily the result of burgeoning demand for new rules, primarily from the securities industry but also from governments and regulators, to deal with evolving market practices and events. There is a continuous demand for new rules because, when done properly, rules are good for everybody. Sound rules reduce risk and cost and facilitate transactions. Ronald Coase described this from the economic perspective, observing how securities exchanges originally used private law rules to enable two people who wiggle their fingers at each other across a room to create a sophisticated contract that would automatically and reliably complete within a few days (Spink 2010a, para. 24).

Modern rules reflect basically the same functional policy objectives, principles, and regulatory mechanisms used by the London and New York stock exchanges in 1882 (Spink 2010a, paras. 3(d), 22, 84). They remain principles-based, but over time those principles have become increasingly codified and detailed in response to the continuous demand for clearer articulations of exactly how the principles apply to particular products or transactions and to changing conditions. The need to update existing rules means the demand is not only continuous but continuously increasing. Securities regulation is therefore essentially a constant law-reform process that applies basic policy principles to a rapidly evolving securities industry.

The next section focuses more specifically on how Canadian securities regulators met this growing demand for policy and law reform as an example of "federalism as process." It examines how the process evolved in response to the demand for more and better securities regulation by improving the system's dynamic efficiency.

Dynamic Efficiency and Rule-Making

Dynamic efficiency is basically the ability of a system to innovate, adapt, and respond appropriately to market developments. It has been aptly described as "the acid test of a good regulatory regime" (Lortie 2010, 22). There are many examples of the dynamic efficiency of the existing system (Anand and Klein 2005; Lortie 2010; Courchene 2010a, 2010b), but here I focus on how the rule-making process evolved to become more dynamically efficient.

In 1988, every securities commission in Canada was basically a department of government, each responsible for its respective act and regulations. It was already obvious that conventional processes for amending legislation or making regulations were ill-suited to the demands of securities regulation because elected officials, however well intentioned, could not be expected to deal with the volume, rapidity, and complexity of issues arising in this area. Regulators tried to meet the demand for new rules by issuing policy statements in ever-increasing numbers, but policy statements did not have the force of law. Eventually, one was struck down (*Ainsley* 1993), triggering major changes to give securities regulators:

- more authority: the power to make rules (legally equivalent to regulations passed by government);
- more autonomy: several major commissions (starting with the Alberta Securities Commission in 1995) were removed from government and converted to provincial corporations managed by a CEO, with directors appointed by government; and
- more resources: major commissions became self-funding, using regulatory fees to fund their operations.

These changes gave securities regulators significantly more responsibility and capacity and deliberately insulated them from elected officials. They recognized the risks associated with politically motivated regulatory decisions and attempted to reduce those risks by having most decisions made by expert regulators instead of elected officials. The precise balance and accountability mechanisms were different in each jurisdiction; the only constant was that every regulator reported to a minister who reported to a legislative body.

There was earnest debate about the merits of rule-making (MacIntosh 1994), and the models continue to evolve, but the overarching functional purpose has always been the same: to provide a more responsive, transparent, consultative, and non-partisan policy-development process. Rule-making processes were designed to facilitate more rigorous, better-informed debate on technical or specialized issues than was possible with conventional legislative processes. The processes enabled the use of explanatory "companion policies," which do not have the force of law but promote better understanding and compliance with the rules. The objective was to produce better-quality policy.

Rule-making enabled policy development and implementation to move either faster or slower than was possible with conventional legislation. Faster action is sometimes useful, but the more significant advantage of rule-making is that it enabled the policy-development process to be sustained over much longer periods than with conventional legislative processes. That longer attention span is a necessity for dealing with the complex issues that abound in securities regulation.

Rule-making facilitated harmonization in some areas and regulatory competition in others. The volume of change and consultation increased so that securities regulators now hear complaints of "regulatory fatigue" from stakeholders struggling to keep up with requests for comments on proposed new rules. That seems a necessary and small price to pay for a more rigorous, transparent consultation process and resulting dynamic efficiency. It belies suggestions that our policy-making processes are too slow and reminds us again that the critical objective is not speed but quality.

Competitive Federalism and Innovation

Securities regulation provides many concrete examples of the "theory of competitive federalism" described by Breton (1986). Competitive federalism "brings to the operations of governments some of the innovation and dynamic efficiency associated with the operation of decentralized markets in the private sector" (Courchene 2010b, 6). A colourful example was described in a 2007 speech by the then-chair of the British Columbia Securities Commission:

> A few months ago, I attended a presentation by an eminent professor from Columbia University, who told the audience that the SEC has ramped up the pace of its policy processes. As an example, he pointed out that the SEC had concluded that rapid dissemination of corporate disclosure through the internet meant the traditional one-year hold period for private placements was unnecessarily long. As a result, the SEC had published a proposal to reduce the hold period to six months. If Canada's regulators can't keep up with this kind of innovation, he thundered, Canadian markets will become even more uncompetitive.
>
> It might surprise the good professor to learn that Canadian regulators actually noticed the internet some years ago, and that we came to the same conclusion. As a result, we reduced our hold period from 12 months to 4 months. That was in 2001. We aren't too worried about falling behind our US colleagues on this one!
>
> Indeed, Alberta and British Columbia pioneered this change in 1998. Demonstrating one of the strengths of our decentralized system—innovation—our successful implementation in the west led to national adoption a few years later, (Hyndman 2007, 8-9)

The evidence filed in the securities references included other examples of how decentralization and competitive federalism foster dynamic efficiency and innovation (which centralization sacrifices for uniformity), and how the SEC's recent failures may be seen as the result of "excessive centralization" (Macey 2010a, 61; Courchene 2010b, 18-19) facilitating regulatory capture, complacency, and error (Courchene 2010b, 21; Suret and Carpentier 2010, 96-105; Choi 2010, paras. 75-8). The evidence also described how the risk of regulatory capture for a single regulator in Canada would be particularly high because our financial sector is so concentrated (Suret and Carpentier 2010, 96-105; Choi 2010, paras. 75-8).

MacIntosh (2012b, 259) describes how decentralized policy-making produces superior policy outcomes in securities regulation because it is a process of Bayesian updating where "making good legislation is essentially a never-ending iterative process" in which "regulation experiences rapid and essentially continuous evolution." Before considering some specific examples of such evolution, it is useful to examine the incentives for securities regulators and the concern about a "race to the bottom."

Why There Is No Race to the Bottom

Concerns about provincial autonomy resulting in a race to the bottom reflect certain misconceptions about the incentives facing securities regulators. For example, evidence in the references suggested that:

- securities regulators have incentives to impose "negative jurisdictional externalities" such as allowing a local factory to pollute rivers flowing into other provinces; ignoring or discounting the effects of consumer fraud perpetrated by local firms against consumers in other provinces; and preserving a local monopoly (Trebilcock 2010, para. 22);
- provinces are largely powerless against such externalities because it is difficult to negotiate interprovincial cooperation and coordination to "avoid these kinds of beggar-thy-neighbour effects" and avoid "some form of 'race to the bottom' where all provinces choose to ignore jurisdictional externalities" (Trebilcock 2010, para. 24);
- "[a] principle of decision-making by consensus or unanimity means that 'hold-out' provinces can credibly threaten to undermine efforts at coordinated responses to inter-jurisdictional externalities" (Trebilcock 2010, para. 24); and
- jurisdictional externalities from a decentralized system of provincial securities regulation are pervasive and lead to dysfunctional, costly and inefficient regulatory regimes (Trebilcock 2010, para. 7).

Although a regulatory "race to the bottom" is hypothetically possible, the evidence demonstrates quite the opposite. Securities markets have always been international, inherently receptive to free trade, and relatively borderless by comparison with markets in tangible goods (Spink 2010c, para. 11). It has long been understood that "the larger the pool of investors bidding on a company's securities, the more efficiently the price of those securities will be set and the more liquid the market for them will be" (Tafara and Peterson 2007, 46). The normal incentives for regulators are to pursue the most efficient market possible while maintaining a primary focus on investor protection, thereby maximizing the benefits for investors and issuers both locally and outside the jurisdiction (Spink 2010c, para. 11). These incentives drive securities regulators to produce positive externalities through continuous improvement and innovations that respond to local conditions (Spink 2010c, paras. 12-6; Macey 2010a, 30-4, 2010b, 2-3; Choi 2010, paras. 65-80).

Canada has of course experienced its share of regulatory errors and failures. Armstrong (1997, 2001) examines the history of securities regulation from 1870 to 1980, including fascinating details about regulatory failures such as the epic struggle to control Toronto boiler rooms. Those details reveal no race to the bottom but rather a steady inclination toward better regulatory policy in which failure normally consisted of not advancing quickly enough or in exactly the right direction. This pursuit of better regulatory policy was the reason that interprovincial cooperation was formalized in 1937 through the Canadian Securities Administrators (CSA) and is evident in every CSA harmonization initiative and every example of innovation, experimentation, or diversity since (Rousseau 2010a, 90-8, 115-48).

Experimentation enables individual jurisdictions to maximize their positive externalities (by exporting successful innovations) while limiting the risks associated with unsuccessful experiments. For example, Alberta's Junior Capital Pool (JCP) program was initially problematic. The very first JCP in 1986 generated a massive scandal and the bankruptcy of a brokerage firm, resulting in many regulatory and criminal proceedings; my first job as a securities regulator was largely occupied by taking enforcement action against violators of that original JCP policy. The problems pointed regulators in the direction of reform. The policy was modified several times and since 2002 has operated across Canada as the Capital Pool Company program with considerable success (TSX Venture Exchange 2012, 3). The crucial point is that the process that created the JCP policy and modified it until it became a success was dynamically efficient.

JCPs illustrate why it is simplistic to suggest that federal legislation might usefully set "minimum standards." Sometimes it makes sense to reduce regulatory requirements, or to do away with them altogether (Aitken 2005). So-called minimum standards would actually just ossify a single standard, preventing innovations or improvements by individual jurisdictions such as JCPs (Suret and Carpentier 2010, 41-2; Choi 2010, paras. 22-4; Rice 2010, para. 172e).

JCPs were also a pivotal factor in the failure of the federal government's proposals for a single securities regulator in the mid-1990s—the MOU proposals, named after numerous draft memoranda of understanding (MOUs) between the federal government and provinces. Parallels between the failure of the MOU proposals and failure of the federal government in the securities references are described in the next section.

WHY THE MOU PROPOSALS FAILED

The MOU proposals started in 1994 (Canada 1994), collapsed, were revived in 1996, and collapsed again in early 1997 (MacIntosh 1997; Harris 2002, 27-36; MacIntosh 2012a, 179-80; MacIntosh 2012b, 265). They were presented as a constitutionally neutral initiative focused on improving the efficiency of the system by reducing costs and eliminating duplication (Sawiak et al.1996). Alberta was initially open to the proposals and considered them seriously. The MOU proposals generated intense critical scrutiny of our existing system (CSA 1995a).

Similar to what occurred in the securities references, scrutiny revealed that the system was already quite efficient. It became evident that a single regulator was going to cost more than our existing system because transition costs would be significant and a single regulator (in whatever form) would inevitably be bigger than the existing system. Although presented as reducing overlap and duplication, the MOU proposals were recognized as a source of overlap and duplication (CSA 1995a, para. 2.1.6). Since no other policy goals had been articulated for the MOU proposals (CSA 1995a, paras. 2.3.3, 6.2.3), their inability to improve efficiency may alone have been enough to cause their failure.

Alberta's paramount concern, however, was that a single regulator would eliminate the most valuable feature of our existing system: innovative regional initiatives such as JCPs (Alberta Hansard 1996, 2244). Although the federal government agreed in principle that regional innovation should be accommodated, it was impossible to envision how JCPs, or any other significant regional innovations, could be achieved under a single regulator. This issue crystallized Alberta's opposition, and other provinces had similar concerns about forced uniformity.

The MOU initiative was never formally pronounced dead, but discussions ended early in 1997 after Ontario agreed to a federal securities commission on the understanding that a majority of the commissioners would be selected from Ontario (McIntosh 2007). From today's perspective it seems astonishing that such a significant issue with the governance of the proposed federal regulator would surface so late in the process, but it reflects how the initiative had until then been focused narrowly on the possibility of improved efficiency.

The parallels between the MOU proposals and the securities references seem significant: functional improvements were claimed but not supported by empirical evidence; scrutiny of the existing system revealed strengths that a single regulator could not replicate; and in the end, only Ontario supported the federal proposals. The next section examines how our regulatory system evolved in the aftermath of the MOU proposals and considers whether that evolutionary trajectory will continue in the aftermath of the securities references.

THE PASSPORT SYSTEM: THE EVOLUTION OF PROCESS

We can trace the evolutionary trajectory of today's passport system directly back to the failure of the MOU proposals (CSA 1995b, 18). While the proposals foundered, the Alberta and British Columbia securities commissions signed a regulatory accord designed to increase coordination and cooperation on regulatory initiatives, policy development, and securities enforcement (ASC/BCSC 1996). That accord was the next step in refining the prospectus-review process, which in 1999 evolved into the Mutual Reliance Review System (MRRS) (Rousseau 2010a, 93-7). Each of these incremental functional improvements was an evolutionary step toward our current passport system.

The passport system is a mutual-recognition process functionally similar to the Multijurisdictional Disclosure System adopted by the SEC and Canadian jurisdictions in 1991. Mutual recognition basically means that each jurisdiction accepts the others' disclosure and approvals, nobody gives up jurisdiction, and everyone's anti-fraud provisions continue to apply. Mutual recognition enables practically free trade in securities without compromising each jurisdiction's overarching objective of investor protection. It is the most obvious functional model for globalized free trade in securities (Spink 2010c, para. 23; Selinger 2007).

The term "passport system" is simply the label attached to the most recent set of functional improvements to regulatory process that have been evolving constantly since the 1930s (Spink 2010c, para. 24). The key innovation enabling mutual recognition (dubbed "operation of law") is quite narrow and technical, applying to only certain portions of our securities regulatory system (Spink 2010c, para. 23; Rousseau 2010a, 112-4), but has resulted in significant functional improvements.

FUNCTIONAL IMPROVEMENTS

It is important to recognize that the passport system, like the vast bulk of policy initiatives throughout the history of securities regulation, focused strictly upon making incremental functional improvements to the existing system. It is therefore incorrect to refer to our entire securities regulatory system as the "passport model," or to view the passport system as a structural model or evolutionary endpoint. The passport initiative deliberately expressed no conclusion on regulatory structure and was neutral to the significant structural differences among regulators in the passport jurisdictions.

Constitutional rhetoric portrayed the passport system as a "virtual single regulator," implying that it was an inadequate attempt to emulate the functional superiority of a single regulator (Spink 2010b, paras. 46-8). In fact, the passport system was conceived as potentially superior to a single regulator (CSA 1995a; CSA 1995b). It was designed to provide a "single window of access to market participants"—as a single regulator would—with respect to areas where securities law is highly harmonized, but to outperform a single regulator by preserving the essential elements of consensus-based policy making and the ability of jurisdictions "to innovate and test new and unique initiatives" (Alberta et al. 2004, paras. 5.1, 5.10).

Accountability

The passport system illustrates how accountability mechanisms have evolved and how relatively subtle changes can have significant effects. It changed the dynamics of policy-making by creating the Council of Ministers of Securities Regulation and giving it a role in the existing consensus-building process. This produced "unprecedented levels of co-ordination and consensus among provincial and territorial governments and the Canadian Securities Administrators to streamline and improve securities regulation," and a large volume of National Instruments and complementary legislative reforms including entirely new and harmonized securities acts in several jurisdictions (Selinger 2007).

The council was perhaps the most successful innovation of the passport system in terms of improving the quality and pace of policy development. In each jurisdiction there are three distinct policy inputs on securities regulatory issues: 1) the securities regulator; 2) ministry officials; and 3) the minister. Basically, the council improved the process by which those inputs were coordinated so that, when consensus is possible it is reached more quickly and, when there is no consensus, the reasons are clearer and discussions are better informed. Better coordination of policy and legislative timetables at the ministerial level, together with a shift toward "platform legislation" (retaining fundamental principles in the act but removing detailed provisions to be addressed through rule-making) makes the continuous reform process more efficient for everyone. It is easier for smaller jurisdictions to develop and maintain harmonized securities legislation and to actively participate in policy discussions. Jurisdictions choosing to simply monitor policy discussions and harmonize their legislation obtain all the benefits of the process at low cost. Each jurisdiction remains locally accountable and free to innovate. The council continues to allow each province to customize its internal accountability and policy arrangements with its securities regulator. These arrangements vary significantly across Canada and are another form of regulatory competition, reflecting:

- fundamentally different public policy or regulatory philosophies, such as Quebec's "communitarian capitalism" versus Anglo-American "individualist capitalism" (Courchene 2010a, paras. 34-40);
- more nuanced policy differences such as exempt market regulation; and
- even more nuanced structural/substantive/policy differences such as the independent securities tribunals in Quebec and New Brunswick (Rousseau 2010a, 178-85; Spink 2010b, para. 8, n.7).

These changes to the accountability mechanisms are subtle. Although they give elected officials an increased role in managing the process by which regulatory decisions are made, they remain intended to reduce the possibility of unwise political regulatory decisions by making political influences more transparent and subjecting them to more rigorous policy scrutiny. The council is not perfect, but it appears to provide the most productive level of political accountability for securities regulation that has evolved to date in Canada.

THE PASSPORT SYSTEM IN PERSPECTIVE

Although the passport system has been a significant functional improvement, it is just the latest innovation in our continuously evolving securities regulatory system and would have gone largely unnoticed except for Ontario's refusal to participate and the ensuing constitutional references. Thrusting it into the spotlight revealed in extraordinary detail how the passport system evolved and why it seems to work so well. Looking back along that evolutionary trajectory, the following points seem evident:

- The objectives and principles of securities regulation have not changed significantly over time; what has changed continuously are technology and products in the securities industry and the details of securities legislation.
- The process for continuous reform of securities legislation evolved primarily in pursuit of better-quality regulatory policy and dynamic efficiency.
- Regulatory competition, experimentation, innovation, and diverse perspectives tend to produce better-quality regulatory policy and dynamic efficiency, whether or not the result is harmonization.
- Securities markets have always been international, so harmonization (as distinct from uniformity) and mutual recognition are the most promising bases for enabling international free trade in securities while preserving healthy regulatory competition.
- Our current passport system is a world leader in terms of the achieving the functional policy objectives of securities regulation, illustrating what Courchene has described more broadly as Canadians being "masters of the art of federalism" (Courchene 2010a, para. 11) and excelling at "federalism as process" (Courchene 2010b, 6).
- Regulators can never rest on their laurels but must continually innovate and pursue functional improvements. The most important regulatory challenge is always the next one.

Ontario and the Passport System

From a functional perspective, it has always been clear that Ontario should join the passport system and harmonize its securities legislation with that of the other provinces (Selinger 2008). In 2003, Ontario supported consulting on a passport system based on the view that, if implemented, it would represent an incremental improvement to the current securities regulatory framework. However, it refused to sign the Passport Memorandum of Understanding in 2004 because "for Ontario, the passport system was not an end unto itself, but rather a step towards the creation of a national securities regulatory system" (Rousseau 2010a, 107-8). Ontario officials were concerned that joining the passport system would "not do anything for Ontario" but would result in the loss of political momentum for a single regulator (Ontario Hansard 2004).

After the Supreme Court's decision, Ontario's finance minister was quoted as saying, "The passport system itself does not serve the interests of the Ontario market, particularly" (Howlett 2011). A new political consideration is that joining the passport system now may be seen as final capitulation by Ontario (MacIntosh 2011), the federal government's only provincial ally in the securities references. Since Ontario and the federal government have been aligned politically on this subject for some time, Ontario's position on the passport system seems unlikely to change except in tandem with the position of the federal government.

Ontario's refusal to join the passport system raises interesting questions about its particular vision of federalism and about the capacity of a single province to alter the course of federalism. The functional superiority of the passport system was always the most plausible explanation for Ontario's refusal to participate (Spink 2010b, para. 48), and it is extremely unusual in my experience for political considerations to prevail over functional considerations in this way (Spink 2010c, para. 13). The fact that political considerations have prevailed in Ontario illustrates what I will refer to as "constitutional risk"—the risk that a constitutional agenda may generate incentives for retrograde policy that override normal functional policy considerations.

TURF WARS AND CONSTITUTIONAL RISK

The realization that the long struggle over securities regulation has always been a constitutional turf war is sobering. One wonders how history may have been written if Canada had replaced its world-leading securities regulatory system with an inferior model based on constitutional rhetoric. The securities references illustrate how toxic this kind of constitutional turf war can be to functional policy development and implementation, and how preposterous the supportive myths can be—an extreme example of constitutional risk.

My first exposure to constitutional risk was in the 1990s when I described how a constitutional turf war and agenda impeded the process of modernizing our securities transfer legislation (Spink 1997). It still does. That particular constitutional agenda (and supportive myth that securities transfer legislation is a matter of corporate law, not property and civil rights) significantly obstructed the reform process and frustrated functional policy objectives—including the reduction of systemic risk—by clinging to obsolete concepts deliberately rejected by other jurisdictions (Spink 2007, 194-5; Spink 2010a, paras. 66-8; Gray and Scavone 2012). Although the proper constitutional characterization of securities transfer legislation seems clear (Geva 2004), these toxic policies were necessary to hold a line in the constitutional turf war by delaying action on securities transfers pending the federal government's anticipated victory in the securities references, whereupon securities transfers could be subsumed under the trade and commerce power as a matter of "economic efficiency" (Puri and Lan 2007, 30). This history of retrograde policy and the artificiality of the supporting myths are the antithesis of evidence-based policy and epitomize constitutional risk.

Another example of constitutional risk has been chattel-security law. Ziegel (2012) described this as an area "where federal-provincial co-operation has failed conspicuously." The federal government has resisted almost-unanimous calls for elimination of Bank Act security provisions with "a very short and unpersuasive explanation" (Wood 2012, 256), producing outcomes that "are not commercially sensible" and an approach which "undermines several foundational features of modern secured transactions law and makes it necessary for secured parties to adopt more costly practices" (270). Because the federal government evidently has constitutional jurisdiction over Bank Act security, this is a slightly different type of turf war and constitutional risk—the risk that federal jurisdiction may be used to prevent provincial law from reaching its policy objectives, perpetuating a "tortured and dysfunctional relationship" between the federal and provincial regimes (248).

A striking example of constitutional risk invoked by the securities references was the epic constitutional turf war where "for many years the federal government mounted a repeated campaign to assume the national regulation of the insurance industry [and the] federal efforts were rejected on every occasion" (*Reference ABCA* 2011, para. 42; Armstrong 1976; Armstrong 1981, 100-13). There are many important parallels between securities and insurance regulation. Perhaps the most significant fact concerning the war over insurance regulation is how that war was conducted not by the federal government but by federal bureaucrats. Gray (1946, 483) observed that Parliament had not understood the policy of the failed federal insurance legislation because that policy "was made in the offices of the Dominion Insurance Department on Rideau Street, Ottawa, irrespective of the party or the minister for the time being nominally responsible for Dominion legislative policy. This fact is the key to what is regarded as a series of unfortunate judicial defeats for Dominion jurisdiction by those who persistently seek to establish at Ottawa a centralized control of Canada's business economy."

In retrospect, it seems axiomatic that decades-long, strategic, constitutional turf wars must be conducted by bureaucrats or not conducted at all. Cooper observed that "senior bureaucrats in the [federal] Department of Finance have for generations sought to control and regulate securities [and] still harbor secret (or not-so-secret) desires in that direction" (Cooper 2012, 16). As discussed in the next section, the turf war over securities regulation has continued and seems almost certain to produce a sequel to the securities references and perhaps even a series of constitutional battles like those over insurance regulation.

THE WAY FORWARD

Elsewhere I have observed that the "victorious" provinces did not seek this battle and gained nothing from the securities references except affirmation of the constitutional status quo (Spink 2012, 185). On the other hand, the reference decisions were a crushing blow to the federal government, because obtaining jurisdiction over securities regulation was evidently part of a larger constitutional agenda that began to unravel after the references.

For example, there have long been questions about constitutional validity of Part 1 of the federal Personal Information Protection and Electronic Documents Act (PIPEDA), which "sprang from an ambitious—some have said cynical and aggressive—attempt to stake out expanded jurisdiction for federal policy-makers" (Chester 2004, 52). The federal government's constitutional arguments in support of PIPEDA (*State Farm* 2010, para. 42) were practically identical to those that later failed in the securities references. After the references, former Supreme Court Justice Michel Bastarache described "compelling reasons to believe that PIPEDA, as enacted, would not be upheld as constitutional" (Bastarache 2012, 17). The references also cast doubt on the constitutionality of certain federal copyright provisions (Geist 2012; Crowne-Mohammed and Rozenszajn 2009).

Recent amendments to the Payment Clearing and Settlement Act (PCSA) are remarkable because they purported to shift reliance from banking to the first branch of the trade and commerce power, asserting jurisdiction based on the mere fact of cross-border activity (Canada 2011, 8:33). This subtle change arguably represents an even bolder and more aggressive expansion of the trade and commerce power than was attempted in the securities references. It clearly anticipated a federal victory in the securities references and might have succeeded in that event, completing the categorical transfer of jurisdiction from the provinces to the federal government under the banner of trade and commerce. Now conspicuously *ultra vires*, these amendments reopen longstanding concerns over the constitutionality of portions of the PCSA (Rousseau 2010a, 72-6). Moreover, these amendments are a particularly dangerous manifestation of constitutional risk because the PCSA plays an important role within the larger legal framework aimed at reducing systemic risks, and that framework obviously cannot operate properly unless every legislative component of it is constitutionally valid.

A Systemic-Risk Reference?

With so much at stake, the federal government was naturally reluctant to accept the results of the securities references as a defeat. Instead, it decided to "forge ahead" toward "the goal of establishing a national securities regulator" (Fraiberg 2012b) based upon *obiter* comments in the Supreme Court's decision regarding systemic risks.

The current argument is essentially that "the federal side did not lose," because the decision "recognizes, for the first time, a significant role for the federal government in securities regulation, particularly in regulating systemic risk" (Jamal 2012, 96-7). Partisans of federal regulation urged the federal government not to "throw in the towel" but to "address a glaring regulatory gap with respect to systemic risk" (Anand and Bishop 2012) by creating a new federal systemic-risk regulator

(Fraiberg 2012a, 178; Puri 2012a, 195-6; Sarra 2012; Ford and Gill 2012; Anand 2012b). The Canadian Bankers' Association (2013) objected to proposed securities regulation intended to reduce systemic risk in derivatives markets on the basis that the Supreme Court "confirmed the federal government's exclusive jurisdiction to regulate systemic risk in Canada, including systemic risk as it relates to OTC derivatives transactions."

The 2013 Federal Budget threatened to unilaterally propose federal systemic-risk legislation unless a "timely agreement" could be reached with the provinces on a "cooperatively established common securities regulator" (Canada 2013a, 143). In September 2013 an "Agreement in Principle [AIP] to Create a Cooperative Capital Markets Regulatory System" was signed by representatives of the governments of Canada, Ontario, and British Columbia. The AIP contemplates as-yet-unseen uniform provincial securities legislation and complementary federal legislation asserting authority to "make regulations of national application (including in non-participating jurisdictions) related to systemic risk in national capital markets" (Canada 2013b, s. 4). The Government of Quebec has indicated that it will challenge the constitutional validity of such federal legislation the moment it is tabled in Parliament (Séguin 2013) so, assuming such legislation sees the light of day, there will presumably be a "systemic-risk reference."

Some of the weaknesses in the federal systemic-risk arguments have been discussed elsewhere (Spink 2012; Rousseau 2012a, 2012b; Cooper 2012; MacIntosh 2012b; Allaire 2013), and I agree with MacIntosh that the "argument about systemic risk was never more than an adventitiously concocted flying buttress cooked up in the wake of the credit meltdown to support an inherently unsupportable case," and "to the extent the feds actually believe their argument about systemic risk, it is a triumph of ideology over reason" (MacIntosh 2011). This chapter focuses narrowly on how the federal systemic-risk arguments reflect traditional constitutional rhetoric and false assumptions about systemic risks that are, essentially, extensions of the transformation rhetoric that failed in the securities references.

Systemic risk was an integral part of the argument that "this area of economic activity has been so transformed that it now falls to be regulated under a different head of power" (*Reference SCC* 2011 para. 116). The federal government asserted that systemic risk is a relatively new phenomenon that only became relevant to securities regulators in 1998 and requires "national, if not international, regulation" (Canada 2010, paras. 27-9, 82, 84, 119). These and similar assertions that "securities regulation has not historically included concerns relating to systemic risk" (Anand 2010a, 7) are unfounded. In fact, systemic risks are as old as the markets themselves and have been regulated in the securities industry since the 1800s using the same property-and-civil-rights mechanisms now being applied to reduce systemic risk arising from over-the-counter derivatives and other sources (Spink 2010a, paras. 84-5; Spink 2012, 184; IOSCO 2011a, 2013). Reducing systemic risk has always been one of the core objectives of securities regulation because it overlaps and is often practically synonymous with protecting investors and ensuring that markets are fair, efficient, and transparent (IOSCO 2003a, 5-7; Spink 2010a, paras. 5-12; IOSCO 2011a, 6). What that means, of course, is that if "systemic-risk regulation" was a constitutional head of power, and it was federal, then federal systemic-risk regulation could replicate and subsume provincial securities regulation.

The securities references make clear, however, that federal legislation cannot validly replicate existing securities legislation because, in the absence of "constitutionally significant transformation" (*Reference SCC* 2011, para. 115) it is impossible to show a new or different constitutional purpose for such duplicative law. There has been no transformation—the thousands of pages of existing securities regulation are properly characterized as property and civil rights (Rousseau 2012b), as future generations of such regulation will be. Federal trade-and-commerce legislation is thus confined to qualitatively different legislation (Edinger 2013, 16). Although such legislation related to systemic risk is hypothetically possible, it remains abstract because, until we see it, all we can say about it is that it must be qualitatively different from valid provincial legislation and of a type that the provinces could not effectively achieve—unlike existing securities regulation.

Significantly, despite the strong incentives to do so, the federal government presented no new approach to systemic risk in the securities references, nor in connection with the AIP. It is not surprising that the federal government has been unable to devise qualitatively different legislation or to present evidence showing a policy need for such legislation. The Supreme Court described a hypothetical "constitutional gap" that could only be filled by qualitatively different federal legislation, which is a correct statement of constitutional law but not a description of specific legislation nor a policy suggestion. Until qualitatively different federal legislation is presented, there is no reason to assume it will ever exist. Recent developments (IOSCO 2013) and the evolution of our regulatory system to date strongly suggest that future measures to reduce systemic risks will not be qualitatively different from existing law but will take the form of incremental policy initiatives developed within the existing legal framework (Spink 2012, 184).

In the absence of qualitatively different legislation, we should heed Lederman's (1965, 94) admonitions that "when classifying to distribute legislative powers, we approach the facts of life only through their legal aspects, that is, only to the extent that such facts have been incorporated in rules of law as the typical fact-situations contemplated by those rules"; "vague general questions about legislative jurisdiction cannot be answered with any real clarity or precision." Lederman emphasized the importance of understanding the division of powers in terms of "classes of laws, not classes of facts" and seemed to foresee the current discussion of systemic risks: "It is impossible for instance to look at a set of economic facts and say that the activity is trade and commerce within section 91(2) and therefore any law concerning it must be federal law. Rather, one must take a specific law … which is relevant to those facts and then ask if that rule is classifiable as a trade or commercial law" (1953, 246).

Lederman's points are illustrated by existing federal and provincial laws related to systemic risks. Some (such as prudential regulation of banks, or the enforcement of close-out netting of derivatives) are properly characterized as matters of banking or bankruptcy and insolvency, while others (such as securities regulation or securities transfer laws) are properly characterized as matters of property and civil rights. It is therefore naïve, even dangerous, to discuss "systemic risk" as though it were a constitutional head of power. The same can be said of "derivatives."

The dangers of vague general discussions about legislative jurisdiction were highlighted in the securities references when Saskatchewan and British Columbia (which had previously expressed some political support for the federal initiative before seeing the proposed legislation) eventually joined with the other provinces in condemning the proposed legislation, leaving Ontario as the sole provincial supporter. Many intriguing questions arise from those events: what was Ontario's understanding with the federal government; what was the misunderstanding with Saskatchewan and British Columbia; and would the federal government have acted differently if it had known it would eventually stand alone with Ontario against six other provinces? The fundamental lessons seem clear: specific legislation is necessary to any meaningful discussion of jurisdiction; political agreements about jurisdiction made without reference to specific legislation are meaningless; and provinces cannot agree to proposals that would amend the division of powers except by constitutional amendment. As the Supreme Court said, "notwithstanding the Court's promotion of cooperative and flexible federalism the constitutional boundaries that underlie the division of powers must be respected"; "the backbone of these [cooperative] schemes is the respect that each level of government has for each other's own sphere of jurisdiction" (*Reference SCC* 2011, paras. 62, 133).

IOSCO's (2013) review of the implementation of new principles relating to systemic risk and the perimeter of securities regulation suggests that Canada has relatively advanced regulatory mechanisms for addressing systemic risk, including cooperation and coordination systems between the relevant federal and provincial regulators. The AIP appears to be another constitutionally driven structural initiative disguised as a policy initiative, destined to fail for essentially the same reasons that federal securities legislation failed in the securities references (Spink 2012, 184-5): lack of evidence supporting the asserted transformation, inability to present a qualitatively different approach, and inability to demonstrate provincial incapacity.

THE NEED FOR A MORE TRANSPARENT PROCESS

It is depressing to think of how many resources have been spent over the decades on artificial criticisms of our securities regulatory system, confusing the public and tarnishing Canada's reputation globally—all in order to advance a constitutional agenda. These wasted resources and the constitutional risks illustrated by the securities references and ongoing campaign for a federal securities regulator demonstrate the need for a more transparent process to deal with proposed constitutional changes.

When a constitutional paradigm shift is proposed, it seems reasonable that the public ought to know what constitutional chips are on the table, where all those chips might go, and what is being exchanged for what. I knew none of that in the securities references, even though I was a relative insider. It was clear that many constitutional chips were on the table but, except for securities regulation, no one knew exactly what other chips were in the pile. There were political arrangements between the federal government and some of the provinces, but the details of those arrangements were unclear, even to the governments involved. Such confusion about a constitutional paradigm shift seems like an unacceptable risk, and increased transparency seems the best way to prevent it.

The reference process worked perfectly in this instance and was a credit to our judiciary. However, the reference process was forced to overcome the lack of transparency in the larger process for dealing with constitutional change. For example, the first official statement of the federal government's constitutional position on its proposed securities legislation was its 1 November 2010 factum filed with the Quebec Court of Appeal—released only 11 weeks before the Quebec hearing and less than six months before the Supreme Court hearing. Litigation strategy is understandable, but it seems unwise to have such a short fuse on such a potent constitutional device.

A more transparent process would reduce constitutional risk by ensuring that constitutional proposals are clearly identified and assessed as such—not disguised as policy proposals as they were in the securities references and in the brewing systemic-risk reference. We should be encouraged by the courts' scepticism about conjecture, insistence on evidence, and rejection of constitutional rhetoric in the securities references. The courts demonstrated the importance of transparency by "letting the cat out of the bag" in the securities references. We should anticipate a similar result in the systemic-risk reference and hope that will cause future constitutional initiatives to be scrutinized even more carefully.

REFERENCES

Ainsley Financial Corp. v. Ontario (Securities Commission). [1993]. 106 D.L.R. (4th) 507 (Gen. Div.).

Aitken, B. 2005. "Another Way Forward for Securities Reform." British Columbia Securities Commission presentation to the Task Force to Modernize Securities Legislation in Canada. 14 October. http://www.bcsc.bc.ca/uploadedFiles/Aitken_Presentation_IDA_Oct2005.pdf.

Alberta. 1938. *The Case for Alberta*. Edmonton: King's Printer.

Alberta et al. 2004. *A Provincial/Territorial Memorandum of Understanding Regarding Securities Regulation*. http://www.securitiescanada.org/2004_0930_mou_english.pdf.

Alberta and British Columbia Securities Commissions. 1996. *Letter of Accord*. 9 December. http://www.bcsc.bc.ca/release.aspx?id=523.

Alberta Hansard. 1996. 20 August, 2244.

Alberta Securities Commission (ASC). 2004. *The Alberta Capital Market: Exempt Market Study*, March 2004. http://www.albertasecurities.com/news/Publications/Documents/11394__1478198_v12_-_ACMP_PART_2_-_EXCERPT_FOR_PUBLICATION.pdf.

Allaire, Y. 2013. "Systemic Federal Risk: Canada Has No Need of National Securities Regulator." *Financial Post*, 9 October. http://opinion.financialpost.com/2013/10/09/systemic-federal-risk-canada-has-no-need-of-national-securities-regulator/.

Anand, A. 2005. "Securities Regulation at an Impasse: Developing Effective Regulation in an Ineffective Regulatory Regime." *Banking and Finance Law Review* 20 (2): 191-216.

—. 2010a. "Is Systemic Risk Relevant to Securities Regulation?" *University of Toronto Law Journal* 60 (4): 941-81.

—. 2010b. "The Real Evidence on a National Securities Regulator." Mowat Centre. http://www.mowatcentre.ca/opinions.php?opinionID=47.

—. ed. 2012a. *What's Next for Canada? Securities Regulation after the Reference*. Toronto: Irwin Law.

—. 2102b. "After the Reference: Regulating Systemic Risk in Canadian Financial Markets." In *What's Next For Canada? Securities Regulation after the Reference*, edited by A. Anand, 197-221. Toronto: Irwin Law.

Anand, A., and G. Bishop. 2012. "Don't Throw in the Towel: Systemic Risk in Securities Markets Must Be Federally Regulated." 17 February. http://utorontolaw.typepad.com/faculty_blog/2012/02/dont-throw-in-the-towel-systemic-risk-in-securities-markets-must-be-federally-regulated.html.

Anand, A., and A. Green. 2010. "Why Is This Taking So Long? The Move towards a National Securities Regulator." *University of Toronto Law Journal* 60 (2): 663-86.

—. 2011. "Side-Payments, Opt-Ins and Power: Creating a National Securities Regulator in Canada." *Canadian Business Law Journal* 51 (1): 1-26.

Anand, A., and P.C. Klein. 2005. "Inefficiency and Path Dependency in Canada's Securities Regulatory System: Towards a Reform Agenda." *Canadian Business Law Journal* 42 (1): 41-72.

Anisman, P. 1981. "The Proposals for a Securities Market Law for Canada: Purpose and Process." *Osgoode Hall Law Journal* 19 (3): 329-67.

—. 1986. "The Regulation of the Securities Market and the Harmonization of Provincial Laws." In *Harmonization of Business Law in Canada*, edited by R.C.C. Cumming, 77-168. Toronto: University of Toronto Press.

Anisman, P., and P.W. Hogg. 1979. "Constitutional Aspects of Federal Securities Legislation." In *Proposals for a Securities Market Law for Canada*, vol. 1, 137-220. Ottawa: Minister of Supply and Services.

Armstrong, C. 1976. "Federalism and Government Regulation: The Case of the Canadian Insurance Industry, 1927–34." *Canadian Public Administration* 19: 88-101.

—. 1981. *The Politics of Federalism: Ontario's Relations with the Federal Government, 1867–1942*. Toronto: University of Toronto Press.

—. 1997. *Blue Skies and Boiler Rooms: Buying and Selling Securities in Canada, 1870–1940*. Toronto: University of Toronto Press.

—. 2001. *Moose Pastures and Mergers: The Ontario Securities Commission and the Regulation of Share Markets in Canada, 1940–1980*. Toronto: University of Toronto Press.

Ascah, R.L. 1999. *Politics and Public Debt: The Dominion, the Banks, and Alberta's Social Credit*. Edmonton: University of Alberta Press.

Banwell, P.T. 1968. "Proposals for a National Securities Commission." *Queen's Intramural Law Journal* 1: 3-35.

Bastarache, M. 2012. "The Constitutionality of PIPEDA: A Re-consideration in the Wake of the Supreme Court of Canada's Reference re *Securities Act*." June. http://accessprivacy. s3.amazonaws.com/M-Bastarache-June-2012-Constitiutionality-PIPEDA-Paper-2.pdf.

Breton, A. 1986. Supplementary Statement to the *Report of the Royal Commission on the Economic Union and Development Prospects for Canada*, vol. 3, 486-526. Toronto: University of Toronto Press.

Canada. 1935. *Report of the Royal Commission on Price Spreads*. Ottawa: King's Printer.

—. 1964. *Report of the Royal Commission on Banking and Finance*. Ottawa: Queen's Printer.

—. 1979. *Proposals for a Securities Market Law for Canada*, vols. 1-3. Ottawa: Minister of Supply and Services.

—. 1994. *Draft Memorandum of Understanding Regarding the Regulation of Securities in Canada*. Reference Record *(Attorney General Of Canada Materials)*, vol. 2, 49-57. http:// www.valeursmobilieres.net/pdf/VolumeIIReferenceRecordAGCanada.pdf.

—. 2010. Factum of the Attorney General of Canada in the Supreme Court of Canada. http:// www.valeursmobilieres.net/pdf/Factum%20AG%20Canada%20Eng%20version.pdf.

—. 2011. *Proceedings of the Standing Senate Committee on Banking Trade and Commerce* No. 8, 15 December. http://www.parl.gc.ca/Content/SEN/Committee/411/banc/ pdf/08issue.pdf.

—. 2013a. *Jobs, Growth and Long-Term Prosperity – Economic Action Plan 2013*. http:// www.budget.gc.ca/2013/doc/plan/budget2013-eng.pdf.

—. 2013b. *Agreement in Principle to Move Towards a Cooperative Capital Markets Regulatory System*. http://www.fin.gc.ca/pub/ccmrs-scrmc/agreement-principle-entente-principe-eng.asp.

Canadian Securities Administrators and Provincial Officials Working Group (CSA). 1995a. *Issues and Alternatives in Securities Regulation*. 6 March. Reference Record of the Attorney General of Alberta in the Supreme Court of Canada, vol. 20, 154-191. http:// www.valeursmobilieres.net/pdf/VolumeXXReferenceRecordAGAlberta.pdf.

—. 1995b. *Survey of Possible Improvements to Provincial Securities Regulation*. 6 March. Reference Record of the Attorney General of Alberta in the Supreme Court of Canada, vol. 20, 192-218. http://www.valeursmobilieres.net/pdf/VolumeXXReferenceRecordAGAlberta. pdf.

Chester, S. 2004. "PIPEDA Reference Raises Vital Constitutional Questions." *Canadian Privacy Law Review* 1 (5): 52-5.

Choi, S. 2010. "The Benefits of Provincial Securities Regulation in Canada." 23 June. Documentation du Procureur Général du Québec in the Supreme Court of Canada, vol. 11, 8. http://www.valeursmobilieres.net/pdf/VolumeXIReferenceRecordAGQuebec.pdf.

Citizens Insurance Company v. Parsons. (1881.) 7 A.C. 96 (PC), affirming (1880), 4 S.C.R. 215 (*Parsons*).

Cooper, B. 2012. "A Return to Classical Federalism? The Significance of the Securities Reference Decision." Frontier Centre for Public Policy, Policy Series No. 129. February. http://www.fcpp.org/files/1/PS129_ClassicFed_FB22F1.pdf.

Corcoran, A. 2010. "International Standatds Affecting Securities Regulators and Regulation as Applicable to Québec." 23 June. Documentation du Procureur Général du Québec in the Supreme Court of Canada, vol. 12, 126. http://www.valeursmobilieres.net/pdf/VolumeXIIReferenceRecordAGQuebec.pdf.

Courchene, T.J. 1986. *Economic Management and the Division of Powers*. Toronto: University of Toronto Press.

—. 2010a. "A Single National Securities Regulator? Public Policy and Political Economy Perspectives." 26 June. Reference Record of the Attorney General of Alberta in the Supreme Court of Canada, vol. 18, 260. http://www.valeursmobilieres.net/pdf/VolumeXVIIIReferenceRecordAGAlberta.pdf.

—. 2010b. "The Economic Integration Continuum and the Canadian Securities Industry: In Praise of the Status Quo." 27 October. Reference Record of the Attorney General of Alberta in the Supreme Court of Canada, vol. 22, 110. http://www.valeursmobilieres.net/pdf/VolumeXXIIReferenceRecordAGAlberta.pdf.

Crowne-Mohammed, E.A. and Y. Rozenszajn, 2009. "DRM Roll Please: Is Digital Rights Management Legislation Unconstitutional in Canada?" *Journal of Information, Law & Technology* 2. http://go.warwick.ac.uk/jilt/2009_2/cmr.

Daniels, R.J. 1992. "How 'Broke' Is the System of Provincial Securities Regulation?" *Canadian Investment Review* 5 (1): 89-98.

Danson v. Ontario (Attorney General). [1990]. 2 S.C.R. 1086.

Doyle, K.M. 1996. "Securities Regulation in Canada: Status, Issues and Prospects." http://digitool.library.mcgill.ca/webclient/StreamGate?folder_id=0&dvs=1388622440842~681.

Edinger, E. 2013. "*Reference re Securities Act*: If Wishes Were Horses, Then Beggars Would Ride." *Canadian Business Law Journal* 54 (1): 1-16.

Expert Panel on Securities Regulation. 2009. *Final Report and Recommendations*. Ottawa: Department of Finance.

Financial Stability Board. 2012. *Peer Review of Canada*. http://www.financialstabilityboard.org/publications/r_120130.pdf.

Fluker, S. 2009. "The Counterview to a National Securities Regulator in Canada." 17 January. http://ablawg.ca/wp-content/uploads/2009/10/blog_sf_securities_jan2009.pdf.

Ford, C., and H. Gill. 2012. "A National Systemic Risk Clearinghouse?" In *What's Next For Canada? Securities Regulation after the Reference*, edited by A. Anand, 145-84. Toronto: Irwin Law.

Fraiberg, J. 2012a. "A National Securities Regulator: The Road Ahead." *Canadian Business Law Journal* 52 (2): 174-81.

—. 2012b. "Finding Common Cause: The Renewed Quest for a National Securities Regulator." C.D. Howe Institute E-brief, 28 June. http://cdhowe.org/pdf/e-brief_136.pdf.

Geist, M. 2012. "Are Canada's Digital Laws Unconstitutional?" 11 January. http://www.michaelgeist.ca/content/view/6231/135/.

General Motors of Canada v. City National Leasing. [1989.] 1 S.C.R. 641.

Geva, B. 2004. "Legislative Power in Relation to Transfers of Securities: The Case for Provincial Jurisdiction in Canada." *Banking & Finance Law Review* 19 (3): 393-423.

Grammond, S. 2011. "Flaherty's Supreme Court Loss Is Federalism's Gain." 22 December. http://fullcomment.nationalpost.com/2011/12/22/sebastien-grammond -flahertys-supreme-court-loss-is-federalisms-gain/.

Gray, V.E. 1946. "More on the Regulation of Insurance." *Canadian Bar Review* 24 (6): 481-8.

Gray, W., and R.M. Scavone. 2012. "Retreat from a Federal Securities Transfer Presence: Next Stage in the Development of the Canadian Securities Settlement System." *Banking & Finance Law Review* 27 (3): 375-405.

Harris, A.D. 2002. "White Paper – A Symposium on Canadian Securities Regulation: Harmonization or Nationalization?" Toronto: University of Toronto Capital Markets Institute.

—. 2003. "Securities Regulatory Structure in Canada: The Way Forward." *Canadian Business Law Journal* 38 (1): 57-124.

—. 2005. "'Once More into the Breach': A Comment on James C. Baillie, 'The Wise Persons' Committee Report: Another Attempt to Revolutionize Canadian Securities Regulation.'" *Canadian Business Law Journal* 41 (2-3): 461-70.

Hjartarson, J. 2010. "One Economic Market or a Collection of Jealous Rivals?" Mowat Centre. http://www.mowatcentre.ca/research-topic-mowat.php?mowatResearchID=19.

Hogg, P.W. 1974. "The Constitutionality of Federal Regulation of Mutual Funds." In *Proposals for a Mutual Fund Law for Canada*, vol.1, 75-87. Ottawa: Information Canada.

Howlett, K. 2011. "Ontario to Push for Reforms to Fragmented Securities System." 22 December. http://www.theglobeandmail.com/globe-investor/ontario-to-push-for-reforms-to-fragmented-securities-system/article2281169/.

Hyndman, D. 2007. "Separating Fact from Fiction – Canadian Securities Regulation in the 21st Century." Delivered to Economic Club of Toronto, 19 September 2007. http://www. bcsc.bc.ca/uploadedFiles/SeparatingFactFromFiction.pdf.

International Monetary Fund. 2013. *Canada: 2012 Article IV Consultation*. IMF Country Report No. 13/40. http://www.imf.org/external/pubs/ft/scr/2013/cr1340.pdf.

International Monetary Fund FSAP. 2008. *Canada: Financial Sector Assessment Program – Detailed Assessment of the Level of Implementation of the IOSCO Principles and Objectives of Securities Regulation*. IMF Country Report No. 08/61. http://www.imf.org/external/pubs/ft/scr/2008/cr0861.pdf. (IMF FSAP 2008)

International Monetary Fund FSSA. 2008. *Canada: Financial System Stability Assessment – Update*. IMF Country Report No. 08/59. http://www.imf.org/external/pubs/ft/scr/2008/cr0859.pdf.

International Organization of Securities Commissions. 2003a. *Objectives and Principles of Securities Regulation*. http://www.iosco.org/library/pubdocs/pdf/IOSCOPD154.pdf.

—. 2003b. *Methodology for Assessing Implementation of the IOSCO Objectives and Principles of Securities Regulation*. http://www.iosco.org/library/pubdocs/pdf/IOSCOPD155.pdf.

—. 2008. *Methodology for Assessing Implementation of the IOSCO Objectives and Principles of Securities Regulation*. http://www.iosco.org/library/pubdocs/pdf/IOSCOPD266.pdf.

—. 2010. *Objectives and Principles of Securities Regulation*. http://www.iosco.org/library/pubdocs/pdf/IOSCOPD323.pdf.

—. 2011a. "Mitigating Systemic Risk: A Role for Securities Regulators – Discussion Paper." http://www.iosco.org/library/pubdocs/pdf/IOSCOPD347.pdf.

—. 2011b. *Methodology for Assessing Implementation of the IOSCO Objectives and Principles of Securities Regulation*. http://www.iosco.org/library/pubdocs/pdf/IOSCOPD359.pdf.

—. 2013. *Thematic Review of the Implementation of Principles 6 and 7 of the IOSCO Objectives and Principles of Securities Regulation*. http://www.iosco.org/library/pubdocs/pdf/IOSCOPD424.pdf.

Jackman, H.N.R. 2011. "The Onus Is on Ottawa." *National Post*, 26 July, A8. http://article.wn.com/view/2011/07/26/The_onus_is_on_Ottawa/#/related_news.

Jamal, M. 2012. "*Reference Re Securities Act*: Comment on Lee and Schneiderman." In *What's Next for Canada? Securities Regulation after the Reference*, edited by A. Anand, 95-9. Toronto: Irwin Law.

Jenah, S.W. 2007. "Commentary on *A Blueprint for Cross-Border Access to U.S. Investors: A New International Framework*." *Harvard International Law Journal* 48 (1): 69-83.

Karazivan, J., and J-F. Gaudreault-DesBiens. 2010. "On Polyphony and Paradoxes in the Regulation of Securities within the Canadian Federation." *Canadian Business Law Journal* 49 (1): 1-39.

Kennedy, W.P.M. 1937. "The British North America Act: Past and Future." *Canadian Bar Review* 15 (6): 393-400.

Leckey, R., and E. Ward. 1999. "Taking Stock: Securities Markets and the Division of Powers." *Dalhousie Law Journal* 22: 250-91.

Leclair, J. 2003. "The Supreme Court of Canada's Understanding of Federalism: Efficiency at the Expense of Diversity." *Queen's Law Journal* 28: 411-53.

—. 2010. "'Please, Draw Me a Field of Jurisdiction': Regulating Securities, Securing Federalism." *Supreme Court Law Review* (2d) 51: 555-91.

Lederman, W.R. 1953. "Classification of Laws and the British North America Act." Reprinted in W.R. Lederman, 1981, *Continuing Constitutional Dilemmas*.Toronto: Butterworths, 229-49.

—. 1965. "The Balanced Interpretation of the Federal Distribution of Legislative Powers in Canada." In *The Future of Canadian Federalism*, edited by P.A. Crepeau and C.B. MacPherson, 91-112. Toronto: University of Toronto Press.

Lee, I.B. 2011. "Balancing and Its Alternatives: Jurisprudential Choice, Federal Securities Legislation and the Trade and Commerce Power." *Canadian Business Law Journal* 50 (1): 72-105.

Lehman, J. 1999. "The Bre-X Stock Debacle: Why the Enactment of Canadian Federal Securities Legislation Would Be Good as Gold." *Brooklyn Journal of International Law* 24 (3): 823-53.

Leong, B. 2012. "Inspiring Investor Confidence: Building Competitive and Innovative Capital Markets in BC." Delivered to Vancouver Board of Trade, 30 October. http://www.bcsc. bc.ca/uploadedFiles/Inspiring_Investor_Confidence_Oct_30_final(1).pdf.

Lortie, P. 2010. "Securities Regulation in Canada at the Crossroads." SPP Research Paper. Calgary: University of Calgary, School of Public Policy. http://policyschool.ucalgary.ca/ sites/default/files/research/lortie-online.pdf.

—. 2011. "Securities Regulation in Canada: The Case for Effectiveness." Institute for Research on Public Policy Study, No. 19. http://www.irpp.org/pubs/IRPPstudy/IRPP_ Study_no19.pdf.

MacDonald, V.C. 1937. "The Canadian Constitution Seventy Years After." *Canadian Bar Review* 15 (6): 401-27.

Macey, J. 2010a. "An Analysis of the Canadian Federal Government's Initiative to Create a National Securities Regulator." 23 June. Documentation du Procureur Général du Québec in the Supreme Court of Canada, vol. 12, 37. http://www.valeursmobilieres.net/ pdf/VolumeXIIReferenceRecordAGQuebec.pdf.

—. 2010b. "Supplemental Analysis of the Canadian Federal Government's Initiative to Create a National Securities Regulator." 26 October. Documentation du Procureur Général du Québec in the Supreme Court of Canada, vol. 12, 110. http://www.valeursmobilieres.net/ pdf/VolumeXIIReferenceRecordAGQuebec.pdf.

MacIntosh, J.G. 1994. "Securities Regulation and the Public Interest: Of Politics, Procedures and Policy Statements – Part I." *Canadian Business Law Journal* 24 (1): 77-120; Part II, *Canadian Business Law Journal* 24 (2): 287-314.

—. 1997. "A National Securities Commission for Canada?" In *Reforming the Canadian Financial Sector: Canada in Global Perspective*, edited by T.J. Courchene and E.H Neave, 185-239. Kingston: John Deutsch Institute for the Study of Public Policy.

—. 2011. "Not Even Close." *Financial Post*, 22 December 2011, FP 11. http://opinion. financialpost.com/2011/12/22/not-even-close/.

—. 2012a. "Politics, Not Law." *Canadian Business Law Journal* 52 (2): 179-81.

—. 2012b. "A National Securities Commission? The Headless Horseman Rides Again." In *What's Next for Canada? Securities Regulation after the Reference*, edited by A. Anand, 223-77. Toronto: Irwin Law.

Mallory, J.R. 1954. *Social Credit and the Federal Power in Canada*. Toronto: University of Toronto Press.

McIntosh, G. 2007. "National Securities Agency Gets Ont. Nod." *Edmonton Journal*, 13 February, G8.

Milken Institute. 2010. *2009 Capital Access Index: Best Markets for Access to Business Capital*. http://www.milkeninstitute.org/publications/publications.taf?cat=ResRep&fun ction=detail&ID=38801238.

Monahan, P. 2010. "Provincial Challenges to a National Securities Regulator Are Mere Sideshows." *Globe and Mail*, 1 December. http://www.theglobeandmail.com/globe-debate/provincial-challenges-to-a-national-securities-regulator-are-mere-sideshows/ article1316337/.

OECD. Going for Growth 2006 and *Economics Department Working Paper* No. 506. http:// www.oecd.org/document/24/0,3343,en_2649_34117_41665624_1_1_1_1,00.html.

Ontario Hansard. 2004. 18 August, F-908. http://www.ontla.on.ca/committee-proceedings/transcripts/files_pdf/2004-08-18_pdfF024.pdf.

Pidruchney, W.T. 1985. "The Challenge of Dynamism." In *Canadian Financial Institutions: Changing the Regulatory Environment*, edited by J. Ziegel, L. Waverman, and D.W. Conklin, 179-86. Toronto: Ontario Economic Council.

Puri, P. 2010. "The Capital Markets Perspective on a National Securities Regulator." *Supreme Court Law Review* (2d) 51: 603-23.

—. 2012a. "The Supreme Court's Securities Act Reference Fails to Demonstrate an Understanding of the Canadian Capital Markets." *Canadian Business Law Journal* 52 (2): 190-6.

—. 2012b. "Twenty Years of Supreme Court Reference Decisions: Putting the *Securities Reference* Decision in Context." In *What's Next For Canada? Securities Regulation after the Reference*, edited by A. Anand, 13-48. Toronto: Irwin Law.

Puri, P., and G. Lan. 2007. "Who Needs Paper Anymore? Rationalizing and Allocation of Government Responsibility for the Transfer of Securities." *Banking & Finance Law Review* 23 (1): 1-49.

Québec (Procureure générale) c. Canada (Procureure générale). 2011. QCCA 591, unofficial English translation, CanLII. (*QCCA Reference* 2011).

Rabson, M. 2010. "Power Grab?" 27 May. http://www.winnipegfreepress.com/business/power-grab-94999589.html?path=/business&id=94999589&sortBy=newest.

Rice, W.S. 2010. "Affidavit of William S. Rice." 29 June 2010. Reference Record of the Attorney General of Alberta in the Supreme Court of Canada, vol. 18, 8. http://www.valeursmobilieres.net/pdf/VolumeXVIIIReferenceRecordAGAlberta.pdf.

Reference Re Securities Act (Canada). 2011. ABCA 77. (*Reference ABCA* 2011).

Reference Re Securities Act. 2011. SCC 66. (*Reference SCC* 2011).

Robinson, M.J., and T.J. Cottrell. 2007. "Investment Patterns of Informal Investors in the Alberta Private Equity Market." *Journal of Small Business Management* 2007 45 (1): 47-67.

Rousseau, S. 2010a. "Securities Regulation in Québec and the Debate about a Single Securities Commission." 22 June. Documentation du Procureur Général du Québec in the Supreme Court of Canada, vol. 6, 8. http://www.valeursmobilieres.net/pdf/VolumeVIReferenceRecordAGQuebec.pdf; vol. 7, 8; http://www.valeursmobilieres.net/pdf/VolumeVIIReferenceRecordAGQuebec.pdf.

—. 2010b. "Rapport complémentaire: Commentaires sur les affidavits de M. Ermanno Pascutto, M. Robert Christie et M. Ian W. Russell." 26 November. Documentation du Procureur Général du Québec in the Supreme Court of Canada, vol. 7, 139. http://www.valeursmobilieres.net/pdf/VolumeVIIReferenceRecordAGQuebec.pdf.

—. 2012a. "Endgame: The Impact of *Reference re Securities Act* on the Project to Create a National Securities Regulator." *Canadian Business Law Journal* 52 (2): 186-9.

—. 2012b. "The Provinces' Competence over Securities Regulation in Canada: Taking Stock of the Supreme Court's Opinion." In *What's Next For Canada? Securities Regulation after the Reference*, edited by A. Anand, 279-89. Toronto: Irwin Law.

Roy, N. 1986. *Mobility of Capital in the Canadian Economic Union*. Toronto: University of Toronto Press.

Russell, I.C.W. 2010. "Affidavit of Ian C.W. Russell." 28 October. Reference Record – Investment Industry of Canada Materials in the Supreme Court of Canada, vol. 31, 70.

Sarra, J. 2012. "Assuring Independence and Expertise in Financial Services Law: Regulatory Oversight in Light of the Supreme Court of Canada *Securities Reference* Judgment." In *What's Next for Canada? Securities Regulation after the Reference*, edited by A. Anand, 111-43. Toronto: Irwin Law.

Sawiak, G.V., et al. 1996. *The Transaction Costs of a Decentralized System of Securities Regulation*. Report to the Standing Senate Committee on Banking, Trade and Commerce, April 1996.

Schultz, A., and A. Alexandroff, eds. 1985. *Economic Regulation and the Federal System*. Toronto: University of Toronto Press.

Scott, F.R. 1937. "The Consequences of the Privy Council Decisions." *Canadian Bar Review* 15 (6): 485-94.

Séguin, R. 2013. "Quebec to Challenge Proposed Federal Securities Regulator." 13 December. http://www.theglobeandmail.com/news/politics/quebec-to-challenge-proposed-federal-securities-regulator/article15969108/.

Selinger, G. 2007. "Passport Still Valid." *Financial Post*, 26 October. http://www.securities canada.org/2007_1026_national_fin_post_hon_selinger.pdf.

—. 2008. "Where's Ontario?" *Financial Post*. 26 March. http://www.securitiescanada. org/2008_0326_national_fin_post_hon_selinger.pdf.

Siems, M. 2005. "What Does Not Work in Comparing Securities Laws: A Critique on La Porta et al.'s Methodology." *International Company and Commercial Law Review* (2005): 300-5.

Spink, E. 1997. "Can the Law Catch Up to Securities Market Practices? *Verdun v. Toronto Dominion Bank*." *Banking & Finance Law Review* 12 (3): 439-65.

—. 2007. "The Securities Transfer Act – Fitting New Concepts in Canadian Law." *Canadian Business Law Journal* 45 (2): 167-223.

—. 2010a "Securities Regulation as Property Law." 28 June. Reference Record of the Attorney General of Alberta in the Supreme Court of Canada, vol. 19, 1. http://www. valeursmobilieres.net/pdf/VolumeXIXReferenceRecordAGAlberta.pdf.

—. 2010b. "Distinguishing Functional and Structural Opinions." 29 September. Reference Record of the Attorney General of Alberta in the Supreme Court of Canada, vol. 21, 274. http://www.valeursmobilieres.net/pdf/VolumeXXIReferenceRecordAGAlberta.pdf.

—. 2010c. "Report in Reply to the Reports of Michael J. Trebilcock Dated May 20 and August 23, 2010." 27 October. Reference Record of the Attorney General of Alberta in the Supreme Court of Canada, vol. 22, 135. http://www.valeursmobilieres.net/pdf/ VolumeXXIIReferenceRecordAGAlberta.pdf.

—. 2010d. "Report in reply to the Affidavit of Ian C.W. Russell sworn October 28, 2010." 26 November, Reference Record of the Attorney General of Alberta in the Supreme Court of Canada, vol. 23, 158. http://www.valeursmobilieres.net/pdf/ VolumeXXIIIReferenceRecordAGAlberta.pdf.

—. 2012. "Reacting to the Status Quo in Securities Regulation." *Canadian Business Law Journal* 52 (2): 182-5.

—. 2013. "Our Securities Model Works." 26 March. http://opinion.financialpost. com/2013/03/26/our-securities-model-works/.

State Farm Mutual Automobile Insurance Company v. Privacy Commissioner of Canada, 2010 FC 736.

Suret, J-M., and C. Carpentier. 2010. "Securities Regulation in Canada: Re-examination of Arguments in Support of a Single Securities Commission." 22 June. Documentation du Procureur Général du Québec in the Supreme Court of Canada, vol. 9, 8. http://www. valeursmobilieres.net/pdf/VolumeIXReferenceRecordAGQuebec.pdf.

Swinton, K. 1990. *The Supreme Court and Canadian Federalism*. Toronto: Carswell.

—. 1992. "Federalism under Fire: The Role of the Supreme Court of Canada." *Law and Contemporary Problems* 55 (1): 121-45.

Tafara, E., and R.J. Peterson. 2007. "A Blueprint for Cross-Border Access to U.S. Investors: A New International Framework." *Harvard International Law Journal* 48 (1): 31-68.

Tedesco, T. 2011. "Flaherty Still Pursuing National Securities Regulator, Transcript Shows." 26 January. http://business.financialpost.com/2012/01/26/ flaherty-still-pursuing-national-securities-regulator/.

Trebilcock, M.J. 2010. "National Securities Regulator Report." 20 May. Reference Record – Attorney General of Canada Materials in the Supreme Court of Canada, vol. 1, 222. http://www.valeursmobilieres.net/pdf/VolumeIReferenceRecordAGCanada.pdf.

—. 2012. "More Questions Than Answers: The Supreme Court of Canada's Decision in the National *Securities Reference*." In *What's Next For Canada? Securities Regulation after the Reference*, edited by A. Anand, 37-48. Toronto: Irwin Law.

Tse, D. 1994. "Establishing a Federal Securities Commission." *Saskatchewan Law Review* 58: 427-45.

TSX Venture Exchange Inc. 2012. *CPC Insight*, No. 3. http://www.tmx.com/en/pdf/ CPC_newsletter_issue3.pdf.

Wilbur, R. 1969. *The Bennett Administration, 1930–1935*. Ottawa: Canadian Historical Association Booklets, No. 24.

Wise Persons' Committee. 2003. *It's Time*. Ottawa: Department of Finance.

Wood, R. 2012. "Bank Act – PPSA Interaction: Still Waiting for Solutions." *Canadian Business Law Journal* 52 (2): 248-70.

World Bank. 2013. *Ease of Doing Business in Canada*. http://www.doingbusiness.org/data/ exploreeconomies/canada/.

Ziegel, J. 2012. "Where Federal-Provincial Cooperation Has Failed Conspicuously." *Canadian Business Law Journal* 52 (2): 171-3.

9

CANADIAN FEDERALISM AND INTERNATIONAL TRADE: A SMALL STEP WHILE WAITING FOR THE GIANT LEAP[1]

Patrick Fafard and Patrick Leblond

In the twentieth century, promoting trade between countries was focused, for the most part, on tariffs and associated non-tariff barriers. In the twenty-first century, that focus has shifted to a much broader agenda, so that we no longer speak of "trade" agreements per se but rather of "economic and trade" agreements or "second-generation" trade agreements. As a small open economy, Canada is now at the forefront of this trend and is currently negotiating, as well as contemplating, a wide range of bilateral and multilateral second-generation agreements with a diverse set of countries around the world (Clark 2012).[2] However, as the agenda expands beyond tariffs, the complexity of the agreements also expands. Even if a trade agreement like the North American Free Trade Agreement (NAFTA) is complex, newer agreements seek to address a wider range of issues including labour mobility, investor protection, public procurement, electronic commerce, and intellectual property. Negotiating such second-generation agreements requires some minimal degree of collaboration with provincial governments, which have jurisdiction and responsibilities that are critical to the successful conclusion and implementation of a given agreement.

As a result of the increased complexity of trade agreements, we would expect to see a greater involvement of the provinces in trade negotiations. In fact, this is

---

[1] Parts of this chapter draw on Fafard and Leblond (2012).

[2] An overview of Canadian international trade agreements and current negotiations can be found at http://www.international.gc.ca/trade-agreements-accords-commerciaux/agr-acc/index.aspx?view=d.

precisely what has been happening with respect to the Comprehensive Economic and Trade Agreement (CETA) that Canada and the European Union (EU) began negotiating in the fall of 2009 (Hübner 2011; Leblond 2010).[3] From the beginning, the provinces (and to a more limited extent the territories) were directly participating in the negotiations, beyond their traditional (and more limited) involvement through the federal Department of Foreign Affairs, Trade and Development's C-Trade committee system (C-Trade).[4] Their direct participation came about because, as CETA's name implies, it goes well beyond reducing tariffs and non-tariff barriers (NTBs) and seeks to address a range of issues with a view to increasing trade, labour, and investment flows between Canada and the EU. This innovation is the result both of the substantive nature of the issues being discussed and to a direct and specific request from the EU. The Europeans understood that it made little sense to negotiate trade and economic issues falling under provincial jurisdiction without the provinces being at the negotiating table rather than just being consulted by federal negotiators. In October 2013, Canada and the EU announced that they had concluded negotiations of an agreement-in-principle, and Canada subsequently released a "technical summary" of the negotiated outcomes.[5] In the days following the announcement, several provinces, including Quebec, Ontario, and Saskatchewan, indicated they would support the CETA.

The direct involvement of the provinces in the negotiations of trade and economic agreements represents a significant change to the prevailing practices of Canadian intergovernmental relations. However, we need to ask whether the change represents a giant leap forward or just a small step. The analysis of the CETA negotiations presented in this chapter suggests the latter. To detail this argument, the chapter is structured in three parts. The first section traces the historical evolution of the provinces in Canadian trade policy. The second section examines the provincial governments' involvement in the CETA negotiations. The third and final section concludes on the implications for Canada's international trade policy of the federal system taking a "small step" rather than a "giant leap."

---

[3] Basic information on the CETA is available at http://www.international.gc.ca/trade-agreements-accords-commerciaux/agr-acc/eu-ue/can-eu.aspx?lang=eng&view=d.

[4] So as to avoid awkward references to both provincial and territorial governments, this paper uses the terms "provinces" and "provincial" to designate not just provincial governments but also the governments of the three northern territories.

[5] At the time of writing, December 2013, the full legal text of the CETA had yet to be released.

HISTORICAL EVOLUTION OF THE ROLE OF PROVINCIAL GOVERNMENTS IN CANADIAN TRADE POLICY

Whether and how to involve provincial governments in trade negotiations is by no means a new issue. However, the current debate about the provinces' role is difficult to understand without some reference to the "free trade" negotiations with the United States and later Mexico. These negotiations led to a modest role for provincial governments while reaffirming the fact that the federal government remains the signatory of international trade agreements and, by extension, is responsible for implementation and any financial penalties associated with non-compliance.

A Look Back: Federalism and North American Trade Negotiations

In 1985, the Royal Commission on the Economic Union and Development Prospects for Canada, known more commonly as the Macdonald Commission, issued a major report that made a wide range of recommendations dealing not only with economic policy but also with Canadian political institutions (Inwood 2005). However, the Macdonald Commission is remembered primarily for having recommended that Canada negotiate a bilateral trade agreement with the United States. The recommendation set the stage for the decision by the government of Brian Mulroney to launch negotiations that led to the Canada-United States Free Trade Agreement (CUSFTA) in 1989 and the North American Free Trade Agreement (NAFTA) in 1994, the latter being a trilateral arrangement that includes Mexico.

Free, or at least freer trade, first with the United States and then extended to Mexico, had profound implications for the Canadian economy. Opening up Canadian markets to foreign competition, while perhaps beneficial overall, required significant restructuring and adjustment, particularly in Ontario (Inwood 2005; Courchene 1998). Not surprisingly, the Government of Ontario (along with Manitoba and Prince Edward Island) staked out an aggressive position against the proposed free trade agreement with the United States and, in the advent of an agreement, called on the Government of Canada to provide considerable financial assistance to sectors, firms, and workers negatively affected. Other provincial governments also raised concerns. On the other hand, some provinces, notably Alberta and Saskatchewan, came out strongly in favour of a trade deal with the United States (Inwood 2005; Kukucha 2008). While a free trade agreement also meant painful restructuring in Quebec, its provincial government expressed cautious support for the FTA for a number of reasons. Premier Bourassa's training in economics made him particularly aware of the virtues of freer trade and the strategic opportunity provided by the FTA negotiations to bolster Quebec's role in Canadian intergovernmental affairs (Kukucha 2008). Others have argued that, on balance, increased economic integration with United States was a high priority for successive Quebec governments, which helps explain Quebec's support for the FTA (Bernier and Thérien 1994).

In general, the prospect of a free trade agreement with the United States and the subsequent transformation of the Canadian economy generated considerable pressure on provincial governments to defend those sectors that might be negatively affected. For its part, the Government of Canada needed mechanisms to manage the politics of free trade and underscore the fact that while some provincial governments were opposed to at least some aspects of a bilateral trade deal, others were strongly supportive. Moreover, while the final text of the CUSFTA and the NAFTA had limited direct impact on areas of provincial jurisdiction, at the outset of the first set of bilateral negotiations with the United States, a free trade agreement was thought to potentially have a major impact on provinces. The result was a decision to convene regular meetings between the prime minister and provincial premiers to discuss the CUSFTA negotiations (Hulsemeyer 2004).

At a more technical level, the federal government also needed input from provincial governments with respect to a few areas where provincial governments had either information or jurisdiction. Moreover, Ottawa was interested in sharing at least some information on the evolution of the negotiations with provincial governments. In effect, the CUSFTA negotiations precipitated the deepening of an existing set of arrangements that brought together federal and provincial officials to discuss trade issues. The result was the Continuing Committee on Trade Negotiations (CCTN), which later evolved into what today is known as the C-Trade committee system. C-Trade involves meetings between federal and provincial officials, usually four times each year. It is not a negotiating vehicle nor even a particularly effective means of consultation, but it is a forum for information sharing (Kukucha 2008, 54). In the case of the NAFTA, the C-Trade process became particularly important when, in order to secure congressional approval, it was necessary to develop "side deals" on environment and labour policy, areas of shared or predominantly provincial jurisdiction.

However, while the federal government engaged extensively and publicly with provincial governments during the negotiations leading to the FTA and the NAFTA, provincial governments were never formally part of the negotiations—largely because the final CUSFTA had little direct impact on areas of provincial jurisdiction. At best, provinces were consulted and encouraged to provide information and analysis of the impact of various possible elements of an agreement. Even here, provincial governments were not given privileged access; the federal government engaged in similar consultations with the business community during the negotiations leading to both the CUSFTA and the NAFTA.

Even when the NAFTA negotiations moved more squarely into areas of provincial jurisdiction because of the labour and environment side deals, provinces were consulted but there was no requirement for all them to agree. In fact, only three provinces (Quebec, Alberta, and Manitoba) formally signed onto both agreements. Moreover, the significance of their formally adhering to the side agreements is unclear and may amount to nothing more than a political commitment to be bound by the terms of the agreement, a commitment that may or may not be used by the federal government at some future date (Kukucha 2008).

The downside of a limited provincial role in approving both NAFTA and trade agreements in general is demonstrated by three bilateral trade disputes with the United States, two involving NAFTA-related financial penalties paid by the Government of Canada, the other involving the recent bilateral negotiations between Canada and the United States with respect to government procurement.

Provinces and Recent Canadian Trade Disputes

Under the terms of Chapter 11 of the NAFTA, governments agreed to a set of provisions designed to provide investors with a predictable, rules-based investment climate, as well as dispute settlement procedures. The forest-products company AbitibiBowater used these provisions to challenge the 2008 decision of the Government of Newfoundland and Labrador to expropriate the majority of the company's assets in the province after the company announced the closure of its last operating mill in Grand Fall-Windsor (Best 2010). However, because provincial governments are not parties to the NAFTA, the Government of Canada was left to try to defend the decision and pay any penalties arising from the dispute settlement process. In June 2010, the federal government agreed to settle the claim and announced its intention to reimburse Abitibi for the expropriation in the amount of $130 million, much less than the $500 million sought. And while the federal government indicated it would not try to recoup the $130 million from the province, the prime minister did indicate that it was the intention of his government to create a mechanism to be able to do so in future (CBC News 2010). However, it would appear that no such mechanism has been created.

More recently, a NAFTA tribunal ruled in favour of two US-based oil companies in a dispute over research and development expenditure requirements imposed by Newfoundland and Labrador (Hepburn 2012; Gray 2012). While the oil companies asked for $50 million in compensation, the final amount awarded has not been made public so far (Public Citizen 2013, 15-16). What is clear is that the federal government is responsible for paying any compensation. In effect, these cases suggest that, in the absence of the explicit adherence of a provincial government to a trade agreement or a bilateral agreement with the Government of Canada to implement a trade agreement, the only recourse open to the federal government is to try to monetize the problem.

A somewhat similar dynamic is evident with respect to government procurement. In response to a wave of protectionist measures in the United States following the recession that began in 2008 (i.e., limiting local and state government procurement to US based suppliers), the Canadian and American governments entered into negotiations that eventually led to a formal agreement. In this agreement, the provinces agreed for the first time to allow US firms to bid on provincial or municipal procurement contracts.[6] However, what is of interest is the mechanism by which provinces indicate their consent. Essentially, all provincial and territorial governments with the exception of Nunavut agreed to be bound by the terms of the WTO plurilateral Agreement on Government Procurement (GPA). However, provinces did not sign the GPA as such; rather, they agreed to be included in the list of Canadian government entities to be subject to the terms of the agreement (Cox and Palmer 2010).[7] The Government of Canada remains the signatory to the agreement, and there is no formal indication of provincial consent to be bound by the GPA. The implication of this arrangement is that, in the event that a province or municipality were to discriminate against a US-based supplier in violation of the 2010 agreement between Canada and the United States, Canada would be subject to any retaliation or penalties arising from the violation. Moreover, absent an agreement between the federal government and provinces, it would appear that Ottawa would have no way of sanctioning the recalcitrant provincial government or recouping any financial penalties that might arise.

In general the prospect of a free trade agreement with the United States and then Mexico led to greater information sharing and, to a lesser extent, consultation, by the federal government with provinces (and the private sector). However, the legacy of these negotiations is that the role of provincial governments in trade negotiations remains limited. The Government of Canada is the signatory to trade agreements and has the authority to decide what role, if any, to give provinces in negotiations. Moreover, if a province takes actions deemed to be in violation of a trade agreement (even if otherwise justifiable), there is no mechanism to sanction said province. Most important of all, none of this is set to change with the CETA.

---

[6] Agreement between the Government of Canada and the Government of the America on Government Procurement. The text of the agreement can be found at http://www. international.gc.ca/trade-agreements-accords-commerciaux/assets/pdfs/ENG-Canada-USA_Government_Procurement.pdf. This agreement was signed in order for Canadian businesses to be exempted from the Buy American provisions of the American Recovery and Reinvestment Act (i.e., the American stimulus package).

[7] The list of provincial and territorial commitments under the GPA can be found at http://www.wto.org/english/tratop_e/gproc_e/can2e.doc.

THE CANADA-EUROPEAN UNION (EU) COMPREHENSIVE ECONOMIC AND TRADE AGREEMENT (CETA)

Given the direct involvement of provincial governments in the CETA negotiations, it is important to understand what CETA is and why it makes sense for the provinces to be at the negotiating table. Furthermore, it is necessary to determine the scope of the provinces' participation in the negotiations and, therefore, the influence that they can exert on them. The issue of ratification and implementation is also relevant in this context, since the provinces will ultimately have to make sure their laws, regulations, and actions are in line with the parts of CETA that touch upon their competencies.

What Is CETA?

CETA is known as a second-generation trade agreement because its emphasis is on non-tariff barriers such as standards, regulations, and procedures. Such "behind the border" (as opposed to "at the border") barriers have become the main source of impediments to international trade since tariffs are now quite low, especially between rich countries, as a result of the successive rounds of tariff reductions within the General Agreement on Tariffs and Trade (GATT) since the 1950s and the creation of the World Trade Organization (WTO) in 1995. For instance, in 2007, Canadian goods faced an average tariff of 2.2 percent when they entered the EU, whereas at that time European goods were hit with an average tariff of 3.5 percent to enter the Canadian market. Since then, Canadian tariffs on many imported goods have been reduced to zero. In addition to trade in goods and services, CETA aims to encourage investment between Canada and the EU—for example, by providing greater protection of firms' assets in each jurisdiction or by facilitating access to public procurement contracts. This is why, after free trade with the United States, CETA is the most important bilateral trade agreement ever negotiated by Canada.[8]

---

[8] A joint study conducted by the European Commission and Government of Canada (2008) concluded that a second-generation type of economic partnership agreement would allow Canada to increase its exports of goods and services to the EU by $12.5 billion, while in return the EU would be able to increase its exports to Canada by $25 billion. The report also suggested that the EU's and Canada's GDPs would increase by $17 billion and $12 billion, respectively.

From the EU's perspective there is a hope that CETA will be a stepping stone to a free trade zone across the (northern) Atlantic (Woolcock 2011, 23-4).[9]

At the beginning of the negotiations, it was decided that no sector of the economy would be excluded a priori and that both tariff and non-tariff barriers would be examined.[10] For instance, in spite of the agreement's second-generation nature, the elimination of tariffs on traded goods remains a key negotiation issue. According to the joint study, a quarter to a third of the benefits arising from a partnership agreement would come from getting rid of such duties. Both sides made it clear that no tariff lines were to be excluded from the negotiations, even on agricultural goods.

Barriers to trade in services were also high on the negotiating agenda. The objective in this case was to improve market access and eliminate discrimination in favour of national service providers. For example, the agreement provides a framework for the mutual recognition of professional qualifications across the Atlantic, making it easier for firms to send Canadians to Europe (or Europeans to Canada) to work with subsidiaries and/or business partners. The overall intention here is to build on the two partners' existing WTO commitments under the aegis of the General Agreement on Trade in Services (GATS).

Both Canada and the EU were also keen on eliminating NTBs in areas other than services. For instance, building on the WTO's Agreement on Sanitary and Phytosanitary (SPS) Measures as well as the Canada-EU Veterinary Agreement the CETA establishes a framework for cooperation on issues relating to animal and plant health and food safety, specifically issues that could be deemed to restrict trade in goods and services. In addition, there was a need for transatlantic cooperation with respect to conformity assessments. The same logic applies to customs procedures, where, for example, both sides agreed to cooperate in order to ensure compliance with rules-of-origin provisions. In this case, CETA would build on the existing Canada-European Community (i.e., EU) Agreement on Customs Cooperation and Mutual Assistance in Customs Matters. Finally, concerning non-tariff barriers, the agreement promotes market access and puts in place non-discrimination measures in matters of investment and government procurement while also increasing the protection and enforcement of intellectual property rights by improving on the WTO's Agreement on Trade-Related Aspects of Intellectual Property Rights (TRIPS).

In addition to eliminating tariffs on goods and services as well as reducing the impact of non-tariff barriers through harmonization and regulatory cooperation

---

[9] The EU and the United States began negotiating a bilateral Transatlantic Trade and Investment Partnership in the summer for 2013. For an explanation of the difficulties associated with interregionalism between Europe and North America, see Aggarwal and Fogarty (2005).

[10] The Joint Report on the EU-Canada Scoping Exercise can be found at http://trade. ec.europa.eu/doclib/docs/2009/march/tradoc_142470.pdf.

measures, the CETA negotiations addressed a range of other topics including a dispute-settlement mechanism, competition policy, free movement of persons, labour, and the environment. The CUSFTA was the first bilateral free trade deal to put dispute settlement at the centre of the negotiations. Since then, most bilateral and multilateral trade liberalizing agreements have included such mechanisms in order to render the agreements more effective. Such a mechanism is planned for the CETA. As for competition policy, there is a growing recognition that state aid and other forms of government intervention in the economy (e.g., regulating monopolies) can distort the competitive nature of markets and, as a result, create barriers to trade and investment. So, for example, Canada and the EU agree in the CETA to prohibit agricultural export subsidies. The CETA also aims to facilitate the temporary movement of labour for trade and investment purposes and includes provisions to facilitate temporary entry for Canadians (Europeans) working in the EU (Canada). Finally, as with most bilateral trade agreements involving rich countries these days, the CETA includes chapters on sustainable-development trade and environment, and trade and labour, designed to ensure that Canadian and European labour and environmental laws and standards do not give one side or the other unfair trade or investment advantages.[11]

CETA and the Provinces

Owing to its comprehensive nature, CETA affects several matters of provincial jurisdiction (shared or not shared with the federal government). For example, CETA covers fields such as energy, the environment, education, transportation, science, and technology. It aims, among other things, to encourage workforce mobility between Canada and the EU, which entails the recognition of professional skills obtained on either side of the Atlantic. It also aims to eliminate discrimination against foreign companies in favour of local ones in the awarding of contracts by provincial and (especially) municipal governments.

Given that such negotiation issues fall under exclusive or shared provincial and territorial jurisdiction, and that provinces will ultimately be responsible for implementing many of the agreement's provisions, the EU requested that provincial governments actively participate in the CETA negotiations and credibly commit to the agreement. While customs duties (i.e., tariffs) and intellectual property are clearly under federal jurisdiction, many issues such as agriculture, labour, health, the environment, and energy are either shared with or under the exclusive jurisdiction of the provinces. To avoid devoting time and energy to negotiating the CETA with Canada, only to find out that many provisions are not being applied or implemented by some or all of the provinces, the EU made the provinces' active participation a

---

[11] On regulatory cooperation between Canada and the EU, see Krstic (2012).

conditio sine qua non to begin the negotiations; the assumption was that it will be difficult for them to renege on elements of agreements that they took active part in negotiating. Apparently, the Europeans felt that the lack of provincial "buy-in" in previous agreements between Canada and the EU was a great impediment to success (Kukucha 2011).

In addition to their traditional involvement through the C-Trade committee system, Canadian provinces directly participated in many of the negotiating groups within the overall CETA negotiations. According to Kukucha (2011, 134), the provinces were involved in six and often seven of the 12 groups set up at the beginning of the talks. They were also present at most of the negotiation rounds. Provincial participation led to the somewhat paradoxical situation in which the Canadian delegation—led by the chief negotiator Steve Verheul, from the federal Department of Foreign Affairs, Trade and Development—numbered more than 100 persons, while there were less than a dozen people on the EU side, represented solely by the European Commission.[12] (It should be noted that the provinces were not actually negotiating alongside the federal government's negotiators; they were present in the room during the negotiations only in cases where the issues being discussed fall under provincial jurisdiction. Otherwise, the provinces were subsequently briefed on the results of such negotiations, following the more traditional C-Trade committee system.)

Since NAFTA, Canada has not negotiated an important international economic agreement equivalent to the proposed CETA. Given CETA's multifaceted nature, including the fact that many of the issues under negotiation are areas of provincial jurisdiction, it made sense to closely involve the provinces in the agreement's negotiations. This is why the provinces were invited to sit in on negotiation sessions touching on issues over which they have shared or full jurisdiction within the Canadian federation. Provincial governments were thus more closely involved in developing negotiating positions for the Canadian side. As a result, it is fair to say that the CETA negotiations represented a step forward in recognizing that many areas of provincial jurisdiction are no longer strictly domestic matters but have international ramifications.[13]

Beyond directly involving the provinces in the negotiations, CETA looks unlikely to advance the effectiveness of Canadian federalism in matters of international trade and investment. This is because there is no mechanism for ensuring that the provinces can be held to the commitments that they made inside the negotiating room. A provincial government may wish to pursue a policy direction, perhaps for

---

[12] For an overview of how trade negotiations are structured within the EU, see Fafard and Leblond (2012).

[13] Energy and the environment are other policy areas falling under provincial jurisdiction, which now have a strong international dimension (e.g., Jegen 2011; Schreurs 2011).

good reasons, that is at risk of being deemed in contravention of the CETA. Given that the federal government has sole jurisdiction over international treaties within the Canadian federal system, the provinces are in fact at liberty to ignore CETA, in parts or in its entirety, without facing any of the sanctions included in the agreement, just as in the case of NAFTA. Although the provinces' active involvement in the negotiations may limit the need for such behaviour, assuming that CETA actually reflects the provinces' commitments, future political pressures or the arrival of a new government in power with different political interests could lead to parts of CETA not being implemented by the provinces. And there would be no way to prevent them from doing so, other than naming and shaming them. This situation represents a serious constraint on CETA's effectiveness and ultimate success.

Further Evidence of Small Steps: The Curious Case of Pharmaceutical Drug Pricing

One of the more controversial issues that formed part of the CETA negotiations are the rules governing intellectual property (IP), specifically as these rules affect the pricing of pharmaceutical drugs. While the issue is very complex, in essence the negotiations turn on the fact that the European IP regime offers stronger patent protection to research-based pharmaceutical companies. As part of the CETA negotiations, the European Union was seeking changes to the Canadian IP regime that would have the effect of extending the monopoly power of some drug companies operating in Canada (Gagnon 2012).

The benefit for Canada of moving closer to the European approach would be the promise of increased pharmaceutical research and development spending in Canada. One study estimated that increase to be in the order of $345 million per year. Given the structure of the Canadian pharmaceutical industry, the bulk of this investment would occur in Quebec and to a lesser extent in Ontario (Grootendorst and Hollis 2011). However, it is not clear that this investment will, in fact, take place given the long term decline in pharmaceutical research and development in Canada (Lexchin and Gagnon 2013). Moreover, there are also significant costs associated with this change. These same studies estimate that those who pay for pharmaceutical drugs—individuals, insurance companies, and especially provincial governments—would be faced with a significant increase in costs in the order of as much as $2.8 billion per year (Grootendorst and Hollis 2011). Moreover, as with benefits, these costs would not be evenly distributed across the country. For example, Ontario payers would be required to come up with an estimated $1.2 billion per year. Given that provincial governments cover on average just under 40 percent of all expenditures on prescription drugs (Canadian Institute for Health Information 2012), the proposed IP changes in the CETA could cost provinces upwards of $1.1

billion per year.[14] While the final cost to provincial treasuries will not be known for some time, when the CETA agreement-in-principle was announced in October 2013 the Government of Ontario, among others, was careful to indicate that its support for the agreement was conditional on some form of compensation from Ottawa to address higher pharmaceutical drug costs (Benzie 2013).

Even though provinces will be asked to bear the bulk of the costs associated with this change in Canada's IP regime, and precisely because IP is nominally a matter of federal jurisdiction, provincial governments were not part of the Canadian delegation for this aspect of the negotiations with the European Union. Nor was there a formal mechanism, beyond the C-Trade process, to allow provinces to participate in the deliberations about how to balance the associated benefits and costs. The result is that the provinces were forced to rely on more informal ways of lobbying the federal government. So, in marked contrast to the CUSFTA negotiations that included a series of First Ministers' Conferences, in the case of the IP aspects of the CETA negotiations, provincial governments had to resort to a letter-writing campaign. In June 2012, British Columbia Premier Christy Clark revealed that she and the other provincial premiers had agreed to each write the federal government "urging federal negotiators not to agree to anything that would drive up the cost of pharmaceuticals" (Scofield 2012).

The EU's request that Canada change its IP regime as it applies to pharmaceutical products is but one example of the interconnected nature of contemporary trade policy that makes it difficult to limit provincial involvement to those issues that are only directly a matter of provincial jurisdiction. Provincial governments have an interest in a wide range of issues that are part of the CETA negotiations, even though some of those issues are formally matters of exclusive federal jurisdiction. Provincial participation is confined to those negotiations that deal with areas of provincial jurisdiction, and the provinces have not been accorded any formal means of influencing the final text of an agreement (with the inevitable trade-offs). It is precisely these very real limits on the role of provincial governments that underline the modest nature of the changes to intergovernmental relations and trade policy triggered by the CETA negotiations.

CONCLUSION

The scope of the second-generation international economic and trade agreements goes much beyond tariffs that have formed the basis of bilateral (or regional) trade agreements signed by Canada until now, including the North American Free Trade

---

[14] Not surprisingly, the conclusions of this study have been challenged by RX&D: Canada's Research-Based Pharmaceutical Companies. For an overview, see Picard (2011) and Diebel (2011).

Agreement. A major concern of these twenty-first century agreements is non-tariff barriers such as, *inter alia*, labour mobility, regulations and standards, investment, public procurement, and intellectual property rights, as well as scientific and administrative cooperation between both private and public entities (private-private, public-public, and public-private). Because so many of the issues are areas of exclusive jurisdiction for the provincial and territorial governments, or are areas of shared responsibility with Ottawa, second-generation agreements, by definition, require a more extensive role for provinces.

In the negotiations of the Comprehensive Economic and Trade Agreement, for perhaps the first time[15] provincial governments were actively involved in the negotiations of an international trade agreement, not just consulted or informed like any other stakeholder. However, the analysis presented here suggests that it would be a mistake to characterize this change as a major shift in Canadian intergovernmental relations as they pertain to trade policy. Rather than a giant leap, the provincial role in the CETA negotiations is but a small step forward. First, there is no indication that the provinces' direct participation in the CETA negotiations has become institutionalized such that this approach has now been extended to other negotiations of trade and economic agreements. Second, there is no institutional mechanism, even in the context of CETA, that provides for the provinces to finalize/approve (i.e., sign and ratify) as well as implement a trade and economic agreement in which they have participated as negotiators. Only if the provinces' direct involvement in the negotiations of trade and economic agreements became formal and institutionalized, and if a mechanism were established to ensure that the provinces were legally bound by their commitments during the negotiations, could we talk of a giant leap having been taken by Canada's federal system.

That inability to take a giant leap is likely to negatively impact Canada's international trade policy. First, if the role of provinces is not institutionalized, it remains unclear whether, for any given bilateral or multilateral negotiation, provinces will play a formal and direct role. Canada and the provinces thus have to reinvent the wheel every time there is a second-generation agreement to be negotiated. As a result, there are no institutional economies of scale (i.e., no learning) to be reaped over time from the provinces' direct participation in trade and economic negotiations, as is the case in the EU (Meunier 2005), where every negotiation is "*un éternel recommencement*." Second, the absence of any mechanism to ensure the provinces' implementation of agreements may make other countries reticent to negotiate trade and economic agreements with Canada, unless the scope is limited to areas where

---

[15] In the 1980s the EU raised concerns about provincial liquor board practices. The EU initiated a complaint against Canada under the dispute resolution processes of the General Agreement on Tariffs and Trade. Resolution of this disagreement required extensive bilateral negotiations that, of necessity, included provincial government representatives (Kukucha 2008).

the federal government has sole jurisdiction, thereby making Canada a less appealing trade and economic partner. As a result, the current government of Canada could find it difficult to realize its stated international trade strategy with respect to bilateral and multilateral trade and economic agreements. Finally, even if Canada manages to negotiate and ratify an agreement with one or more of its partners, the uncertainty related to provincial implementation could limit the benefits associated with such an agreement. Firms, whether in Canada or abroad, may decide to wait and see how the agreement is implemented before signing commercial contracts and/or investing important amounts of money.

In sum, the current small step that Canadian federalism has taken with the CETA is largely insufficient for the federal and provincial governments to maximize the economic benefits associated with bilateral and multilateral trade and economic agreements.

REFERENCES

Aggarwal, V.K., and E.A. Fogarty. 2005. "The Limits of Interregionalism: The EU and North America." *Journal of European Integration* 27 (3): 327-46.

Benzie, R. 2013. "CETA: Wynne Hails 'Very Good Deal,' but Warns Ontario Has Concerns." *Toronto Star*, 8 October. http://www.thestar.com/news/canada/2013/10/18/ceta_wynne_hails_very_good_deal_but_warns_ontario_has_concerns.html.

Bernier, I., and J.P. Thérien. 1994. "Le comportement international du Québec, de l'Ontario et de l'Alberta dans le domaine économique." *Études internationales* 25 (3): 453-86.

Best, C. 2010. "The Federal Government Settles AbitibiBowater's NAFTA Claim." *The Court*, 27 August. http://www.thecourt.ca/2010/08/27/canada-settles-abitibibowaters-nafta-claim/.

Canadian Institute for Health Information. 2012. "Drug Expenditure in Canada, 1984 to 2011." Accessed 6 September 2012. https://secure.cihi.ca/estore/productSeries.htm?locale=en&pc=PCC103.

CBC News. 2010. "Provinces Should Pay for NAFTA Losses: PM." 2010. *CBC News Online*, 26 August. Accessed 31 August 2012. http://www.cbc.ca/news/politics/story/2010/08/26/nl-harper-abitibi-826.html.

Clark, P. 2012. "Clear the Tracks for Stephen Harper's Free Trade Express." *iPolitics*, 23 January. http://www.ipolitics.ca/2012/01/23/peter-clark-clear-the-tracks-for-the-harper-free-trade-express/.

Courchene, T.J. 1998. *From Heartland to North American Region State: The Social, Fiscal and Federal Evolution of Ontario: An Interpretive Essay*. With C.R. Telmer. Toronto: Centre for Public Management, Faculty of Management, University of Toronto.

Cox and Palmer. 2010. "Update: Canada-US Agreement on Government Procurement." http://www.coxandpalmerlaw.com/en/home/publications/updatecanadausagreementongovernmentprocurement.aspx.

Diebel, L. 2011. "Studies Warn Drug Prices Will Rise under Trade Deal." *Toronto Star*, 24 June. http://www.thestar.com/news/canada/politics/article/1014637--studies-warn-drug-prices-will-rise-under-trade-deal.

European Commission and Government of Canada. 2008. "Assessing the Costs and Benefits of a Closer EU-Canada Economic Partnership, Brussels and Ottawa: Directorate-General Trade and Department of Foreign Affairs and International Trade." Accessed 31 August 2012. http://www.international.gc.ca/trade-agreements-accords-commerciaux/assets/pdfs/EU-CanadaJointStudy-en.pdf.

Fafard, P., and P. Leblond. 2012. "Twenty-First Century Trade Agreements: Challenges for Canadian Federalism." The Federal Idea, Montreal. http://ideefederale.ca/documents/challenges.pdf.

Gagnon, M.-A. 2012. "Patent Protection for Drugs Should Come at a Price." *Winnipeg Free Press*, 28 August. http://archive.is/d8w5S.

Gray, J. 2012. "Canada Loses NAFTA Battle to Exxon." *Globe and Mail*, 18 June. http://m.theglobeandmail.com/globe-investor/canada-loses-nafta-case-against-exxon/article2449446/?service=mobile.

Grootendorst, P., and A. Hollis. 2011. "The 2011 Canada-European Union Comprehensive Economic and Trade Agreement: An Economic Impact Assessment of the EU's Proposed Pharmaceutical Intellectual Property Provisions." *Journal of Generic Medicines* 8 (2): 81-103.

Hepburn, J. 2012. "Canada Loses NAFTA Claim; Provincial R&D Obligations Imposed on US Oil Companies Held to Constitute Prohibited Performance Requirements." *Investment Arbitration Reporter*. http://www.iareporter.com/articles/20120601/print.

Hübner, K. 2011. *Europe, Canada, and the Comprehensive Economic and Trade Agreement*. New York: Routledge.

Hulsemeyer, A. 2004. *Globalization and Institutional Adjustment: Federalism as an Obstacle?* Aldershot, UK: Ashgate.

Inwood, G.J. 2005. *Continentalizing Canada: The Politics and Legacy of the MacDonald Royal Commission*. Toronto: University of Toronto Press.

Jegen, M. 2011. "Two Paths to Energy Security: The EU and NAFTA." *International Journal* 66 (1): 73-90.

Krstic, S.S. 2012. "Regulatory Cooperation to Remove Non-Tariff Barriers to Trade in Products: Key Challenges and Opportunities for the Canada-EU Comprehensive Trade Agreement." *Legal Issues of Economic Integration* 39 (1): 3-28.

Kukucha, C.J. 2008. *The Provinces and Canadian Foreign Trade Policy*. Vancouver: UBC Press.

—. 2011. "Provincial Pitfalls: Canadian Provinces and the Canada-EU Trade Negotiations." In *Europe, Canada, and the Comprehensive Economic and Trade Agreement*, edited by K. Hübner, 130-50. New York: Routledge.

Leblond, P. 2010. "The Canada-EU Comprehensive Economic and Trade Agreement: More to It Than Meets the Eye." *Policy Options* 31 (7): 74-8.

Lexchin, J., and M-A. Gagnon. 2013. "CETA and Pharmaceuticals: Impact of the Trade Agreement between Europe and Canada on the Costs of Patented Drugs." Toronto: Canadian Centre for Policy Alternatives. http://www.policyalternatives.ca/publications/reports/ceta-and-pharmaceuticals.

Meunier, S. 2005. *Trading Voices: The European Union in International Commercial Negotiations*. Princeton: Princeton University Press.

Picard, A. 2011. "EU Trade Deal Could Cost Canadian Drug Plans Billions." *Globe and Mail*, 23 August. http://m.theglobeandmail.com/life/health-and-fitness/eu-trade-deal-could-cost-canadian-drug-plans-billions/article572488/?service=mobile.

Public Citizen. 2013. "Table of Foreign Investor-State Cases and Claims under NAFTA and other U.S. 'Trade' Deals." August. Washington. Accessed 10 December 2013. http://www.citizen.org/documents/investor-state-chart1.pdf

Schreurs, M.A. 2011. "Federalism and the Climate: Canada and the EU." *International Journal* 66 (1): 91-108.

Scofield, H. 2012. "Premiers Wary of EU Drug Patents." *Halifax Chronicle Herald*, 4 June. http://thechronicleherald.ca/canada/103446-premiers-wary-of-eu-drug-patents.

Woolcock, S.B. 2011. "European Union Trade Policy: The Canada-EU Comprehensive Economic and Trade Agreement (CETA) towards a New Generation of FTAs?" In *Europe, Canada, and the Comprehensive Economic and Trade Agreement*, edited by K. Hübner, 21-40. New York: Routledge.

IV

THE PROVINCES AND THE NORTH: GROWING IN IMPORTANCE?

SOMETHING OLD OR SOMETHING NEW? TERRITORIAL DEVELOPMENT AND INFLUENCE WITHIN THE CANADIAN FEDERATION[1]

George Braden, Christopher Alcantara, and Michael Morden

The election of Stephen Harper and his Conservative Party in 2006 was supposed to be an important turning point for the territorial North. After years of perceived neglect, commentators believed, the Canadian government was finally going to prioritize the needs and issues of the region. Indeed, in the 2007 Speech from the Throne, the Government of Canada announced:

> The Arctic is an essential part of Canada's history. One of our Fathers of Confederation, D'Arcy McGee, spoke of Canada as a northern nation, bounded by the blue rim of the ocean. Canadians see in our North an expression of our deepest aspirations: our sense of exploration, the beauty and the bounty of our land, and our limitless potential. But the North needs new attention. New opportunities are emerging across the Arctic, and new challenges from other shores. Our government will bring forward an integrated northern strategy focusing on strengthening Canada's sovereignty, protecting our environmental heritage, promoting economic and social development, and improving and devolving governance, so that northerners have greater control over their destinies. (Canada 2007c)

---

[1] This research was funded by a SSHRC Strategic Research Grant – Northern Communities: Towards Social and Economic Prosperity, grant #866-2008-0003. References in this chapter to devolution in the Northwest Territories do not discuss recent federal/territorial legislative initiatives to implement the Canada-NWT devolution agreement-in-principle signed in 2011.

In many ways, this "new" federal interest in the North reflects a number of lingering historical forces that have plagued the region for much of its history. It also reflects the rapid and substantial changes that are being wrought on the region by global warming. The sea ice, for instance, is retreating at alarmingly high rates, opening the Northwest Passage as a viable route for commercial shipping between Asia and parts of North America and Europe. Moreover, the melting ice is creating new access to potentially massive unexploited and previously inaccessible resource stores (Abele et. al. 2009, 567). As a result, Canada has become involved in a quiet struggle for positioning, along with the United States, Russia, and other Arctic nations, over who can own and use what in the region.

There are, therefore, both political and structural reasons for why the North has suddenly become a region of interest among politicians and policy-makers in the South. As well, Canadian citizens have become more attuned to the issues of the Canadian North. A recent public opinion poll, for instance, showed that a majority of Canadians rank Arctic sovereignty as the top foreign policy priority for the country (Mahoney 2011). As such, the current federal government has access to significant political capital to address the issues of the North, should it choose to do so.

Yet it would be a mistake to analyze these recent trends in northern policy without considering them in historical context. Generally speaking, federal interest in the North has waxed and waned over time. The Arctic sovereignty question in particular has been given renewed significance with climate change, but it is hardly a product of the twenty-first century. Coates, Lackenbauer, Morrison, and Poelzer argue that the Canadian North, and especially Arctic sovereignty, is akin to a "zombie—the dead issue that refuses to stay dead—of Canadian public affairs. You think it's settled, killed and buried, and then every decade or so it rises from the grave and totters into view again" (Coates et al. 2008, 1). Conflicts over sovereignty and economic resources date back at least to the Yukon Gold Rush in the 1890s, and the desire to exploit the natural wealth of the region has been a preoccupation of the federal government at different points throughout our history, right up through to the government of John Diefenbaker and into the present.

The broad theme of this volume is that a "new" Canadian federal environment has emerged and that perhaps the roles of the provinces and territories in the federation have been altered as a result. Our task is to address this theme as it relates to the territorial North. To do so, we begin by reviewing recent trends in the territorial North that have contributed to the sense that a new Canadian federal environment has emerged. We argue that these trends are simply the latest stage of a longer historical process of federal interest and development in the territorial North. Next, we analyze the extent to which these new and historical forces have shaped the governance structures and processes of devolution for the territorial governments. Finally, we assess the extent to which the territorial governments historically, and in this new, evolving federal environment, are able to exert their influence effectively within a variety of intergovernmental fora. Overall, our analysis suggests that the "new" Canadian federal environment has had both positive and negative effects on the development and influence of territorial governments in the Canadian federation.

THE NEW PRIMACY OF ARCTIC POLITICS

According to most commentators, the main reason that the North now garners increased attention from both policy-makers and publics in the South is the geo-ecological transformation wrought by climate change. Between 1969 and 2001, the Canadian Ice Service reported that ice coverage during the summer months had shrunk at a rate of 15 percent (Griffiths 2003, 5). This long-term dwindling of sea-ice is actually incremental compared to trends post-2001. In 2007, for instance, the Arctic witnessed "a great and cataclysmic change ... one that would remove any doubts that the ice was in danger" (Anderson 2009, 4). During that year, an enormous area of sea ice dissolved faster than anyone anticipated was possible—an extra 625,000 square miles from the previous summer (Anderson 2009, 4). As a result, many scientists revised their predictions about climate change and Arctic melt to reflect a much faster process.

This trend has substantial geopolitical consequences for the region, primarily for two reasons. First, the melting ice improves the area significantly for marine transportation, raising the stakes for unresolved issues of sovereignty and territorial control. Second, the promise of new access means that the Arctic has become subject to increased and intensive resource exploration and extraction activities. Both of these consequences bring to the region more actors and competing interests.

Sovereignty Claims

Canada is currently engaged in a handful of sovereignty disputes with other Arctic states, some of which are significant to Canadian interests. Chief amongst these is a dispute involving the Northwest Passage, which has become a more viable shipping route as the ice has melted. The sovereignty issue facing Canada in the Northwest Passage does not relate to ownership or title to territory per se. Indeed, Canada's title to the Arctic Archipelago is uncontested (Roth 1990). Rather, there is disagreement over who has control of the Passage. Twice—with the SS *Manhattan* in 1969 and the USCGC *Polar Sea* in 1985—American vessels have travelled through the Passage on test voyages that were perceived as affronts to Canadian functional sovereignty. Officially, Canada views the Passage as an internal waterway and wholly subject to Canadian law, while the United States has maintained that it is an "international strait," meaning that although title belongs to the coastal states, it is open to transit by foreign vessels with little or no restriction (Byers and Lalonde 2009).

Other current disputes range from symbolic to substantive. An example of the former is Hans Island, an uninhabited 1.3 square kilometre patch of land in the

Kennedy Channel that is claimed by both Canada and Denmark. In terms of the latter types of disputes, Canadian and Russian territorial claims overlap at the Lomonosov Ridge, which runs underwater from the East Siberian Shelf to Ellesmere Island (Byers 2009, 93). Title to this ridge carries implications for access to potentially immense stores of valuable resources.

Resource Potential

The opening of the Arctic Ocean also promises access to previously inaccessible non-renewable resources. Early exploration efforts indicate that the Arctic holds the last significant unexploited stores of hydrocarbon in the world (Borgerson 2008, 67). It has been estimated that as much as one-fifth of the remaining oil and gas in the world is under the surface of the Arctic Ocean (Abele et al. 2009, 567). As a result, resource-extraction multinationals have been jostling for position and access to this largely untapped potential. However, because of the high cost of extraction and transportation from the Arctic, interest has been largely fixed to oil prices. In 2008, when oil prices peaked, there was substantial movement towards development. When prices fell again, progress on claiming Arctic oil slowed (Griffiths 2009, 1). Because the extraction industry is so closely tied to the global price of oil, it becomes difficult to predict what form the short-term competition for Arctic resources will take. But while time horizons are ambiguous, it seems likely that at some point global demand will stimulate an "Arctic race" for riches (Abele et al. 2009, 569).

Political Change

In addition to international currents, the present federal government has placed a high priority on Arctic sovereignty in particular, and northern issues in general. In the 2006 federal election, Stephen Harper surprised many by highlighting the state of the North as a cornerstone of his policy agenda (Huebert 2008, 1). This theme has remained constant and prominent in his government's discourse. In the 2007 Speech from the Throne, the announcement of a new northern strategy was accompanied by an appeal to national identity. A similar message was repeated in the 2010 Speech from the Throne: "We are a northern country. Canadians are deeply influenced by the vast expanse of our Arctic and its history and legends. Our Government established the Northern Strategy to realize the potential of Canada's North for northerners and all Canadians" (Canada 2010).

To date, the federal government has backed its rhetoric with an unusual level of substantive policy directed at northern development. Enhancing Canada's military capacity in the North arguably took priority over other policy measures in the first few years of the strategy (Coates et al. 2008, 196). Prime Minister Harper's oft-repeated mantra, "Use it or lose it," means it is important for Canada to demonstrate an active presence in the region to reaffirm its sovereignty claims (Bartenstein 2010). To that end, the government pledged, *inter alia*, the construction of new Arctic patrol vessels and a deep-water naval base in Nanisivik (Canada 2007a; Canada 2007b), the construction of the polar class icebreaker CCGS *John G. Diefenbaker*, and the growth and professionalization of the Canadian Rangers, the largely Indigenous militia that patrols the Arctic.

THE FEDERAL INTEREST AND DEVOLUTION

Despite domestic, geo-political, and ecological changes that have elevated popular awareness of the North, it would be incorrect to conclude that the federal government entirely neglected the region in the past. In fact, we have simply entered the latest stage of a sustained, albeit uneven, southern interest in the territorial North. The Canadian North has long been important to federal policy-makers, not only as the last frontier in the Canadian "nation-building" project but also as a battleground for defending Canadian sovereignty, and for providing resources and revenues for the economies of the South. Encroachment on functional sovereignty during the Yukon Gold Rush, the Second World War, and the Cold War drove federal policy-makers to invest in a larger governmental presence in the North. The allure of the North's untapped resource riches has held Ottawa's attention periodically, at least since Diefenbaker's "Roads to Riches" policy. At times, some of this interest has been expressed symbolically as opposed to substantively, probably because, as Coates and his colleagues have argued, the federal government's preference has been "to spend public money where the votes were, and there [are] not many of these north of the Arctic Circle" (Coates et al 2008, 65). This tendency to sometimes use symbolic action, combined with federal concerns regarding Arctic sovereignty, nation-building, and economic development, has resulted in a disjointed, incremental and sometimes contradictory redefinition of the role and political/constitutional development of territorial governments within the federation.

Nonetheless, historically speaking, territorial governments have largely benefited from federal concerns about protecting Canadian sovereignty in the North. To partially fulfill this goal, the federal government has engaged in devolution, a strategy involving strengthening territorial governments with significant powers, responsibilities, and incentives to flex their governance functions in the region, as a means of more visibly demonstrating Canada's sovereign control. The territories were originally governed as effective fiefdoms by the long arm of distant Ottawa. This relationship began to change after the Second World War, and the pace of change accelerated again in the 1970s and 1980s (Alcantara 2012; Alcantara, Cameron, and Kennedy 2012). The historical trajectories of the three modern territories share important similarities but are different from each other in import-ant ways. What is clear in each case is the link between the federally perceived national interest, and movement towards devolution.

Yukon

The early history of Yukon was profoundly connected to the wax and wane of its resource extraction potential and the sovereignty concerns that these trends created for the federal government. The Klondike gold rush brought large but relatively short-term settlement to the territory during the 1890s. Many of the miners were American, and in the early period of the gold rush, the territory was effectively governed by Western American customary authority—namely, citizens' assemblies called "miners meetings" that existed in the absence of any state apparatus (Coates et al. 2008, 20). It was because of this affront to Canada's functional sovereignty that the federal government first sought to establish a presence in the region, initially with a small RCMP deployment in 1895. In 1898, the territory was of-ficially created by an act of Parliament. It was to be governed by a "Commissioner in Council," which was somewhat equivalent to a pre-responsible government lieutenant-governor aided by an initially appointed, then later elected, executive council (Cameron and White 1995, 17).

In the early twentieth century, the gold rush subsided and the population de-clined steeply, from a peak of 50,000 to only 4,000 in the 1921 census. The federal government ceased to regard the territory as important and scaled back local governance. The Office of the Commissioner, for instance, was consolidated with other administrative bodies and later dissolved, and the council was greatly reduced in membership. This arrangement persisted until the Second World War, when Japanese manoeuvres near Alaska raised concerns about the unprotected north-west flank of the continent. Here again, the national interest dictated establishing a more substantive governance presence and investing more heavily in the North. Among other things, Canada cooperated with the United States in building a road link between northern British Columbia and Alaska, which had an immense impact on the wage and traditional economies of Yukon (Cameron and White 1995, 18).

The infrastructure boom persisted into the 1950s, now linked to a federal awaken-ing to the resource potential of the region. Diefenbaker's "Road to Resources" policy was central to a nation-building strategy that embraced the North. Construction began for the Dempster Highway to link Dawson City with Inuvik and to capitalize on promising new oil and gas exploration. There was also a new push to attract European migrants to the North, also as a function of nation-building. Yukon's then-MP Aubrey Simmons argued, for instance, that "the development, settlement, and opening up of the North will vastly increase our national wealth, and provide work and homes for countless thousands of new Canadians" (Cameron and White 1995, 18).

Renewed interest in the vulnerability, resource potential, and national importance of Yukon coincided with a governance overhaul. The modern "constitution" of
Yukon took form through the Yukon Act, 1953. This legislation created a territorial
council with a jurisdictional range somewhat similar to provincial legislatures
(Cameron and White 1995, 18). The council initially remained subordinate to federal
bureaucrats at the new Department of Northern Affairs and National Resources
(Abele 2009, 27). Serious devolution came later, however, as Yukon's stock as a
vehicle for economic development and nation-building grew in the eyes of federal
policy-makers. In 1979, the famous "Epp Letter," sent by Minister of Indian Affairs
and Northern Development Jake Epp to Commissioner Ione Christensen, expressed
formally that the power to govern resided with the territorial legislature — in short,
that responsible government had reached the North (Alcantara, Cameron, and
Kennedy 2012).

The same period also saw the emergence of Indigenous peoples as central political actors. In the early 1970s, this new assertiveness came into conflict with the
federal government's desire to advance oil and gas exploration (McArthur 2009,
193). The federal government, battle-weary from the ill-conceived White Paper
on Indian Policy that had provoked massive opposition from Indigenous peoples
across the country, and hopeful to move on development, conceded the necessity to
negotiate (McArthur 2009, 193). In 1973, the Council for Yukon Indians issued a
formal claim. In 1993, an Umbrella Final Agreement was concluded, allowing for
First Nation–specific negotiations and final agreements with four of the 14 Yukon
First Nations in 1995. Seven more individual treaties have since been reached. The
result is a complex interplay of Aboriginal governments, the federal government, and
the Yukon territorial government through an array of consociational power-sharing
mechanisms, including resource and wildlife management boards with guaranteed
Indigenous representation (Alcantara, Cameron, and Kennedy 2012; White 2002).

The final step towards quasi-provincial status was taken in 2003, when the
Government of Yukon and the federal government finally completed a devolution
agreement concerning jurisdiction over lands and resources. This final agreement
came long after most of the other "province-type" powers had been devolved and
was done in a way that carefully preserved the interests of the federal government,
as we discuss in greater detail below.

Northwest Territories

The federal government's passing of the Northwest Territory Act of 1875 created
the domestic legal basis for Dominion authority over the region. This legislation
confirmed the interim provisions put in place by the federal government in 1870,
which established direct federal control and delivery of basic services to the region
(Alcantara 2012). In 1905, the NWT Act was amended to create the position of
commissioner as chief executive officer of the region, and established an advisory

Territorial Council made up of four appointed civil servants from Ottawa. In 1919, a precedent that lasted 60 years was established, whereby the deputy minister of the Department of the Interior was appointed commissioner of the territory, solidifying the bureaucratic and Ottawa-centric nature of governance in the territory (Dickerson 1992, 29-30). Without the same pressing concerns relating to sovereignty as had existed with Yukon, the federal government during this period extended public authority in the NWT using mainly incremental and symbolic steps rather than substantive ones. Finally, in 1967, following the advice of the Carrothers Commission, the territorial administration was moved to Yellowknife, the new territorial capital. With a local government finally in place, a period of devolution was kick-started. The sheer size of the territorial government grew profoundly over the next decade, from a staff of about 75 people in 1967 to 2,845 territorial employees by 1979 (Dickerson 1992, 90). The next 30 years saw the gradual expansion of the government of the Northwest Territories' responsibilities to include the provision of health care, social services, and education, the administration of airports, and forest management (Alcantara 2012). As was the case with Yukon, devolution was tied to the deepening interest of the federal government in the territory.

The development of the Northwest Territories was also fundamentally impacted by the resurgent political presence of Indigenous peoples. New Aboriginal assertiveness was brought resoundingly to the attention of the federal government when Dene, Métis, and Inuvialuit groups organized to resist the construction of a natural gas pipeline in the Mackenzie Valley. These activities directly infringed on federal interests and demanded a response (Abele 2009, 31). As with Yukon, the pressure exerted by Indigenous peoples for self-determination created a more complex political dynamic for devolution. The treaty negotiation process unfolded very differently than it had in Yukon, however. Comprehensive land claims agreements were concluded with the Inuvialuit (1984), Gwich'in (1992), Sahtu Dene and Métis (1994), and more recently, the Tlicho (2005). Unlike the settlements with the Yukon First Nations, and with the exception of the Tlicho, these agreements did not contain self-government provisions. The most dramatic modern treaty, at least in terms of redrawing the map of Canada, was the one that partitioned the NWT and created the territory of Nunavut.

In 2004, long after social policy and other expensive jurisdictional items had been devolved, a framework agreement was reached to devolve the last "provincial-type" powers exercised by the Department of Indian and Northern Development (DIAND) in the territory, namely resource management and the control of Crown land. Initially, a tight deadline of June 2005 was set to reach a final agreement, but the process broke down and remained unresolved for some time (Feehan 2009, 350). Finally, in early 2011, the premier of the NWT, Floyd Roland, signed an agreement-in-principle (AIP) with the federal government. This agreement, however, remains highly contentious, with some Indigenous leaders in the territory opposed to the devolution arrangement. Four of the seven Aboriginal groups in the territory, the Inuvialuit Regional Corporation, the NWT Métis Nation, the

Sahtu Secretariat Incorporated, and the Gwich'in Tribal Council, have indicated their support, signing the Devolution AIP 2011 (IRC and Métis) and 2012 (Sahtu and Gwich'in), but the other three groups remain opposed. Debate continues as well amongst non-Aboriginals in the NWT about whether the framework agreement adequately protects the territorial interest or concedes too much to the federal government (Alcantara 2012).

Nunavut

If there is one feature of the modern transformation of the North that can be identified readily by most southern Canadians, it is surely the birth of a new territory in the eastern Arctic. This process began in earnest in 1976 amidst the formation and growing assertiveness of a variety of Indigenous political organizations across the country. At that time, the main Inuit organization in the region, the Inuit Tapirisat, submitted a claim that then included the Inuvialuit people, but the Inuvialuit later withdrew from the Nunavut process and reached an independent settlement within the Northwest Territories (Wilson and Alcantara 2012). The Nunavut claim was settled in 1993, and the self-governing territory of Nunavut was proclaimed in 1999. Significantly, settling the claim allowed the federal government to obtain legal title to the territory, thereby bolstering its position in international Arctic sovereignty disputes (Byers and Lalonde 2009).

As with the other territories, devolution for Nunavut has first meant the transfer of expensive governmental responsibilities. The challenges posed to the nascent jurisdiction in adopting these new responsibilities are summarized by Graham White: "The [Government of Nunavut] must deliver a host of public services and programs critical to Nunavummiut: everything from the timely distribution of welfare cheques, to air ambulance services, to the recruitment of nurses ... design of primary school curricula ... [etc.]. At the same time, it must address a substantial deficit in basic organizational capacity—a lack of the human, financial and organizational resources that large modern governments need to perform their functions adequately" (White 2009, 301). These challenges are compounded in Nunavut by the significant health, social, and economic problems faced by its population—amongst the most severe in Canada—from a lack of housing to national highs in suicide rates to a private sector that is dwarfed in size by the civil service (White 2009, 301).

Devolution has unfolded slowly in Nunavut since 1999. Like the government of the NWT, the government of Nunavut does not control its land and resource management; the federal government continues to retain these responsibilities. Nonetheless, Nunavut does still exercise some influence on these matters, via the members it appoints to the various co-management institutions of public government that were created with the Nunavut Land Claims Agreement, including the Impact Review Board, the Planning Commission, the Water Board, and others. Further constitutional devolution relating to lands and resources remains in its early stages.

In 2007, the Mayer Report on Nunavut Devolution expressed uncertainty about the readiness of Nunavut to receive a greater share of responsibility, but acknowledged that "the devolution train left the station." He suggested an incremental, "phased" approach to devolution (Mayer 2007, 46). In 2011, Nunavut Premier Eva Aariak used the signing of the agreement-in-principle with the NWT to place greater pressure on the federal government to open meaningful talks. In light of the experiences of the other territories, Premier Aariak appealed to the instrumental economic value of devolution to the territory and country: "There are a lot of positive spinoffs ... the world is looking at Nunavut now in terms of resource development and it will only increase. It is so ... important now for us to at least start the process" (CBC News).

CANADIAN FEDERALISM AND THE FINAL FRONTIER: THE DEVOLUTION OF TERRITORIAL LANDS AND RESOURCES

The purportedly new interest in the North, then, is a less dramatic departure from the past than is often presented. Federal attention to Arctic sovereignty, as well as to the economic opportunities in the North, have waxed and waned over time. The result of more consistent attention over the past four decades has been dramatic political change. Yukon and, now to varying degrees, the NWT and Nunavut have embarked on a transformative process bringing them closer to quasi-provincial status. Devolution has been used federally as a vehicle for realizing the economic potential of the North and for anchoring Canada's regional claims in more solid ground. In this sense, the northern territories have benefited from sustained federal attention, and to a certain extent, federal and territorial interests have converged.

However, the process of devolution has also reflected the federal government's general interest in sometimes limiting its involvement in the region to symbolic action, and more importantly, in ensuring the stability of the economic and fiscal health of the country. Because devolution has been driven primarily by the national interest, it has unfolded in an uneven, partial, and sometimes disadvantageous way, at least from the perspective of territorial and Aboriginal governments. The range of specific jurisdictions transferred over the past 60 years is illustrative of the forces of federal self-interest. Among the first things the federal government transferred were powers that represented a substantial public expenditure—such as education, social assistance, health care, and local government. In contrast, the last items to be devolved have been those items that generate revenue, such as control over lands and natural resources (Alcantara 2012). These varied outcomes demonstrate how federal perceptions of the national importance of the region have had negative as well as positive effects on territorial governments and their place within the federation.

These points can be illustrated by considering why Yukon was able to reach a devolution agreement in 2003, while the NWT was only able to complete an AIP in 2011. The key to explaining these outcomes is to look at the nature of the deals. In particular, the agreements were completed mainly because they transfer a variety of costly programs and jurisdictions to the territories while protecting federal revenue streams stemming from territorial natural resource development. The Yukon deal was achieved more easily because there was less economic value at the time for the federal government to concede (Alcantara 2012).

Under the Yukon devolution agreement, the "net fiscal benefit" clause states that the territorial government is allowed to keep up to an annual maximum of $3 million in revenues from natural resource developments, not including oil and gas, which were already covered by the 1998 Canada-Yukon Oil and Gas Accord. For revenues collected beyond the $3 million cap, there is a dollar-for-dollar reduction in the annual Territorial Formula Financing grant that the federal government provides to the territories to subsidize the cost of social and other programs. Another clause of the devolution deal involved the federal government assuming responsibility for any waste sites approved prior to 2003, while the Government of Yukon would be responsible for waste sites approved after. Should annual resource revenues exceed $3 million, the federal government gets to keep all of the revenues above that ceiling, without having to pay for any of the remediation costs after the development is finished. To put those costs in context, the Faro Mine, approved by the federal government in the 1960s and now inactive, has cost approximately $500 million to remediate—a huge expense. In future, the Government of Yukon will be responsible for the clean-up and administration of Faro-type mines, while the federal government will continue to benefit from significant revenues, effectively cost free (Alcantara 2012). Furthermore, the devolution agreement allows the federal government the recourse of resuming control over Crown land for reasons of national interest (Irlbacher-Fox and Mills 2007, 5).

Interestingly, the Yukon devolution agreement may be subject to change in the near future. The Yukon government has long pushed for changes to the revenue-sharing scheme, and in an August 2011 visit, Prime Minister Harper signalled his willingness to renegotiate these terms (Government of Yukon 2011). To understand what these changes might look like, it is instructive to look more carefully at the net fiscal benefit in the NWT's Agreement-in-Principle.

A final agreement on lands and resources has taken a lot longer to achieve in the NWT, with the negotiating parties only completing an AIP in 2011. Considering the role that the federal interest has played in directing the process, this is not difficult to understand. Historically, the resource sector in Yukon has not generated significant revenue, although this is changing. In 2010, mining and oil and gas extraction accounted for 9.2 percent of Yukon's GDP—up significantly from 5.1 percent in 2008, and about 3 percent in 2006 (Government of Yukon 2010; Feehan 2009, 349). Little development activity was occurring at the time the Yukon devolution deal was signed, but changing circumstances have led Yukon officials to demand that the federal government revisit the deal. In the NWT, on the other hand, the resource sector has always been central to the government's growth and revenue potential. Mining, primarily of diamonds, as well as the exploitation of oil and gas, have consistently represented over one-third of the territory's gross domestic product (Government of Northwest Territories 2010).

Consequently, the NWT government has long opposed any devolution agreement that attempted to mimic's Yukon's, and so devolution has been almost impossible to complete. On the other hand, the federal government has remained firm on reproducing such a deal because it preserves the national interest. Only when territorial officials were willing to adopt a net fiscal benefit that was consistent with federal preferences was an AIP reached in 2011 (Alcantara 2012). Under the NWT AIP, 50 percent of resource revenues are excluded from any offset calculation, "up to an overall fiscal capacity cap equal to 5 percent of the NWT's Gross Expenditure Base" (Northwest Territories Lands and Resources Devolution Agreement-in-Principle 2011). Based on a 2010 Gross Expenditure Base of $1.2 billion, for instance, the cap would have been approximately $60 million. The amount of resource revenue that the Government of NWT would have kept, therefore, would have been much more than Yukon. However, there is still a hard cap in place that is congruent with the economic interests of the federal government, and that potentially limits the revenues that the territorial government might generate from its natural resources (Alcantara 2012).

Three points bear emphasizing. First, while federal interest in the North has arguably ascended to new heights, as a result of structural, ecological, and political change, it is not without precedent. In fact, interest has waxed and waned since Confederation, driven primarily by concerns about challenges to Canadian sovereignty in the Arctic and the immense resource potential of the region. Second, relatively sustained federal interest over the past few decades of the twentieth century has resulted in immense political change. Devolution, seen by the federal government as a means to a certain set of ends, has transformed the territorial governments from colonial fiefdoms into quasi-provinces. Third, because the national interest has provided the impetus behind devolution deal-making, it has unfolded so as to unload the most costly governmental responsibilities to the territories while preserving some of the federal government's ability to derive revenue and offset the costs associated with Territorial Formula Financing (Alcantara 2012).

In short, relatively sustained federal attention to these economic and security questions over the past half-century has brought political transformation to the region. The federal government has used devolution as a vehicle to cement its sovereignty claims and to develop the region to realize its economic potential. The result has been quiet but dramatic constitutional change: large-scale devolution to the territories to such an extent that they have reached the status of quasi-provinces, the negotiation and in some cases settlement of modern treaties with Indigenous peoples, and the emergence of a new governance regime that combines ethno-national power-sharing with "public government." The territories have, in this broad

sense, benefited from federal nation-building. However, the nation-building impera-
tive has also shaped the nature of devolution in a way that has not entirely been in
the interest of Northerners. Preserving the national interest has meant devolving
expensive governmental responsibilities first and revenue generators last—if at all.

Given these realities and contextual factors, to what extent are the territories
able to exert influence within the Canadian federation? Have devolution and the
political/constitutional development of the North been accompanied by an increased
role in federal-provincial intergovernmental arenas?

TERRITORIAL INFLUENCE IN THE FEDERATION

Since World War II, many major national public policy initiatives in Canada have
been determined by the interface and relations between and among governments—
federal, provincial, and more recently, territorial (Cameron and Simeon 2002). This
section examines and assesses the role of territorial governments in the federation
from three perspectives:

- Federal-Territorial (FT) relations, which includes Aboriginal relations, given
  the emergence of Aboriginal land rights and institutions of self-government
  in the territories;
- Provincial-Territorial (PT) relations, taking into account bilateral agreements
  between territorial and provincial governments and territorial participation
  in Annual Premiers Conferences, now the Council of the Federation, and
  Western Premiers Conferences; and
- Federal-Provincial-Territorial (FPT) relations, which includes territorial
  participation in the full range of FPT meetings and their intergovernmental
  dynamics.

Before dealing with each of these topics, a brief review of where territorial governments fit into the intergovernmental interface of this country starting in the late
1960s and early 1970s will provide some important context.

Put simply, territorial governments were not involved in PT and FPT meetings
in the 1960s and most of the 1970s. In large part, this was because full responsible government did not arrive in Yukon until the late 1970s and in pre-division
Northwest Territories (NWT) until the early 1980s (Alcantara, Cameron, and
Kennedy 2012). Until full responsible government was attained, the executive
branches of government in the two territories included federally appointed commissioners and senior civil servants who were accountable to the commissioners
and not to an elected executive branch of government. There were no premiers,
ministers, or deputy ministers and therefore no one to participate on behalf of the
territories in PT and FPT fora. In any discussion of territorial interests or issues in
FPT fora, for example, the federal government spoke on behalf of the territorial
governments.

Nevertheless, there were bilateral agreements between the territorial governments and some of the provinces. In the NWT, for example, federal civil servants were the bureaucracy of the territorial government up until the late 1960s (Dickerson 1992). During that time, they negotiated agreements with Alberta education and medical institutions so that territorial students could attend Alberta technical or post-secondary education facilities, and residents requiring medical services not provided in the territory could get treatment in Edmonton hospitals.

What happened to change these circumstances? The mid to late 1970s saw the gradual introduction of responsible government in the territories (Cameron and White 1995, 49). Setting aside how it was achieved in Yukon and the NWT, we begin to see the appointment of ministers from the Legislative Assemblies to serve in the executive branches of the territorial governments (Alcantara, Cameron, and Kennedy 2012). We also see the gradual erosion of the authority of the federally appointed commissioners. These changes became reflected in provincial and federal-provincial intergovernmental arenas. While initially there was some reluctance in provincial fora to include the territories, likely because provincial governments did not understand the evolving role of ministers in territorial governments, eventually territorial governments became players in most PT sectoral fora where officials and ministers regularly met to deal with common issues and to plot strategies for how to deal with the federal government. At the FPT level during this period, territorial officials and ministers were eventually invited and participated in all FPT sectoral fora, with the exceptions of finance and energy, mines, and resources. In the NWT, for example, where there were only five and eventually seven ministers between 1979 and 1984, attending all the PT and FPT sectoral meetings across the country was challenging. Yet it was critically important for territorial governments to make this commitment, as demanding as it was and continues to be, to demonstrate that they were prepared to participate in intergovernmental meetings that dealt with areas of exclusive provincial and territorial jurisdiction or where federal legislative or policy and program initiatives had implications for the provinces and territories.

By the early 1990s, territorial ministers and officials were invited to participate in FPT and PT fora dealing with finance and energy, mines, and resources sectors. During the time when territorial finance ministers were not invited by the federal minister to participate in FPT finance ministers' meetings, the territorial minister for the NWT sat in on meetings as a member of a provincial delegation. As federal-territorial formula financing arrangements came to resemble, in part, equalization agreements with the provinces, the territories were accorded full status at finance meetings. Moreover, when it became apparent that the federal government could not unilaterally make decisions on territorial resource matters, ministers and officials from the North were invited into sectoral meetings on energy, mines, and resource issues.

Despite these positive developments, it took several years before territorial government leaders and premiers became players at provincial premiers' conferences or first ministers meetings and conferences involving the prime minister. Territorial government leaders started out as observers at Annual Premiers Conferences (APCs) and Western Premiers Conferences (WPCs), eventually gaining the opportunity to speak and finally to be full participants. At an APC in Nova Scotia in 1982, held in the province's legislative chambers, territorial leaders observed from the visitors' gallery. In 1983, at the APC hosted by Ontario, territorial leaders sat with officials and were invited to make short statements on their economies to an audience that included premiers Lougheed, Blakeney, Lévesque, Davis, and Peckford, all key players in the constitutional debates of the early 1980s. On a humorous note, to accommodate those premiers who did not fully support territorial participation at APCs, two official photographs were taken at an APC. One included just the premiers from the provinces; the second included the premiers plus the two "book-end" territorial leaders, one on the extreme left and the other on the extreme right of the photograph. At the first ministers level, territorial leaders and their officials were full participants in the Aboriginal constitutional round convened by Prime Minister Trudeau in the mid 1980s, but did not become full players in other FMMs or FMCs until the Mulroney years. While excluded for the majority of Meech Lake Constitutional Accord meetings, territorial premiers, ministers, and officials were at the tables for all Charlottetown Accord meetings and have been in all first ministers conferences and meetings since then (Alcantara 2013).

What explains the expansion of territorial governments' participation in all PT and FPT fora to the full members that they are today? First, with the introduction of responsible government and elected MLAs serving as ministers, it became difficult for provincial and federal governments to ignore or oppose territorial participation in PT and FPT sectoral fora. While the NWT's non-partisan consensus-style government, for example, may have been a curious anomaly in a country where partisan politics reigned in the federal and provincial governments, responsible and representative government existed in the two territories. Exclusion had make sense when the territories were governed by federally appointed officials. But democracy had now reached the North.

Second, provincial governments came to realize that territorial governments experienced many of the same challenges that they did, and that if the provincial premiers, ministers, and officials truly wanted to reflect the interests of all of Canada in their deliberations, it made sense to include the territories. A simple example illustrates this point. Transportation ministers and officials regularly make recommendations on a wide range of transportation issues, including, for example, a common set of wide-load signs used by trucks on major highway grids. For many years, most of the highways in the NWT did not meet provincial standards for width (some still do not). NWT ministers and officials made the case for national standards, which would also apply to the narrower highways in the territory.

Third, given their bilateral agreements with some key provinces such as British Columbia, Alberta, Manitoba, Quebec, and Newfoundland, territorial governments had allies that helped to convince other provinces that the territories could not be ignored. Over the years, these agreements have expanded beyond purchasing education and medical services to include addressing common interests relating to economic development, transportation, and environmental issues.

Fourth, given the decline in the status of federally appointed commissioners, the more active role of other federal departments in territorial affairs, and the corresponding reduction in the role of the Department of Indian Affairs and Northern Development (DIAND)—now Aboriginal Affairs and Northern Development Canada (AANDC)—territorial governments, rather than DIAND, were seen as the legitimate representatives of their constituents and their interests (Cameron and White 1995).

Finally, in the premiers and first ministers fora, successive territorial leaders became full participants, in part because of political affiliations and also because territorial governments had become very effective players in the intergovernmental interface, sensitive to their place in the "pecking order" but also astute enough to know where and how to build alliances (see Alcantara 2013).

With this background in mind, the remainder of this section examines in more detail each of the three intergovernmental arenas in which the territories participate. Despite small populations and limited representation in Canada's institutions of intrastate federalism, territorial governments have been quite successful in influencing the course of the federation and making their voices heard within the federal system.

Federal-Territorial Relations

As earlier sections of this chapter have described, the territories are no longer an isolated Arctic wilderness, governed as colonies by far-away Ottawa, with little or no connection to the rest of Canada. As territorial governments have evolved over time, so too has their ability to influence federal decision-making relating to the regions. For example:

- Yukon made the move to party politics in the late 1970s and eventually convinced the Joe Clark Conservative government to instruct the Yukon commissioner to act on instructions of the Yukon Cabinet, thus establishing responsible government in the territory (Alcantara, Cameron, and Kennedy 2012).
- NWT Aboriginal peoples, admittedly more than the territorial government of the day, convinced Prime Minister Trudeau's Liberal government to impose a ten-year moratorium on oil, gas, and pipeline development in the Mackenzie Valley until Aboriginal land rights were settled (Abele 2009, 31).
- In the late 1970s, the NWT Legislative Assembly and Cabinet worked with Inuit leaders from the eastern Arctic to convince the federal government to create a new territory. In 1999, the map of Canada was changed forever with the establishment of Nunavut (Henderson 2007).

- Since the late 1970s when negotiations started on the first comprehensive claim in the territories, the NWT and Yukon governments have been active participants in Aboriginal land rights and self-government negotiations and their implementation—empowering Aboriginal people through land ownership and participation in resource management and development decision-making (McArthur 2009).
- National parks are no longer established because prime ministers or their spouses think preserving large pieces of the territories will be good for Canada.
- More recently, the federal government concluded that the ad hoc approach to federal decision-making in the territories had to be changed, and it developed a Northern Strategy to guide its decisions there, including the establishment of a northern economic development agency, CanNor, to provide a more focused approach to a number of federal economic development programs North of 60 (Coates et al. 2008, 196).

There are numerous other milestones that demonstrate that territorial governments and the residents of the North have exerted significant influence on federal decision-making related to federal-territorial relations. For instance, the territories have shaped federal policy relating to territorial formula financing; the devolution of provincial-type jurisdiction over resources management and development; and input on circumpolar Arctic issues through the Arctic Council, among other things.

What explains these successes, especially in light of the fact that only three members of Parliament represent the 111,500 residents of the three territories in Ottawa? First, court decisions and national attention forced the federal government to deal with Aboriginal rights issues (Abele 2009, 31-3). In the case of the NWT, for example, where the majority of the territory's Legislative Assembly and government were Aboriginal, both forces exerted significant influence on key issues where federal action on Aboriginal issues could no longer be delayed or ignored. Second, in the case of Yukon, partisan relationships between Conservative or Liberal governments in Whitehorse and Ottawa contributed to decisions favouring the territory, such as responsible government under Joe Clark and devolution under Jean Chrétien, both coinciding with Conservative and Liberal governments in Whitehorse, respectively. Third, while historically not all territorial MPs were unknown backbenchers in the federal machine (Yukon MP Eric Nielsen being an example), in recent years MPs like the NWT's Ethel Blondin-Andrew, Nunavut's Leona Aglukkaq, and Yukon's Larry Bagnell have had a high profile within the federal ministry; Bagnell served as parliamentary secretary, Blondin-Andrew as minister of state, and Aglukkaq as minister of health. Having territorial representation in Cabinet has no doubt been helpful in advancing territorial interests. Furthermore, the creation of a regional minister for the North has helped to raise the political profile of the region within the governing party of the day.

Fourth, the declining roles of the federally appointed commissioner and the minister and Department of Northern Development signalled that the territorial ministers of transportation, for example, had to now deal directly with their federal counterparts. Eventually, with a few exceptions, the minister and Department of Northern Development lost their mandate in Ottawa on everything northern. Finally, during the past decade in particular, the territories have started to realize their resource potential and have been taking a more active role in responding to environmental issues resulting from resource development. With INAC/AANDC no longer the lead northern player, a variety of federal ministers and departments now have to deal directly with their territorial counterparts, as well as take into account Aboriginal land rights and self- government institutions.

Provincial-Territorial Relations

Long gone are the days when BC Premier Bill "Wacky" Bennett wanted to annex Yukon and its resources to his province. Nevertheless, as noted above, some provincial governments have had long-standing bilateral relations with territorial governments dating back decades to when provincial governments and their education and medical institutions provided services that were not available in the North. Furthermore, resource development in the North was of obvious interest to some provinces that benefited from providing goods and services, primarily to territorial mining and oil and gas activities, or from processing ore from northern base metal mines.

Relations at the political level did not materialize until responsible government came to the territories. Alberta and British Columbia, for example, designated their Intergovernmental Affairs ministers to liaise with their territorial counterparts in the 1980s. As the territories became more aggressive during the 1980s and 1990s in attending provincial sectoral fora, the linkages between provincial and territorial governments began to grow and deepen.

Some present-day examples of provincial-territorial relations where territorial governments exert influence include the following:

- The Nunavut and Quebec governments are engaged over polar bear harvesting and conservation of the species in the Baffin Region and Northern Quebec. The Nunavut and Newfoundland governments also have an interest in how fishing quotas are allocated in the North Atlantic.
- The Nunavut and Manitoba governments have for a number of years been examining the feasibility of building a highway from northern Manitoba into the Kivalliq region of Nunavut, primarily to tap into resource potential in the Kivalliq and maximize Manitoba's resupply status.
- Alberta has long recognized that the oil and gas potential of the NWT's Mackenzie Valley has long-term significance for the province's petro-chemical industry, and for the province's long-standing role in providing goods and services to the NWT.

- Similarly, British Columbia and, to some extent, Alberta benefit directly from resource development activity in Yukon.
- Finally, the NWT is moving aggressively to express concerns over the impact that Alberta's oil sands and BC's Peace River hydro development activity have been having on downstream water quality in NWT rivers and lakes.

So what can we learn about provincial-territorial dynamics as they have evolved over the past four decades? First, while provincial governments may have been reluctant to engage with territorial governments prior to the 1960s, the introduction of responsible government and aggressive efforts by territorial governments to become players in PT sectoral fora has resulted in territorial ministers and eventually territorial government leaders and premiers becoming participants with full status. Second, beyond providing medical and educational services, some provincial governments have obvious economic interests in territorial resource development activity or providing goods and services, and therefore it is in their interest to establish bilateral relations with the northern territories. Finally, Annual Premiers Conferences and now the Council of the Federation have realized that they are not complete without territorial participation and, furthermore, that it helps to have the three territories on side when they want to make a strong case to Ottawa.

Federal-Provincial-Territorial Relations

With this background in mind, it is not surprising that territorial governments are now participants in all FPT fora, even though in some meetings the territories do not have the same status as provinces. For example, while territories are not participants in equalization, they still participate in FPT finance ministers' conferences. Also, while NWT and Nunavut do not have administrative jurisdiction over resources, they still participate in energy, mines, and environment ministers conferences. The major breakthrough at the FPT first ministers level happened during the Charlottetown Accord constitutional round, when territorial leaders were accepted into the first ministers club. To their credit, Prime Minister Mulroney and the premiers accepted their territorial counterparts as full players at the table, and since then prime ministers and provincial premiers have shown no hesitation about including territorial leaders in bilateral and multilateral discussions.

What accounts for the broader acceptance of territorial premiers in first ministers meetings? First, territorial leaders have been constructive and, as noted, have acted carefully to understand their place in the pecking order of the federation. Their agendas are similar at times to the agendas of the federal and provincial governments, and they bring to the table extensive experience with Aboriginal issues. Indeed, the territories can take some credit over the past four decades for raising the profile of Aboriginal issues among federal and provincial governments. Also, territorial leaders know there is nothing to be gained by asking for or discussing provincial status. Second, the recurring theme of responsible government also applies here. Who are the prime minister and premiers going to dialogue with on territorial issues or on the territorial perspective on national issues? It can only be the duly elected leader of each territory, rather than the federally appointed commissioner or the minister of AANDC. Third, the Canadian public and the national media are not willing to accept that the territorial governments are mere extensions of a federal government department. They are now seen as the legitimate, representative, and responsible institutions representing one-third of the territorial mass of Canada. To their credit, Ottawa and the provinces recognized this reality many years ago and have ensured that their territorial counterparts are included as equals in the PT and FPT exchanges that are so critical in charting the course of the country and its regions.

CONCLUSION

Territorial governments and their premiers have made remarkable progress in the three intergovernmental fora examined above. The three territorial governments are currently accorded the internal legitimacy necessary to demonstrate that they are the legitimate representatives of their constituents' interests on a wide variety of issues dealt with in FT, FPT, and PT intergovernmental dynamics. For Yukon, it is likely that the premier, ministers, and government officials will continue to have the legitimacy to represent the territory in intergovernmental fora. While the Yukon government may from time to time express positions in intergovernmental meetings that are not supported by emerging Yukon First Nations governments, it is unlikely that Yukon's ability to represent the territory will ever be questioned.

Similarly, in Nunavut, it can be expected that the Nunavut government will be able to represent the interests of all Nunavummiut, including the powerful territorial and regional Inuit land claim organizations, in intergovernmental arenas without having its legitimacy questioned. It is important to note that there are no Inuit Aboriginal governments similar to those found in the NWT and Yukon.

The challenge will be in the NWT, where it will be critical for the NWT premier, ministers, and government to ensure that, on key issues, they have the support of real and emerging First Nation, Inuvialuit, and Métis self-government institutions in the territory, or that they are accurately reflecting those interests (Braden 2009, 264). The PT meetings with national Aboriginal leaders prior to Western Premiers Conference and Council of the Federation meetings aside, it is doubtful that an Aboriginal regional government from the NWT will ever be accorded a seat at the PT tables. So the NWT government will need to ensure that it can come to the intergovernmental tables knowing that it will not be denounced by Aboriginal governments back home. Yet these challenges are not unique. Indeed, provincial and federal governments experience them as well when they must sometimes make unpopular commitments at intergovernmental tables.

In closing, when resource management, jurisdiction, and associated revenue-sharing measures are eventually implemented in the NWT and Nunavut, Canada's three territories will have achieved most of the features of a province, the Constitution's amending formula aside. The political/constitutional development of Canada's three northern territories has more or less been achieved in the Canadian tradition, incrementally and over time, with a minimum of acrimony and the gradual building of trust and respect. It has happened partly as a result of the federal government's interest in solidifying its sovereign claims to the region and of harnessing the region's resource potential. These motivations have contributed to an uneven process of devolution. Yet territorial initiative has also been important, especially as territorial governments have matured and exercised their influence more frequently within the institutions of Canadian federalism. By relationship-building with federal and provincial ministries, maintaining the pecking order, and establishing themselves as the legitimate loci of political participation and representation in the North, territorial governments have become near-full participants in the all-important myriad arenas of intergovernmental relations. This bidirectional process has resulted in a quiet but profound constitutional change north of 60.

REFERENCES

Abele, F. 2009. "Northern Development: Past, Present and Future." In *Northern Exposure: Peoples, Powers, and Prospects in Canada's North,* edited by F. Abele, T. Courchene, F.L. Seidle, and F. St-Hilaire, 19-65. Montreal: Institute of Research on Public Policy.

Abele, F., T. Courchene, F.L. Seidle, and F. St-Hilaire. 2009. "The New Northern Policy Universe." In *Northern Exposure: Peoples, Powers, and Prospects in Canada's North,* edited by F. Abele, T. Courchene, F.L. Seidle, and F. St-Hilaire, 561-94. Montreal: Institute of Research on Public Policy.

Alcantara, C. 2012. "Preferences, Perceptions, and Veto Players: Explaining Devolution Negotiation Outcomes in the Canadian Territorial North." *Polar Record.* http://dx.doi.org/10.1017/S0032247412000125.

—. 2013. "Ideas, Executive Federalism and Institutional Change: Explaining Territorial Inclusion in Canadian First Ministers' Conferences." *Canadian Journal of Political Science* 46 (1): 27-48.

Alcantara, C., C. Kirk, and S. Kennedy. 2012. "Assessing Devolution in the Canadian North: A Case Study of the Yukon Territory." *Arctic* 65 (3): 328-38.

Anderson, A. 2009. *After the Ice: Life, Death, and Geopolitics in the New Arctic.* New York: Harper Collins.

Bartenstein, K. 2010. "'Use It or Lose It': An Appropriate and Wise Slogan." *Policy Options* (July/August): 68-73.

Borgerson, S.D. 2008. "Arctic Meltdown: The Economic and Security Implications of Global Warming." *Foreign Affairs* 87 (2): 63-77.

Braden, G. 2009. "Governance in the Western North." In *Northern Exposure: Peoples, Powers and Prospects in Canada's North*, edited by F. Abele, T.J. Courchene, F.L. Seidle, and F. St-Hilaire, 259-65. Montreal: IRPP.

Byers, M. 2009. *Who Owns the Arctic? Understanding Sovereignty Disputes in the North*. Vancouver: Douglas & McIntyre.

Byers, M., and S. Lalonde. 2009. "Who Controls the Northwest Passage?" *Vanderbilt Journal of Transnational Law* 42 (4): 1133-1210.

Cameron, D., and R. Simeon. 2002. "Intergovernmental Relations in Canada: The Emergence of Collaborative Federalism." *Publius* 32 (2): 49-71.

Cameron, K., and G. White. 1995. *Northern Governments in Transition: Political and Constitutional Development in the Yukon, Nunavut and the Northwest Territories*. Montreal: Institute of Research on Public Policy.

Canada. 2007a. "Press Release: Prime Minister Stephen Harper Announces New Arctic Offshore Patrol Ships." 9 July. Accessed 8 November 2011. http://pm.gc.ca/eng/media.asp?id=1742.

—. 2007b. "Press Release: Prime Minister Announces Expansion of Canadian Forces Facilities and Operations in the Arctic." 10 August. Accessed 8 November 2011. http://www.pm.gc.ca/eng/media.asp?category=1&id=1784.

—. 2007c. Text of Governor General Michaelle Jean's Speech from the Throne, 16 October 2007, Ottawa. http://www.sft-ddt.gc.ca.

—. 2008. "Press Release: PM Announces New Polar Class Icebreaker Project to Be Named after Former PM John G. Diefenbaker." 28 August. Accessed 12 November 2011. http://pm.gc.ca/eng/media.asp?id=2251.

—. 2010. Text of Governor General Michaelle Jean's Speech from the Throne, 3 March 2010, Ottawa. http://www.sft-ddt.gc.ca.

CBC News. 2011. "Nunavut Premier Wants Devolution Talks." 27 January. Accessed 8 January 2012. http://www.cbc.ca/news/canada/north/story/2011/01/27/nunavut-devolution-nwt-eva-aariak.html.

Coates, K., P.W. Lackenbauer, B. Morrison, and G. Poelzer. 2008. *Arctic Front: Defending Canada in the Far North*. Markham: Thomas Allen.

Dickerson, M.O. 1992. *Whose North? Political Change, Political Development, and Self-Government in the Northwest Territories*. Vancouver: UBC Press and the Arctic Institute of North America.

Feehan, J.P. 2009. "Natural Resource Devolution in the Territories: Current Status and Unresolved Issues." In *Northern Exposure: Peoples, Powers, and Prospects in Canada's North,* edited by F. Abele, T. Courchene, F.L. Seidle, and F. St-Hilaire, 345-72. Montreal: Institute of Research on Public Policy.

Government of the Northwest Territories. 2010. *Northwest Territories Bureau of Statistics Gross Domestic Product by Industry, 1999 to 2010*. Yellowknife: Bureau of Statistics, Government of the Northwest Territories. Accessed 15 January 2012. http://www.stats.gov.nt.ca/economy/gdp/index.otp.

Government of Yukon. 2010. *Yukon Bureau of Statistics Gross Domestic Product by Industry, 2010*. Executive Council Office, Bureau of Statistics Information Sheet No. 65-17,

December 2011. Whitehorse: Executive Council Office, Bureau of Statistics, Government of Yukon. Accessed 15 January 2012. http://www.eco.gov.yk.ca/stats/pdf/gdp_2010.pdf.

—. 2011. "Press Release: Yukon Welcomes PM's Commitment to Improve Resource Revenue Sharing Agreement." 29 August. Accessed 15 February 2011. http://www.gov. yk.ca/news/11-132.html.

Griffiths, F. 2003. "The Shipping News: Canada's Arctic Sovereignty Not on Thinning Ice." *International Journal* 58 (2): 257-82.

—. 2009. "Towards a Canadian Arctic Strategy." *Foreign Policy for Canada's Tomorrow.* Vol.1, Toronto: Canadian International Council.

Henderson, A. 2007. *Nunvaut: Rethinking Political Culture.* Vancouver: UBC Press.

Huebert, R. 2008. *Canada and the Changing International Arctic: At the Crossroads of Cooperation and Conflict.* Montreal: Institute of Research on Public Policy.

Irlbacher-Fox, S., and S.J. Mills. 2007. *Resource Revenue Sharing in the Canadian North: Achieving Fairness across Generations.* Ottawa: Walter and Duncan Gordon Foundation.

Mahoney, J. 2011. "Canadians Rank Arctic Sovereignty as Top Foreign-Policy Priority." *Globe and Mail.* Accessed 24 January 2011. http://www.theglobeandmail.com/news/politics/canadians-rank-arctic-sovereignty-as-top-foreign-policy-priority/article1881287/.

Mayer, P. 2007. *Mayer Report on Nunavut Devolution.* Ottawa: Fasken Martineau.

McArthur, D. 2009. "The Changing Architecture of Governance in Yukon and the Northwest Territories." In *Northern Exposure: Peoples, Powers, and Prospects in Canada's North,* ed. F. Abele, T. Courchene, F.L. Seidle, and F. St-Hilaire, 187-231. Montreal: Institute of Research on Public Policy.

Northwest Territories Lands and Resources Devolution Agreement-in-Principle. 2011.

Roth, R. 1990. "Sovereignty and Jurisdiction over Arctic Waters." *Alberta Law Review* 28: 845-72.

White, G. 2002. "Treaty Federalism in Northern Canada: Aboriginal-Government Land Claims Boards." *Publius* 32 (3): 89-114.

—. 2009. "Nunavut and the Inuvialuit Settlement Region: Differing Models of Northern Governance." In *Northern Exposure: Peoples, Powers, and Prospects in Canada's North,* edited by F. Abele, T. Courchene, F.L. Seidle, and F. St-Hilaire, 283-313. Montreal: Institute of Research on Public Policy.

Wilson, G., and C. Alcantara. 2012. "Mixing Politics and Business in the Canadian Arctic: Inuit Corporate Governance in Nunavik and the Inuvialuit Settlement Region." *Canadian Journal of Political Science* 45 (4).

11

ON THE RELATIVE NEGLECT OF HORIZONTAL INTERGOVERNMENTAL RELATIONS IN CANADA

Éric Montpetit and Martial Foucault[1]

Premiers disgruntled by reductions in transfer payments in a context of mounting health care costs; a federal government resolute to increase its involvement in health care despite nationalist fervour in Quebec City; several approaching provincial elections: those were the conditions leading to the intergovernmental health deal struck at a First Ministers conference in September 2000. A journalist writing in the *Canadian Medical Association Journal* described the conference as follows: "The unholy alliance between Harris and Bouchard, the exasperation that Harris triggered in Ralph Klein, the unseemly spitting match between the have and have-not provinces—all this revealed that Ottawa bashing is the only activity that unites premiers." She added, "This conference allowed Jean Chrétien to emerge with more moral authority than most of his provincial counterparts" (Gray 2000, 1030).

For many Canadians, intergovernmental relations closely match the writer's imagery. Those relations would be motivated by premiers unhappy with federal policy that interfered with or insufficiently worked toward provincial policy goals. In the end, however, Ottawa's authority would overshadow provincial concerns. Provinces would have a hard time uniting against the federal government. Regional rivalry might occasionally produce alliances of neighbouring provinces, but only to play nasty games making interprovincial harmony impossible. In other words,

[1] This research was funded by the Social Sciences and Humanities Research Council of Canada. The authors would like to thank Jean-Philippe Gauvin, Alison Smith, and Jean-François Godbout for useful comments.

for many Canadians, when they think about intergovernmental relations, they think first and foremost about the vertical relations between the federal and provincial governments. Horizontal relations between provincial governments are viewed as dysfunctional when not entirely ignored.

Unsurprisingly, then, scholars have paid little attention to horizontal intergovernmental relations. Figures about the number of intergovernmental meetings have been put forward to support the argument that vertical relations are important (Bakvis and Skogstad 2002, 9). Few scholars, however, have tried to assess the relative importance of vertical and horizontal intergovernmental relations. Using data on policy priority, we suggest such an assessment in this chapter. We acknowledge that the measure itself is vulnerable to criticisms, but measuring intergovernmental relations comprehensively—however imperfect an exercise it might be—is a worthwhile endeavour. We hope to convince scholars of the value of the exercise, encouraging them to work toward better measurement.

The results produced by our measure are satisfying in many ways. First, they are consistent with the qualitative knowledge of scholars of vertical intergovernmental relations. They also raise serious questions about scholarly neglect of horizontal intergovernmental relations. We find that for every single decade between 1960 and 2010, horizontal relations have been more than, or at least as important as, vertical ones. Moreover, horizontal relations have steadily increased since 1970, while vertical relations go up and down in cycle.

Second, horizontal relations are strongest among provinces from the same geographic region. In other words, Harris and Bouchard unsurprisingly coordinated over the health deal in 2000, but eastern and western premiers did so as well. The rivalry between Ontario and Alberta did not cause much harm to overall horizontal relations. The health deal was concluded in the middle of a long period of continuous strengthening of horizontal intergovernmental relations and at the outset of a period of weakening vertical ones. As we will show in this chapter, the imagery of intergovernmental relations, illustrated above in the press coverage of the 2000 health deal, is misleading on a number of counts.

DEFINING INTERGOVERNMENTAL RELATIONS IN CANADA

Intergovernmental relations can be defined as the relationship between Canadian governments on matters of policy development. The governments involved in intergovernmental relations thus far have been mostly the federal, provincial, and territorial governments. Municipalities have been represented by provincial governments in intergovernmental forums, as local governments fall within provincial constitutional responsibilities. In fact, municipal governments are just beginning to claim an autonomous role in intergovernmental relations (Turgeon 2009). Therefore, intergovernmental relations can be taken to refer to the vertical relationships between the federal and provincial governments and to the horizontal relationships among provincial governments to debate, discuss, negotiate, and resolve conflict or coordinate policy.

The literature frequently distinguishes between political and administrative intergovernmental relations (Johns, O'Reilly, and Inwood 2006; Bakvis and Brown 2010). "Political intergovernmental relations" refers to formal meetings involving ministers or first ministers, generally publicized and covered by the press. The conference leading to the health deal in 2000 is an example of political intergovernmental relations. The annual meeting of the Council of the Federation, created in 2003 to improve provincial coordination, is another example, in this case of horizontal relations. Political intergovernmental relations, however, are only the tip of the iceberg. Less visible, administrative intergovernmental relations in fact play a large role in policy development. Some policy problems requiring intergovernmental coordination are resolved at the administrative level and never end up on the agenda of ministerial intergovernmental meetings. Administrative intergovernmental relations take place on a daily basis, involving civil servants at all levels. They coordinate policy efforts during formal meetings, but also through informal phone calls and other forms of communication. Therefore, an understanding of intergovernmental relations exclusively focused on political intergovernmental relations would miss important aspects of the phenomenon. As Johns, O'Reilly, and Inwood (2007, 22) put it, "Hundreds of meetings each year, millions of dollars' worth of agreements negotiated monthly, countless of informal contacts, and a varied and complex intergovernmental machinery—this is the nature of intergovernmental administrative relations in Canada today."

Yet existing measures of intergovernmental relations unfortunately focus exclusively on the political level, relying only on information—mostly agendas and communiqués—about formal ministerial and prime ministerial meetings (Fafard et al. 2011; Bakvis and Skogstad 2002). Even if they did not mean to provide a precise measure of intergovernmental relations, Inwood, Johns, and O'Reilly (2011, 42) draw some conclusion on patterns of intergovernmental relations from variations in the number of First Ministers Conferences. It could be tempting to treat such measures as indicators of intergovernmental relations writ large, although it is not certain that political intergovernmental relations correlate positively with administrative ones. Administrative intergovernmental relations are so dense in comparison with political ones that the two phenomena are difficult to associate. Intense intergovernmental activities by administrators might reduce the necessity of intense intergovernmental activities by politicians, and vice versa, or they might be unrelated. In any case, we propose in this chapter an indicator just as logically associated with administrative intergovernmental relations as with political ones. In other words, our measure captures both political and administrative intergovernmental relations without assuming that they are related.

CORRELATION OF POLICY PRIOROTIES AND INTERGOVERNMENTAL RELATIONS

We suggest using correlations of policy priorities as indicators of the intensity of intergovernmental relations. A correlation measures the correspondence of a fluctuation of two phenomena. When speaking of correlations of policy priorities, we thus refer to corresponding changes in the priorities of two governments. At first sight, it might appear odd that we use correspondence in changes of priorities as an indicator of intergovernmental relations. After all, intergovernmental relations and policy priorities appear as two distinct and unrelated phenomena. We nevertheless argue that correspondence of priorities among governments indicates with acceptable validity that governments sustain relations. In fact, we assume that dense intergovernmental relations necessarily involve similar structures of government priorities, as governments deepen their relationship with each other when they share a similar interest in a policy area. They do so to resolve conflicts, to improve coordination, or simply to exchange experience and ideas and learn from one another. Inversely, governments with different priority structures are likely to be relatively indifferent to each other. It is indeed reasonable to assume that governments that pay attention to different problems have little incentive to talk to one another.

So far, we have suggested that government priorities drive intergovernmental relations, but this is not an argument that we wish to support against the inverse possibility. In fact, we fully acknowledge that intergovernmental relations might occasionally come before policy priorities. Intergovernmental meetings might inspire governments, encouraging them to pay more attention to the issues that rank high in the priority structure of governments with which they sustain intense relations (Weyland 2007). Our goal is not to identify a direction in the causal relationship. We simply need to establish that a correspondence exists between intergovernmental relations and the structures of priorities of at least two governments to use the latter as an indicator of the former. We reason that intense intergovernmental relations, vertical or horizontal, administrative or political, occur among governments with similar priorities, whatever the particulars of the causal relationship.

To illustrate, the variation of defence in federal priorities between 1960 and 2010 is not correlated with the low rank of defence in provincial priority structures. Moreover, as defence is an uncontested federal jurisdiction, very little intergovernmental relations occurred on this issue between 1960 and 2010. In other words, the indicator accurately indicates the weakness of intergovernmental relations on this issue. In the 1990s, health care gained several ranks in both federal and provincial priorities. The literature also indicates that the intensity of intergovernmental relations over this policy issue increased during that decade. After 2006, health dropped in the priorities of the federal government but less so in the provinces. The weakening of the correlation also matches the beginning of a phase of weaker intergovernmental relations on health.

If governments that have intense intergovernmental relations are logically expected to have positively correlated policy priorities, it might be objected—on an equally logical basis—that nothing requires governments that happen to have similar priorities to sustain a relationship. This reasoning echoes criticisms of dyadic studies of policy diffusion and international relations (Gilardi and Füglister 2008). In fact, priorities form for many reasons beside intergovernmental relations. Similar demographic factors, for example, can encourage two provinces to prioritize health simultaneously. Other factors, including language or political rivalry, might at the same time discourage the two provinces from deepening their relationship over health-policy development. If this latter set of factors effectively discourages intergovernmental relations despite demography pressing the two provinces to increase their attention to health, the correlation of priorities would provide a misleading indicator of intergovernmental relations. This reasoning is convincing enough to make us acknowledge the likelihood of a measurement error associated with our indicator.

However, we believe that the error is small. In any vertical or horizontal dyad of governments in Canada, the likelihood is low that the incentive to develop intergovernmental relations created by similarities in policy priorities will be cancelled out by the effect of factors discouraging intergovernmental relations. To an extent, language can be an obstacle to intergovernmental relations between Quebec, a francophone province, and most of the other provincial governments in which English prevails. But it is by no mean an insurmountable obstacle. If attending to a policy priority requires it, Quebec will find the resources to develop efficient intergovernmental relations with English-speaking provinces. In fact, Quebec has relatively intense intergovernmental relations with the other provinces in most policy domains.

Prejudice in one province against least-known provinces (for example, a large province against remote small provinces) may also work against intergovernmental relations. To an extent, however, intergovernmental relations in Canada are institutionalized (Inwood, Johns, and O'Reilly 2011). That is, each year, all governments are invited to some prescheduled meetings, often at the political level. If those meetings are only the tip of the iceberg of Canadian intergovernmental relations, if they only occur occasionally, if a large proportion of intergovernmental relationships is informal, institutionalized relations nevertheless provide opportunities to revise prejudices and align bilateral relations along similarities in policy concerns. They can also convince a government arriving at the meeting with dissimilar priorities to increase its attention to problems indicated in the priorities of the others. Such a revision of policy priorities would also encourage a deepening of intergovernmental relations, possibly at the administrative level. Through this process, dense informal relationships can develop, despite initial prejudice. In other words, the factors working against intergovernmental relations tend to be weaker than the incentives to develop intergovernmental relations stemming from similarities in policy priorities.

In a book exploring the possibility of a race-to-the-bottom whereby interprovincial competition would lead to a systematic reduction in policy standards, Harrison (2006) reproduces a quote from a provincial civil servant exasperated by the continuous search for new theories of intergovernmental dysfunctions. Putting forward a simple theory, the civil servant confirms that policy priorities and intergovernmental relations go hand in hand: "One of the reasons provincial policies look so much alike, he said, is because we all talk to each other!" (Harrison 2006, 265). This simple theory receives confirmation in various cases found in Harrison's book.

We argue that the correlation of governmental structures of policy priorities provides a valid indicator of intergovernmental relations. When Canadian governments have different priorities, they tend to have weak intergovernmental relations. Or else, when they have weak intergovernmental relations, they normally also have dissimilar priorities. Conversely, growing similarities in priority structures correspond to growing intergovernmental relations. We acknowledge that an indicator closer to the phenomenon that we seek to measure would be ideal (a measure of government officials talking to each other, for example), but the structure of policy priorities has the advantage of facilitating the measurement of political as well as administrative intergovernmental relations, as government priorities activate both politicians and civil servants. Structures of policy priorities also facilitate the measurement of vertical as well as horizontal intergovernmental relations. The only drawback is the measurement error, which we believe to be small owing to the strength of the combined causal effects of similar priorities on intergovernmental relations on the one hand and of intergovernmental relations on similarities in priority structures on the other. Meanwhile, the institutionalization of intergovernmental relations in Canada—the fact that a federal system requires regular relations among governments—requires officials from various governments to talk to each other, and therefore works against forces discouraging the deepening of intergovernmental relations.

STRUCTURES OF POLICY PRIORITIES IN SPEECHES FROM THE THRONE

Canadian governments, federal and provincial, announce their policy priorities at the beginning of legislative sessions in so-called Speeches from the Throne. Policy priorities are thus announced roughly once a year in a relatively consistent manner between the federal and provincial governments but also among provincial governments. As correlations compare priorities from different governments, priorities have to be identified from comparable material. Speeches from the Throne are read on a regular basis for identical ends across provinces and the federal government and therefore they are perfectly suited to the task. In addition, the information that these vehicles provide on policy priorities has been shown to be reliable in Britain, where the tradition originates, and also in Australia (John and Jennings 2010; Montpetit and Foucault 2012; Dowding et al. 2010).

The content of speeches from the Throne was coded following the method elaborated in the Comparative Agendas Project (see, e.g., Frio 2012).[2] The project suggests dividing speeches into quasi-sentences, to determine if a quasi-sentence has policy content and to associate each quasi-sentence containing policy content with a single topic from a list of 25 (see Table 1). A quasi-sentence is most of the time a full sentence, which can be split if it speaks about more than one topic. The structure of policy priorities is given by the percentage of quasi-sentences in a speech going to each topic. To illustrate, Table 1 provides the priority structure for the Newfoundland, Quebec, and British Columbia governments, as revealed in their respective 1975 Throne speeches.

Table 1: Priority Structure of the Newfoundland, Quebec, and British Columbia Governments, 1975

Topic Name	Percentage of Quasi-Sentences		
	NFL	QC	BC
1. Public land and water management	16.7	5.7	2.9
2. Fisheries	10.6	0	0
3. Community development and housing	8.1	4.2	8.0
4. Labour and employment	7.9	11.4	12.3
5. Macroeconomics	6.8	8.0	3.6
6. Agriculture and forestry	6.8	4.6	15.9
7. Energy	6.6	0	1.4
8. Health	5.6	2.3	13.0
9. Banking, finance, and domestic commerce	4.6	7.6	12.3
10. Transportation	4.1	1.9	3.6
11. Education	3.9	3.8	2.9
12. Intergovernmental relations	3.7	4.2	1.4
13. Government operations	3.4	11	2.2
14. Social welfare	3.0	1.9	2.9
15. Law and crime	3.0	4.9	5.8
16. Local government	2.2	3.0	0
17. Environment	1.5	3.4	2.9
18. Culture and entertainment	1.4	8.0	0
19. International affairs and foreign aid	0.3	0	2.9
20. Minority issues and multiculturalism	0	7.6	4.3
21. Native affairs	0	0.8	0.7
22. Defence	0	0	0
23. Foreign trade	0	2.3	0.7
24. Space, science, and technology	0	3.0	0
25. Constitutional and national unity issues	0	0.4	0

Source: Authors' compilations.

---

[2] http://www.comparativeagendas.org/.

We have coded the content of all provincial and federal Speeches from the Throne between 1960 and 2009. In total, 445 speeches containing 116,753 quasi-sentences were coded. As indicated in Table 2, most of the quasi-sentences have policy content (89 percent). The vast quantity of information thus collected from Throne speeches significantly reduces the margins of error in our estimation of priority structures.

The method of correspondence analysis that we use here was adapted from Jones, Larsen-Price, and Wilkerson (2009). The calculation of the correlation of priority structures among governments required the preparation of a first matrix in which each line represents a year and a topic (e.g., 1960/Health) and each column the priorities of a given government (e.g., Newfoundland), expressed in percentage. The percentage ranks a topic in a given year in a priority structure, and as the percentages are not normally distributed, we estimated Spearman coefficients of correlation to establish correspondence between governments' priority structures. Then, for a given five-year period (e.g., 1960–64/ NFL-PEI) these coefficients were transposed in a single column in a second matrix, in which each line represents a dyad of governments, horizontal when involving two provinces and vertical when matching a province with the federal government. Additional columns of coefficients of correlation—calculated by taking into account exclusive federal competencies—provincial and shared competencies, and exclusive provincial competencies, were also produced for analyses controlling divisions of policy responsibilities between the federal and provincial governments. This control is important, as stronger horizontal than vertical correlations could be explained by similarities in provincial competencies and differences between provincial and federal responsibilities.

All the results presented below were produced using the second matrix, organized in dyads. Again, correlations of policy priorities between and among governments in Canada are used here as indicators of intergovernmental relations.

Table 2: Descriptive Statistics on the Coding of Throne Speeches

Government	Number of Speeches	Average Number of Quasi-Sentences	Average % of Policy Content
Newfoundland	44	14,474	90.8
Prince Edward Island	48	15,359	87.2
Nova Scotia	38	8,460	88.5
New Brunswick	47	13,978	91.6
Quebec	29	7,902	87.7
Ontario	37	10,452	89.2
Manitoba	34	7,847	91.5
Saskatchewan	36	7,652	90.8
Alberta	49	10,120	88.6
British Columbia	48	12,362	86.1
Federal	35	8,147	83.3

Source: Authors' compilations.

ANALYSIS OF VERTICAL INTERGOVERNMENTAL RELATIONS

Canadian scholars have produced significant knowledge of vertical intergovernmental relations, identifying patterns of relations between the federal government and provinces in general, ranging from classical federalism, to cooperative federalism, to competitive federalism, to constitutional federalism, to collaborative federalism (Simeon and Robinson 2009). This literature points to cycles in intergovernmental relations—that is, to periods during which intergovernmental relations intensify and periods during which they weaken.

The postwar period up to the end of the 1960s has been depicted as the golden days of vertical intergovernmental relations. This period witnessed the joint construction of the Canadian welfare state by the federal and provincial governments. Shared-cost programs were then designed to advance social objectives, including better access to higher education and health, and assistance to the disadvantaged and the elderly. The period came to an end, so it seems, around 1968, with intergovernmental agreements on health care and social assistance coverage (Banting 1987). Professional civil servants were the main actors in the design and the management of shared-cost and other intergovernmental programs during this period (Dupré 1988). In addition, these programs justified the development of a modern intergovernmental administrative apparatus, which still today provides for an intergovernmental policy capacity in Canada (Inwood, Johns, and O'Reilly 2011). In the 1960s, then, the involvement of cabinet ministers was secondary to that of civil servants. If problems had to be resolved by politicians, they often did so discretely, thanks to their acquaintance with their provincial or federal counterparts. Intergovernmental relations thus intensified between the Second World War and the end of the 1960s in a relatively smooth manner.

One exception to this pattern was Quebec's difficult relationship with Ottawa under Duplessis, who claimed autonomy in areas of provincial competencies (Montpetit 2008). Our empirical analysis, however, does not cover this period. Moreover, relations between Quebec and Ottawa in the first half of the 1960s were comparatively smooth, as were those between other provinces and Ottawa (McRoberts 1997).

This harmony began breaking down at the end of the 1960s, as intergovernmental relations began entering seriously into political considerations. Using intergovernmental relations for political purposes, ministers and first ministers became increasingly involved (Simeon and Robinson 1990, 194). Several premiers came to realize that they could make electoral gains by contesting federal policy, and therefore intergovernmental rivalries increasingly ended up on the public plate (Stevenson 1995, 415; Lemieux 1993, 96-8). The intergovernmental conference held in Victoria in 1971 symbolizes the entry of intergovernmental relations into a more political phase. Visible political conflicts between the federal government and provinces have since Victoria served to undermine the work undertaken by civil

servants to establish cooperative intergovernmental relations. The gradual transformation of shared-cost programs into programs with conditions for the transfer of
federal funds to the provinces was nothing to please provincial civil servants who
began to complain about increasing federal coercion at the expense of cooperation
(Barker 1988). Dupré (1988, 244) wrote of the deterioration in intergovernmental
relations from the end of the 1960s on: "First ministers have become prone to talk
past each other from their respective capitals, rather than with each other on the
basis of their policy interdependence."

Talking past each other was even more tempting in the 1970s, as most provinces
had by then developed state-like capacities. Years of so-called province-building
had enabled provincial governments to begin dealing with Ottawa on a more
equalitarian basis, contesting federal policy more vigorously in areas of provincial competencies, albeit with variations from one province to the next (Young,
Faucher, and Blais 1984). Rising energy prices and provincial ownership of natural
resources launched provinces on promising, yet sufficiently distinctive economic
development paths to encourage hostility toward any national policy (Simeon and
Robinson 2009, 167). The most telling example is Alberta's refusal of the National
Energy Policy in the early 1980s.

In addition to province-building, constitutional disagreements between Ottawa
and Quebec contributed to a relative disinterest in vertical intergovernmental relations in all provinces except Quebec. Relations between Quebec and Ottawa took on
a particular meaning after the election of the Parti Québécois in 1976. Needless to
say, Quebec's relationship with Ottawa during that period was less than harmonious.
The focus on the Constitution, which was mostly seen as unproblematic outside
Quebec and Ottawa, certainly discouraged vertical intergovernmental relations in
several of the other provinces. The relative provincial disinterest in intergovernmental relations lasted up until the election of the Progressive Conservative Party
in Ottawa in 1984.

The 1984 federal elections cooled the tense political relations that had developed between several provinces and Ottawa in the 1970s, that cooling reflecting
Mulroney's pragmatic approach in comparison to that of Trudeau (Aucoin 1986).
Nonetheless, intergovernmental interests on matters other than the Constitution
peaked again in the 1990s, with the federal government's revitalized willingness to
affirm itself as a leader of national policy in areas that matter directly to Canadians.
It did so with new tools, notably those of the New Public Management approach,
presented as softer and less coercive than the previous conditional grant approach
and therefore more acceptable to provincial governments (Simeon and Cameron
2002; Lazar 2000; Bakvis and Skogstad 2002; Montpetit 2006). In the background
of 1994's drastic reductions of federal transfers to the provinces, however, the new
tools did not appease intergovernmental tensions, but they nonetheless required
an intensification of vertical intergovernmental relations at both the political and
administrative levels. This phase of so-called collaborative federalism lasted until
2006.

The Conservative Party of Canada, openly hostile to government intervention and favourable to decentralization, was elected in 2006. Little scholarly work has been published on vertical intergovernmental relations under this government, but commentators have noticed a serious weakening on this front attributable to the attitude of the federal government. On the one hand, the federal government has few national policy projects and shows little inclination to negotiate with provincial governments' budgetary decisions that impact transfers to provinces. On the other hand, the Conservative federal government seeks to respect provincial competencies, adhering to the classical conception of federalism whereby each order of government makes policy exclusively and autonomously in its own spheres of competencies. This latter attitude toward provinces belongs to Open Federalism, the Harper government's strategy to distinguish its conception of Canadian federalism from that of the previous Liberal governments (Montpetit 2007).

This summary of the cycles of vertical relations between the federal and provincial governments will be useful to assess the validity of correlations of priority structures as indicators of intergovernmental relations in Canada. The knowledge summarized here is based on years of qualitative studies by Canadian scholars (with the exception of the most recent period) and can be taken to provide the most accurate depiction of the cycle of vertical intergovernmental relations. Therefore, consistency between this knowledge and the cycle suggested by the indicator provides a first validity test.

Figure 1 presents the evolution of the distribution of vertical correlations among provinces by five-year periods. The bar in the middle of the box represents the median correlation, while the top of the box is the first quartile and the bottom is the third. The dots represent outlying values. The correlations are calculated using percentages of quasi-sentences with a political content for all topics listed in Table 1, but five in which the federal government enjoys near-exclusivity. The latter topics are defence, foreign affairs, foreign trade, banking, and space. We will revisit the issue of the division of competencies between the federal and provincial governments. It makes sense for now to exclude from the analysis those domains in which the two orders of government interact very little at best.

The results in Figure 1 are highly consistent with the narrative of vertical intergovernmental relations presented above. The intensification characterizing the 1960s is clear and has run across all provinces relatively consistently. A weakening of intergovernmental relations started in the 1975–79 period, although vertical relations remained relatively strong in Ontario and in Quebec. In this latter case, constitutional disputes might explain the strength of the vertical relations. In fact, the vertical relations between Quebec and the federal government weakened considerably in the 1980–84 periods, possibly owing to frustration related to the 1982 constitutional deal. The correlation coefficient went from a statistically significant 0.5 (p-value < 0.1) for the 1975–79 period (the outlying value in Figure 1) to a statistically insignificant 0.19 in 1980–84. Between 1980 and 1984, however, Alberta had the weakest relations of all the provinces with the federal government (a correlation coefficient of –0.11, p-value>0.1), possibly also a reaction of frustration following

Figure 1: The Evolution of Vertical Correlations

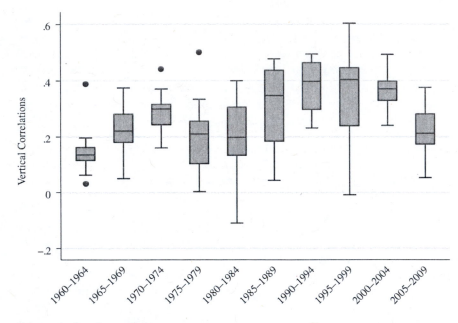

Source: Authors' compilations.

Trudeau's National Energy Policy. The intensification resumed in 1985–89 for several provinces and peaked between 1995 and 1999. This latter period was also characterized by important provincial variations, with Ontario peaking at a significant correlation coefficient of 0.6. Over the entire 1960–2009 period, Ontario has had, most consistently, relatively intensive relations with the federal government in comparison with the other provinces. Lastly, as expected, the correlations dropped consistently across provinces for the 2005–09 period. This level of consistency with qualitative knowledge gives us confidence in the validity of the correlations of priorities as indicators of intergovernmental relations.

MEASUREMENT OF HORIZONTAL INTERGOVERNMENTAL RELATIONS

Confident in our indicator, we can now move on to estimations of horizontal intergovernmental relations about which we have little quantitative and qualitative knowledge. In fact, the scholarly literature does not provide any clues about potential cycles as found for vertical relations, or about the relative importance of horizontal versus vertical relations. Figure 2 thus provides a first direct systematic comparison of horizontal and vertical intergovernmental relations. Horizontal relations dominate clearly.

Figure 2 displays for the same five-year periods the means used in a two-group mean-comparison test. The first group comprised all dyads of vertical relations, the federal government matched with provinces, and the second group comprised all dyads of horizontal relations, that is, every combination of provinces. The tests were repeated for each five-year period. Owing to the use of means, the dashed line shows an accentuated version of the cycle presented in Figure 1. Although the correlations of vertical relations are constantly below those of horizontal relations, the difference drops below a significance level of 0.1 in the peak periods of vertical intergovernmental relations, which is unsurprising given the limited number of vertical dyads. In other words, horizontal intergovernmental relations are generally more intense than vertical ones, although the intensity of vertical relations can almost reach that of horizontal ones during peak periods.

Perhaps even more interesting is the cycle of horizontal intergovernmental relations, which does not mimic the cycle of vertical intergovernmental relations. In fact, after a sharp decline in the 1960s, horizontal intergovernmental relations have steadily increased since 1970.

Figure 2: Mean Differences between Correlations of Horizontal and Vertical Intergovernmental Relations

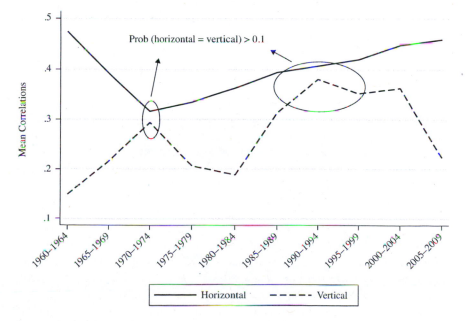

Source: Authors' compilations.

Given the scarcity of a scholarly literature on horizontal intergovernmental relations, we can only offer an exploratory explanation. To make matters worse, the explanation for the 1960s is far from straightforward. As discussed above, increased interest in the development of the welfare state is driven by the growth of vertical intergovernmental relations in the 1960s, and vice versa. As shown in Figure 1, however, some provinces were more interested in welfare state development than others. Interestingly, provinces that did not seek welfare state development also seem to have had too little in common to sustain horizontal relations in other sectors.

The situation began to change in the 1970–74 period. While the constitutional dispute between Quebec and Ottawa began eroding the interest in vertical intergovernmental relations, new concerns emerged on the agenda of provincial governments. Little was known about the policy alternatives to tackle these concerns, and provinces in search of solutions were inclined to share expertise and ideas. Environmental protection provides a good illustration. The Canadian Constitution does not attribute the environment—not foreseen as a domain of government intervention in 1867—clearly to either the provinces or the federal government. Therefore, governments intervene in this domain by extension of their constitutional responsibilities in other domains, the federal government using fisheries, and provinces using natural resources, for instance. As a consequence, while developing environmental policy, provinces have more in common with each other than with the federal government, with which a minimum of coordination nonetheless remains necessary. In any case, in domains in which constitutional authority is attributed in the same manner as in environmental policy, provinces may be naturally drawn toward each other as they likely face similar policy challenges.

In addition, the federal government has displayed at best a weak inclination to become a dominant player in environmental policy (Doern and Conway 1994; Lee and Perl 2003). Provincial governments have therefore frequently been left on their own to puzzle over policy solutions, without help from the federal government (Montpetit 2002). These conditions were favourable to the formation of cooperative ties among several provincial governments. Ties often formed at the administrative level and were oriented toward problem-solving. And they were all the more attractive as they involved none of the turf wars or disputes over resource allocation or threats of unilateralism that often characterize vertical intergovernmental relations. In any case, from the 1970s on, such pooling of provincial minds and expertise occurred in emerging domains, contributing to the steady growth of horizontal intergovernmental relations displayed in Figure 2.

If emerging issues and the need to puzzle over the problems to which they gave rise have driven the growth of horizontal intergovernmental relations since the 1970s, regional variations have likely also played a role. Similar constitutional authority may bring provinces to work toward the development of similar policy, but neighbouring provinces should be particularly drawn toward each other. Not only does geographic proximity facilitate the development of relations but neighbours possibly also face similar problems. Problem-solving among provincial govern- ments of the same region might thus be more attractive than among geographically disparate governments. Figure 3 in fact confirms that horizontal intergovernmental relations, if strong overall in comparison with vertical relations, are even stronger among the provincial governments of the same region. Following common cat- egorization, we included among western provinces British Columbia, Alberta, Saskatchewan, and Manitoba. Eastern provinces are comprised of Newfoundland and Labrador, Prince Edward Island, Nova Scotia, and New Brunswick. Central Canadian provinces are Quebec and Ontario.

Figure 3 was produced following a simple ordinary least square regression an- alysis, using correlations of priorities in domains of shared and provincial authority as the dependent variable.

Figure 3: Marginal Effects of Geographic Proximity on Horizontal Intergovernmental Relations

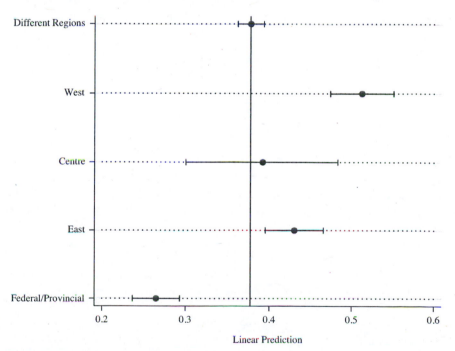

Source: Authors' compilations.

The independent variables are dummies identifying federal/provincial dyads, dyads of eastern provinces, dyads of central provinces, and dyads of western provinces. Dyads of provinces from different regions were used as a reference indicated by the vertical line. Figure 3 thus depicts marginal effects on correlations of moving from dyads of provinces from different regions to all of the other kind of dyads, including dyads of provinces with the federal government.

Results should be interpreted as follows: correlations of provinces from different regions average 0.38, and they are not significantly different from the average correlation of the provinces from central Canada (the margin of error for central Canada is larger, because the region has fewer dyads with only two provinces). Provinces from different regions, however, are significantly different from provinces within western and eastern Canada, which average 0.51 and 0.42 respectively. Western provinces appear to have a particularly strong interest in their mutual relations. In contrast, at 0.25, the federal provincial correlation is significantly lower than all of the horizontal correlations. In other words, even dyads of provinces from different regions display higher average correlation than dyads associating the federal government with every single province.

Figure 3 is consistent with Figure 2, which shows that horizontal intergovernmental relations are stronger than vertical ones. It is also consistent with the intuitive idea that horizontal relations are particularly strong among neighbouring provinces, which in passing adds to our confidence in correlations of priority structures as indicators of intergovernmental relations. Figure 3 can be viewed as a second validity test, passed successfully.

All the correlations presented in the three figures exclude the five topics considered the purview of the federal government, which we identified above. We excluded those topics because we thought that it made sense to do so; that horizontal relations are weak on defence, for example, would surprise no one. Excluding or including them, however, does not modify the results of our analyses. Interestingly, Stevenson (1995, 410) identifies domains that "appear" exclusively provincial: municipalities, education, and some areas of law. We decided to re-examine vertical relations in those domains only and found correlations ranging between 0.15 (Newfoundland and Labrador) and 0.4 (Ontario). The average vertical correlation in the areas that appeared to Stevenson to be of exclusive provincial jurisdiction is 0.26. In contrast, the average vertical correlation in the areas of exclusive federal competencies was near zero at –0.03. Quebec, however, stands out with a correlation of 0.22 in domains of exclusive federal competencies, possibly owing to the province's interest in international affairs, notably la francophonie. In any case, this control for the division of competencies confirms the appropriateness of excluding competencies that are exclusive to the federal government while retaining areas often viewed as exclusively provincial even in calculations of vertical correlations. Ottawa has historically been far more interested in the exclusive areas of provincial competencies than provinces have been in the areas of exclusive federal competencies, a difference confirmed by our analysis.

CONCLUSION

Almost 13 years after the 2000 health deal, the press was still reporting that the premiers of Ontario and Quebec were allying against the federal government, which unilaterally decided to reduce health transfer payments in the winter of 2012. According to the *Globe and Mail*, Quebec premier Jean Charest, during a visit to his counterpart in Toronto in March 2012, referred to history, going as far back as John A. Macdonald's government, "to argue that Mr. Harper is abandoning a long tradition of collaboration with the provinces." Bouchard could have said much the same back in 2000 about Chrétien, and, for that matter, so might have former Ontario premier Bill Davis in the 1970s about Trudeau. Dalton McGuinty, Ontario's premier, was naturally in full agreement with Charest. However, the article goes on to point to a "war of words" between McGuinty and Alberta premier Alison Redford (Howlett 2012, 1). More than a decade after the 2000 health deal, the article suggests, regional rivalries continue undermining horizontal relations among the provinces.

In light of the analysis presented above, some elements of the press coverage of Charest's 2012 visit to Toronto, or of Bouchard's visit in 2000 to Harris, ring true for intergovernmental relations taken more generally. But several other elements are wrong. That the press underlines Ontario and Quebec's cooperative relationship is not surprising: horizontal relations are particularly strong within regional clusters and even more so in Western and Eastern Canada. Nonetheless, horizontal relations between provinces of different regions are not weak. In fact, horizontal relations, even across regions, have grown steadily in intensity since the 1970s. Therefore, the rivalry between Ontario and Alberta occasionally reported in the press probably amounts to nothing more than hiccups.

In fact, provinces have been working with each other with increasing intensity to find policy solutions to common problems. Little scholarly work exists to confirm this trend, but partial evidence suggests that in domains that have emerged since the 1970s, provincial officials, often administrators, have solidified their ties to share their respective experience and benefit from each other's expertise. Therefore, not only have horizontal intergovernmental relations gained in importance but they are different in nature from vertical intergovernmental relations. In contrast with vertical intergovernmental relations, which have been plagued by turf and resource allocation conflicts, horizontal intergovernmental relations aim at problem-solving. Perhaps owing to the erosion of their usefulness, relations between provinces and the federal government have declined since the 1990s. Consequently, Charest's complaint about the current situation seems justified. Contrary to what he suggests, however, vertical intergovernmental relations have often been low in intensity since the 1970s.

Vertical intergovernmental relations occupy central stage in the media as well as in scholarly understandings of intergovernmental relations in Canada, suggesting that they are a prominent feature of the country's political system. The present analysis suggests that those understandings are misleading. It is not that vertical intergovernmental relations are unimportant, but in paying little attention to horizontal intergovernmental relations, we miss an even more important aspect of the functioning of the Canadian federal system. Moreover, the spotlight on vertical intergovernmental relations in depictions of Canada has encouraged perceptions of the country in which conflict is exaggerated. To understand the Canadian federation adequately, the ratio of attention given to horizontal relative to vertical intergovernmental relations should significantly increase.

That being said, studying horizontal intergovernmental relations remains challenging. Horizontal relations are even more dispersed than vertical ones, if only because the starting point of their study is not a single government but ten. In addition, they occur bilaterally, multilaterally, and also regionally. They involve civil servants from various specialized domains more frequently than generalists in central agencies. And they often rest on personal contacts between civil servants, as the size of several provinces in some regions encourages the development of such informal relationships.

To take the measure of the importance of horizontal intergovernmental relations in this context of dispersion, an indicator such as the one proposed in this chapter is necessary. The indicator can certainly be improved, but we are confident that it provides us with a reliable measure—in fact, the only one—of the relative importance of horizontal intergovernmental relations. The knowledge that horizontal intergovernmental relations are important, we hope, will now encourage qualitative studies to better understand their nature.

REFERENCES

Aucoin, P. 1986. "Organization Change in the Canadian Machinery of Government: From Rational Management to Brokerage Politics." *Canadian Journal of Political Science* 19 (1): 3-27.

Bakvis, H., and D. Brown. 2010. "Policy Coordination in Federal Systems: Comparing Intergovernmental Processes and Outcomes in Canada and the United States." *Publius: The Journal of Federalism* 40 (3): 484-507.

Bakvis, H., and G. Skogstad. 2002. "Canadian Federalism: Performance, Effectiveness, and Legitimacy." In *Canadian Federalism: Performance, Effectiveness, and Legitimacy,* edited by H. Bakvis and G. Skogstad. Don Mills, ON: Oxford University Press.

Banting, K.G. 1987. *The Welfare State and Canadian Federalism.* Montreal: McGill-Queen's University Press.

Barker, P. 1988. "The Development of Major Shared-Cost Programs in Canada." In *Perspectives on Canadian Federalism,* edited by R.D. Olling and M.W. Westmascott. Scarborough, ON: Prentice-Hall Canada.

Doern, G.B., and T. Conway. 1994. *The Greening of Canada: Federal Institutions and Decisions.* Toronto: University of Toronto Press.

Dowding, K., A. Hindmoor, R. Iles, and P. John. 2010. "Policy Agendas in Australian Politics: The Governor-General's Speeches, 1945–2008." *Australian Journal of Political Science* 45 (4): 533-57.

Dupré, J.S. 1988. "Reflections on the Workability of Executive Federalism." In *Perspectives on Canadian Federalism,* edited by R.D. Olling and M.W. Westmascott. Scarborough, ON: Prentice-Hall Canada.

Fafard, P., et al. 2011. *Trends and Frequency of Multilateral Meetings: FPT Ministers Meetings, 1997–2011.* Mimeo.

Frio, C. 2012. *Handbook for Coding the British Party Manifestos (1983–2010) for the Comparative Agendas Project.* http://www.academia.edu/2263110/Handbook_for_coding_the_British_Party_Manifestos_1983-2010_for_the_Comparative_Agendas_Project.

Gilardi, F., and K. Füglister. 2008. "Empirical Modeling of Policy Diffusion in Federal States: The Dyadic Approach." *Swiss Political Science Review* 14 (3): 413-50.

Gray, C. 2000. "Everyone Claims Victory in Health Care Deal, but Who Really Won?" *Canadian Medial Association Journal* 163 (8): 1029-30.

Harrison, K. 2006. "Are Canadian Provinces Engaged in a Race to the Bottom? Evidence and Implications." In *Racing to the Bottom? Provincial Interdependence in the Canadian Federation,* edited by K. Harrison. Vancouver: UBC Press.

Howlett, K. 2012. "Don't Balance the Budget on Our Backs, Ontario and Quebec Warn." *Globe and Mail,* 12 March, 1.

Inwood, G.J., C.M. Johns, and P.L. O'Reilly. 2011. *Intergovernmental Policy Capacity in Canada: Inside the Worlds of Finance, Environment, Trade, and Health.* Montreal and Kingston: McGill-Queen's University Press.

John, P., and W. Jennings. 2010. "Punctuations and Turning Points in British Politics: The Policy Agenda of the Queen's Speech, 1940–2005." *British Journal of Political Science* 40 (3): 561-86.

Johns, C.M., P.L. O'Reilly, and G.J. Inwood. 2006. "Intergovernmental Innovation and the Administrative State in Canada." *Governance* 19 (4): 627-49.

—. 2007. "Formal and Informal Dimensions of Intergovernmental Administrative Relations in Canada." *Canadian Public Administration* 50 (1): 21-41.

Jones, B.D., H. Larsen-Price, and J. Wilkerson. 2009. "Representation and American Governing Institutions." *Journal of Politics* 71: 277-90.

Lazar, H. 2000. "In Search of a New Mission Statement for Canadian Fiscal Federalism." In *Canada: The State of the Federation: Non-Constitutional Renewal,* edited by H. Lazar. Kingston, ON: Institute of Intergovernmental Relations, Queen's University.

Lee, E., and A. Perl, eds. 2003. *The Integrity Gap: Canada's Environmental Policy and Institutions.* Vancouver: UBC Press.

Lemieux, V. 1993. *Le Parti libéral du Québec: Alliances, rivalités et neutralité.* Sainte-Foy: Les presses de l'Université Laval.

McRoberts, K. 1997. *Misconceiving Canada: The Struggle for National Unity.* Toronto: Oxford University Press.

Montpetit, É. 2002. "Policy Networks, Federal Arrangements and the Development of Environmental Regulations: A Comparison of the Canadian and American Agricultural Sectors." *Governance* 15: 1-20.

—. 2006. "Declining Legitimacy and Canadian Federalism: An Examination of Policy-Making in Agriculture and Biomedicine." In *Continuity and Change in Canadian Politics*, edited by M. Hans and C. de Clercy. Toronto: University of Toronto Press.

—. 2007. *Le fédéralisme d'ouverture: La recherche d'une légitimité canadienne au Québec.* Quebec: Septentrion.

—. 2008. "Easing Dissatisfaction with Canadian Federalism? The Promise of Disjointed Incrementalism." *Canadian Political Science Review* 2 (3): 12-28.

Montpetit, É., and M. Foucault. 2012. "Canadian Federalism and Change in Policy Attention: A Comparison with the United Kingdom." *Canadian Journal of Political Science* 45 (3): 635-56.

Simeon, R., and D. Cameron. 2002. "Intergovernmental Relations and Democracy: An Oxymoron If There Ever Was One?" In *Canadian Federalism, Performance, Effectiveness and Legitimacy*, edited by H. Bakvis and G. Skogstad. Don Mills, ON: Oxford University Press.

Simeon, R., and I. Robinson. 1990. *State, Society and the Development of Canadian Federalism.* Toronto: University of Toronto Press.

—. 2009. "The Dynamics of Canadian Federalism." In *Canadian Politics*, 5th ed., edited by J. Bickerton and A.-G. Gagnon. Toronto: University of Toronto Press.

Stevenson, G. 1995. "Federalism and Intergovernmental Relations." In *Canadian Politics in the 1990s*, edited by M.S. Whittington and G. Williams. Toronto: Nelson Canada.

Turgeon, L. 2009. "Cities within the Canadian Intergovernmental System." In *Contemporary Canadian Federalism*, edited by A.-G. Gagnon. Toronto: University of Toronto Press.

Weyland, K. 2007. *Bounded Rationality and Policy Diffusion: Social Sector Reform in Latin America.* Princeton: Princeton University Press.

Young, R.A., P. Faucher, and A. Blais. 1984. "The Concept of Province-Building: A Critique." *Canadian Journal of Political Science* 17 (4): 783-818.

12

FROM OLD CANADA, THE NEW EAST: ADJUSTING TO THE CHANGING FEDERAL ENVIRONMENT

Christopher Dunn

The language of Canadian regionalism has become tired and of increasingly limited utility. We are used to thinking in terms like Eastern, Western, and Central Canada in general, and then in increasingly finer distinctions: the Maritimes, the Prairies, Ontario, Quebec—and so the list goes on. At some junctures in Canadian history, however, it is more useful to cast regionalism within larger, more functional categories that catch commonalities and possibilities among unlikely partners. In one such category is the dichotomy of Old Canada and New Canada. This pair of overlooked terms may hold the key to a more creative interprovincialism and federalism in Canada.

Old Canada comprises Quebec, New Brunswick, Nova Scotia, Prince Edward Island, and Newfoundland and Labrador. We call the region "Old Canada" because it is the origin of what we now call Canada. Settled by Europeans largely in the early seventeenth century, this region has the longest traditionally recorded historical memory in the country. Its provinces share significant political, economic, and social characteristics that distinguish them collectively from the rest of the country.

Old Canada increasingly looks to itself rather than to the rest of Canada as the primary frame of reference. Atlantic Canada, which for decades has seen itself as an entity apart from the rest of the country, now increasingly sees itself as a subset of Old Canada. Old Canada is today so compromised by issues of representation, population, and history that relating to other regions is not a priority unless there are broader alliances to be made in the provinces' interest(s).

It is not merely quaint reflections on the past that propel an interest in the region, however. In 2010, Old Canada spent 26 percent of the country's expenditure-based gross domestic product (Statistics Canada 2013). It has 38 percent of the undeveloped hydro potential in the country; the entire West, all four provinces, has 35 percent (EEM 2008). The Atlantic margin has 18 percent of Canada's estimated conventional hydrocarbon resources, the largest amount after the Western Canada Sedimentary Basin, excluding oil sands bitumen (Bott and Carson 2007). The partners in Old Canada have the ability to help each other: Newfoundland and Labrador and Nova Scotia have offshore capabilities Quebec sorely needs as it attempts to develop petroleum resources in the Gulf of St Laurence; Quebec has hydro expertise and marketing ties of which Atlantic provinces could avail.

Old Canada has the potential to synergize its component parts or to drag them down. Pitted against each other as they are in some areas and some eras, the region's provinces suffer. Newfoundland and Labrador needs markets in Central Canada but cannot get access to them through Quebec. Development in the Gulf has suffered from a half-century disagreement on offshore boundaries. Broad labour market policy and industrial subsidies in the area have been segmentalized, to the detriment of area business, a fact belatedly recognized by the June 2012 creation of the Atlantic Workforce Partnership (AWP). This is to say nothing of the loss in social and regional cultural capital that is the bitter fruit of the loss of economic interchange. When all the provinces in Old Canada don't work together, the region doesn't work as a whole. It is not working now. Accordingly, later in this chapter I propose a new working relationship among the partners we call "the New East."

Perhaps it is time to consider what brings Old Canada together and to see if there are modalities for ending, or at least modifying, what separates its component parts.

SHARED POLITICAL CHARACTERISTICS

First of all, Old Canada shares some political characteristics. The decline of what has lately been called "the Laurentian thesis," or "the Laurentian axis," is one such shared reality. The Laurentian thesis posits that the history of Canada for well over a century and a half has been that of the shared fate of Ontario and Quebec. According to Donald Creighton, "the Laurentian theme has its basis in the fact that the St. Lawrence is one of the great river systems … [and] has inspired generations of Canadians to build a great territorial empire, both commercial and political, in the western interior of the continent" (1972, 160-1). David Cameron commented that "a central account of the emergence of modern Canada is the manner in which these two communities, sharing the St. Lawrence River system, sought to advance their interests and prosperity as the country grew" (1994, 112).

Most of the early landmarks of the country, namely, its founding in 1867, the nourishing of the commercial empire of the St Lawrence through St James and Bay streets, the National Policy, westward expansion, the alienation of the hinterland from this centre, were for the benefit of Central Canadian interests—Ontario and

Quebec. In recent times, the policies of the Liberal and old Progressive Conservative Party in areas like constitutional politics, national unity symbols (public broadcasting, bilingualism), the Charter, and social welfare programs that balanced the concerns of Quebec and English Canada (pensions, health care, welfare) carried on the legacy of the Laurentian consensus.

Yet the Laurentian axis has now lost its hold; an Ontario-Western alliance has replaced it. In John Ibbitson's view (2011), a combination of factors has contributed to the former's demise. The economic basis of the consensus has been weakened by the signing of free trade agreements, Ontario becoming part of the Great Lakes region, and the West increasingly orienting to Eastern Asia. New migrants look to governments to reflect their wishes and not push the envelope of new, more liberal, social mores, social causes, and higher taxes.

As well, since the early 1990s Quebec has fundamentally opted out of the consensus. It has consistently forsaken its alliance with Ontario and voted for parties in Opposition. "For better or worse, the province now seems to be permanently outside the governing consensus, regardless of who that government is. Whatever the referendums might have said, Quebec prefers to pursue a separate, if complementary, destiny" (Ibbitson 2011).

The power centre has shifted. The lion's share of seats in Ontario, Manitoba, Saskatchewan, Alberta, and British Columbia—enough to form government—has gone to the Conservatives. In Atlantic Canada, the same can only be said of New Brunswick. The shift seems destined to be long lasting, in light of the disintegration of the Liberals (who have lost vote share in every province and territory since mid-decade) and the shifting regional population figures (see below). For the foreseeable future, governments will be formed from Ontario and the West, and they will have the most important portfolios.

The electoral evidence of the disintegrating consensus has been growing since the 2006 federal election (see Table 1). In 2006, Conservatives were merely the party of rural Ontario; in 2008, that base grew to include suburban Ontario; and in 2011 to this was added the goldmine of most of the "905" seats surrounding Toronto. In every election, the popular vote and seat total of the Conservatives increased. In 2011 they gained two-thirds of the seats in Ontario, where in 2004 they had managed only about a fifth, and their predecessor party, the Alliance, had eked out only two seats in 2000. In Quebec the Conservative seat total has descended to 7 percent and the Liberals to 9 percent (the two basically the same at 16.5 percent and 14.2 percent in popular vote, respectively).

Could Quebec throw its lot in with the new Ontario/West alliance to offset its strategic disadvantages? Conceivably. However, this is unlikely to happen in a country where as one goes westward, the ascendency of more liberal-individualist political philosophies grows, and as one moves eastward, that of social-democratic ones are stronger. Small wonder the West has historically been unfriendly to Quebec aspirations.

Table 1: Election Results, 2011, 2008, and 2006, in Descending Order, in Terms of Popular Vote (PV) and Seats (SE), by Province, and Totals

Prov & % Turnout, 2011, 2008, 2006	Cons PV SE 2011, 2008, 2006		Liberal PV SE 2011, 2008, 2006		NDP PV SE 2011, 2008, 2006		Green PV SE 2011, 2008, 2006		Bloc Québécois PV SE 2011, 2008, 2006		Other PV SE 2011, 2008, 2006		Total SE 2011, 2008, 2006
NL 52.6	28.3	1	37.9	4	32.6	2	0.9	–			0.3		7
47.7	16.6	–	46.8	6	33.7	1	1.7	–			1.3		7
56.7	42.7	3	42.8	4	13.6	–	0.9	–			0.0		7
PEI 73.3	41.2	1	41.0	3	15.4	–	2.4	–			0.1		4
69.0	36.2	1	47.7	3	9.8	–	4.7	–			1.7		4
73.2	33.4	–	52.6	4	9.6	–	3.9	–			0.7		4
NS 62.0	36.7	4	28.9	4	30.3	3	3.9	–			0.1		11
60.3	26.1	3	29.8	5	28.9	2	8.0	–			6.6	1	11
63.9	29.7	3	37.2	6	29.9	2	2.6	–			0.6		11
NB 66.2	43.8	8	22.6	1	29.8	1	3.2	–			0.6		10
62.9	39.4	6	32.5	3	21.9	1	6.1	–			0.2		10
69.2	35.8	3	39.2	6	21.9	1	2.4	–			0.7		10
QU 62.9	16.5	5	14.2	7	42.9	59	2.1	–	23.4	4	0.9		75
61.7	21.7	10	23.7	14	12.1	1	3.5	–	38.1	49	0.8	1	75
63.9	24.6	10	20.8	13	7.5	–	4.0	–	42.1	51	1.2	1	75
ON 61.5	44.4	73	25.3	11	25.6	22	3.8	–			0.9		106
58.6	39.2	51	33.8	38	18.2	17	8.0	–			0.9		106
66.6	35.1	40	39.9	54	19.4	12	4.7	–			0.9		106
MA 59.4	53.5	11	16.6	1	25.8	2	2.6	–			0.6		14
56.1	48.9	9	19.1	1	24.0	4	6.8	–			1.2		14
62.3	42.8	8	26.0	3	25.4	3	3.9	–			2.0		14
SK 63.1	56.3	13	8.5	–	32.3	–	2.6	–			0.2		14
58.7	53.8	13	14.9	1	25.5	–	5.6	–			0.2		14
65.1	49.0	12	22.4	2	24.1	–	3.2	–			1.4		14
AB 55.8	66.8	27	9.3	–	16.8	1	5.2	–			1.9		28
52.4	64.7	27	11.4	–	12.7	–	8.8	–			2.6		28
61.9	65.0	28	15.3	–	11.7	–	6.5	–			1.4		28
BC 60.4	45.6	21	13.4	2	32.5	12	7.7	1			0.8		36
60.1	44.5	22	19.3	5	26.1	9	9.4	–			0.8		36
63.7	37.3	17	27.6	9	28.5	10	5.3	–			1.1		36
NT 53.9	32.1	–	18.4	–	45.8	1	3.1	–			0.8		1
47.7	37.6	–	13.6	1	41.4	1	5.5	–			1.8		1
56.2	19.8	–	40.0	1	42.2	1	2.1	–			0.9		1
NU 45.7	49.9	–	28.7	–	19.4	–	2.0	–			–		1
47.4	34.9	1	29.1	1	27.6	–	8.3	–			–		1
54.1	29.1	–	35.0	–	17.2	–	5.9	–			7.9		1
YU 66.2	33.8	1	32.9	–	14.4	–	18.9	–			–		1
63.2	32.7	–	45.8	1	8.7	–	12.8	–			–		1
66.1	23.7	–	48.5	1	23.8	–	4.0	–			–		1
2011 TOTAL	166		34		103		1		4		0		308
2008 TOTAL	143		77		37		–		49		2		308
2006 TOTAL	124		103		29		–		51		1		308

Source: Elections Canada (2013).

In fact, Christian Leuprecht and Nicolette O'Conner (2005) have constructed an argument to the effect that demographic differentiation is leading to vertical and horizontal "decoupling" in federations. Sub-states that are aging more rapidly (like, say, Old Canada) tend to resist movements away from more centralist, redistributive, and social-democratic policies and regimes; and those aging less rapidly, like New Canada, favour less interventionism and more liberal asymmetry in the federal makeup. In addition, these "like" regions are more likely to strike alliances at the national and supranational levels than are ones that differ. At the same time, a "denationalization" dynamic is at work introducing horizontal cleavages amongst the dissimilar regions (Leuprecht and O'Conner 2005, 221). If this argument holds, it is likely that Quebec will have more in common with the provinces of the Atlantic than the others.

There are several signs of a "vertical decoupling" of the federal and Quebec governments. Increasingly, the province is ignored in national policy-making. The rough proportionality of members of the federal Cabinet from Quebec has not been the working principle of federal cabinet-making that it was a few generations ago (Mallory 1984, 91). In 2013 only five members of Cabinet were from Quebec. To a large extent this exclusion has been self-inflicted by Quebec voters, because of the lack of elected government party members from which to choose in the past 20 years. Yet there is other evidence. The revoking of the long-gun registry, over the protests of Quebec (and the silence over the province's request to be able to use the federal records) is one sign. The introduction of Bill C-10, the omnibus crime bill, and changes to health funding without provincial—notably Quebec—consultation are others.

Issues of symbolic importance have been decided without much attention to Quebec sensitivities. In October 2011, unilingual anglophone Michael Moldaver was appointed to the Supreme Court, even though many of the cases and statutes he would have to deal with are in French. That same month, the government nominated unilingual Michael Ferguson as federal auditor-general, although the job description calls for proficiency in both official languages. The segments of the Canadian Forces have been renamed, Defence Minister Peter McKay announced in August 2011. The Maritime Command and Air Command will revert to names done away with four decades ago—the Royal Canadian Navy and Royal Canadian Air Force. The army, now known as the Land Force Command, will be renamed the Canadian Army. The move was meant to bolster some kind of anglophone nationalism while ignoring Quebec antipathy to monarchical remnants. The CBC noted that "an online poll of 1,016 Canadians conducted by Ipsos Reid between 20 and 27 June 2011 suggested that 67 per cent of Quebecers want to get rid of the monarchy while only 42 per cent of Canadians outside the province support such a move" (CBC News 2011b). Similar results have been noted for years in multiple polls.

The Atlantic provinces share with Quebec the lack of voice in national policy-making. Cabinet members from Atlantic Canada have, since the beginning of the twentieth century, formed a decreasing percentage of total Cabinet numbers. Where once they formed close to a third of cabinets, now they are lucky if they occasionally peak at 15 percent. In 2008, they garnered four of 38 places, or 11 percent; in 2011, the figure was four of 39, or 10 percent—in line with, or actually more than, the region's population. Quebec and the Atlantic provinces share the same Cabinet numbers and the same situation.

SHARED SOCIAL CHARACTERISTICS

The provinces of Old Canada have a number of social characteristics in common. One is diminishing demographic clout. Like the shifting political centre, Canada's population centre of gravity is shifting. Census figures for 2011 (see Figure 1) show that for the first time Quebec and Atlantic Canada's population was less than that of British Columbia and the Prairie provinces: 30.6 percent versus 30.7 percent respectively (Statistics Canada 2011a). In the past 60 years, BC and the Prairies' share of population has increased from 26.5 percent to 30.7 percent, while that of Quebec and the Atlantic provinces has declined from 40.5 percent to 30.6 percent. Quebec and Ontario themselves have gone from a rough parity in population 60 years ago (differing by only 4 percentage points in 1951, namely 28.9 percent versus 32.8 percent, respectively) to a nearly 15 percentage point difference in 2011: 23.6 percent versus 38.4 percent, respectively (Statistics Canada 2011a).

Figure 1: Population Share of Canada's Regions, 1951 to 2011

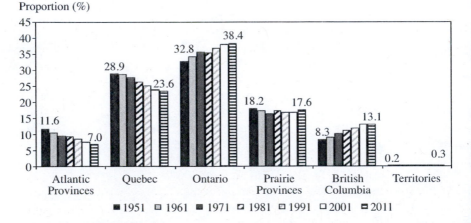

Source: Statistics Canada (2011b).

Urban and related areas in the West have been growing disproportionately faster since 2006:

- Between 2006 and 2011, all census metropolitan areas located in Western Canada have had higher population growth than the national average, except Winnipeg and Victoria.
- Of all census metropolitan areas located in the Prairie provinces and British Columbia, only Winnipeg (+5.1 percent) and Victoria (+4.4 percent) had population growth below the national average (7.4 percent).
- The rate of population growth in almost all census metropolitan areas located in Ontario slowed between 2006 and 2011.
- Between 2006 and 2011, 10 of 15 census agglomerations with the highest population growth were located in Alberta (Statistics Canada 2011c).

The shifting census figures show a likely shift in favour of the political fortunes of the Conservative Party. The figures have provoked a major distribution of Commons seats, in provinces where the Conservatives are already strong. On 27 October 2011, the Harper announced the introduction of the Fair Representation Act. This would see Ontario gain an additional 15 seats (to a total of 121), British Columbia six seats (to 42), Alberta six seats (to 34) and Quebec three seats (to 78). The new House will climb from 308 seats to 338.

Although the new seat totals simply bring these provinces' share of the Commons seats into proportion with their population share, the intra-provincial effects of the 30 new seats are notable. Political commentators have observed that the new seats are likely to be created from suburban areas surrounding cities like Toronto, Vancouver, Calgary and Edmonton where the Conservatives are already strong. Tories hold 26 of the country's 30 largest ridings, from which the newer ones are likely to be carved out by redistribution (Kennedy 2011). More Conservative seats will mean more stacking of the Commons against Quebec (and perhaps Atlantic Canada.)

In addition to size, ethnicity is likely to be a factor. (See Table 2.) The largest ridings went disproportionately Conservative in the 2011 election (13 out of 15), and the largest ridings were disproportionately dominated by visible minorities. Half of the 12 largest Ontario ridings had populations that were over half visible minorities, and eight had over a third. This phenomenon has a compound effect, strengthening both the Conservative hold and weakening the hold of the Laurentian narrative. Matthew Mendelsohn predicts that the 2015 Parliament, the first with the new distribution, will be more multicultural, "more made up of people who have not been historically engaged with the traditional national unity conversation in Canada, which is one of English-French and Quebec-rest-of-Canada. They will now have new narratives of immigrants and multiculturalism" (Mendelsohn, quoted in Kennedy 2012). This is a new story from that of the turn of the century when the new Canadian vote went predominantly Liberal, or even in the 2008 election, when the new Canadian vote was relatively evenly split between Conservatives and Liberals. Even if the Conservatives lose power in the next few years, the terms of the national discussion will have changed.

Table 2: Social and Voting Characteristics of Canada's Largest Ridings, 2006–11

Riding and Population		% Visible Minority, Province and Type	Winning Party and Candidate, 2011	
Brampton West	170,420	53.7% Ontario suburban	Conservative	Kyle Seeback
Oak Ridges–Markham	169,645	41.3% Ontario suburban	Conservative	Paul Calandra
Vaughan	154,215	25.4% Ontario suburban	Conservative	Julian Fantino
Bramalea–Gore–Malton	152,700	64% Ontario suburban	Conservative	Bal Gosal
Halton	151,940	19% Ontario suburban	NDP	Wayne Marston
Mississauga–Erindale	143,360	51.7% Ontario suburban	Conservative	Bob Dechert
Peace River	138,009	2.6% Alberta rural	Conservative	Chris Warkentin
Mississauga–Brampton South	136,470	60% Ontario suburban	Conservative	Eve Adams
Whitby–Oshawa	135,890	14.9% Ontario suburban	Conservative	Jim Flaherty
Nepean–Carleton	133,250	17.4% Ontario suburban	Conservative	Pierre Poilievre
Calgary West	132,155	17% Alberta suburban	Conservative	Robert Anders
Thornhill	131,970	33.3% Ontario suburban	Conservative	Peter Kent
Brampton–Springdale	131,795	56.2% Ontario suburban	Conservative	Parm Gill
Scarborough–Rouge River	130,980	89.4% Ontario suburban	NDP	Rathika Sitsabaiesan
Calgary–Nose Hill	130,945	34.9% Alberta suburban	Conservative	Diane Ablonczy

Source: Statistics Canada (2008); Elections Canada (2013); Mendelsohn and Choudry (2011). The Canadian average size of riding was 102,639, and the average percentage of visible minorities was 16.

All of Old Canada's provinces manifest a declining share of national population. With respect to Quebec, Statistics Canada's most conservative forecast sees it declining over 20 years. "With a population of 7.8 to 8.9 million in 2031, Quebec would see its share of the total population fall from 23.5 percent [in 2005] to 21.6 percent at best" (Statistics Canada 2005). Quebec would, however, still be the second-largest province in terms of population in 20 years. Atlantic Canada would decline as well: between 2.3 and 2.5 million people, or between 5.9 percent and 6.4 percent of Canadians, would be living in one of the four Atlantic provinces in 2031, compared with 2.3 million, or 7.3 percent of the population, in 2005 (Statistics Canada 2005). East of the Ottawa River, therefore, Old Canada will have at best 28 percent of the population, or perhaps less, down from nearly 31 percent of the population 25 years earlier.

Interprovincial migration also contributes to the relative decline of Old Canada. From 2001 to 2010, Quebec lost 66,035 of its population. Newfoundland and Labrador lost 21,016, Nova Scotia 15,768, New Brunswick 12,967, and Prince Edward Island 2,794 (Statistics Canada 2011c). Of course, it is not alone in this phenomenon, since most provinces also experienced drops, but the degree of population loss was greatest in Old Canada.

Aging populations will characterize Old Canada's provinces in particular. Statistics Canada projections indicate that "in almost every scenario, the Atlantic provinces would continue to present the highest median ages in Canada in 2031, while the three territories would have the youngest populations ... Between those two extremes, the median age would be higher than the national median in Quebec and British Columbia and lower in Ontario and the Prairies" (Statistics Canada 2005).

SHARED ECONOMIC CHARACTERISTICS

Old Canada's provinces are alike in another aspect: they are, or have been, fiscally and economically challenged. This situation gives them a different outlook on prospects for the future. It may argue for common cause on future projects.

Old Canada has the highest debt load of all the provinces, as the 2011–12 Quebec Budget Plan observed: "The deficits posted up until the mid-1990s contributed to making Québec the most indebted province in Canada. The projected shortfalls from now until 2013–14, along with public infrastructure investment, will add to Québec's debt load over the coming years and further reduce the government's leeway to fund public services. At $163.3 billion as at March 31, 2010, the gross debt is equivalent to 53.8 percent of GDP, i.e. nearly 26 percentage points more than the average of the other provinces" (the figures for each province being 39.9 for NL, 39.0 ON, 38.9 NS, 31.8 MB, 28.2 PEI, and 25.4 NB, according to figures in the Budget) (Quebec 2011).

The next fiscal year, matters had not improved much for Quebec and most of the other Old Canada provinces. As of 31 March 2011, Quebec's gross debt had increased to 54.3 percent of GDP, PEI's to 28.6 percent, NB's to 28.4, with NS's holding to 38.3 percent; NL's decline to 36.4 percent was due to oil revenues (Quebec 2012, D17).

Old Canada receives most of Canada's equalization payments. In 2011–12, Quebec accounted for 53 percent of equalization. Counted together, Quebec, PEI, NS, and NB accounted for 74 percent of the fund. Old Canada has been relatively "poor" compared to rest of Canada; the GDP per capita for Quebec, PEI, NS, and NB was consistently lower than for Canada as a whole from 2002–03 to 2008–09, and the gap widened as the decade continued (Statistics Canada 2010).

Old Canada ranks as the highest taxer in Canada. In 2011 Quebec had the highest levels for personal income tax for the first, second, and third brackets. The Atlantic provinces are also relatively high taxers, according to Nova Scotia's Finance Department (Nova Scotia 2011).

The disposable personal income per capita for Quebec was virtually identical to that of the three largest Atlantic provinces in 2002–11. However, it was consistently behind Ontario and Western provinces (Institut de la statistique du Québec 2011). Except for the early to mid 1990s, the highest percentage of social assistance beneficiaries has been found in NL and Quebec.

QUEBEC-ATLANTIC TENSIONS, NOT COOPERATION

Such similarities might suggest unity on common fronts—but not in Old Canada. Tensions between Quebec and Atlantic provinces have long been the order of the day on major policy issues. The question is whether the tensions are fatal to future cooperation in the region.

The first issue is economic design. Although it is coming to be increasingly questioned and curtailed, the "Quebec Model" has been the major frame of reference for Quebec's economic policy since the Quiet Revolution. The model featured a number of aspects, but the use of Hydro Quebec (HQ) was arguably the centrepiece of the policy. Hydro Quebec is an integrated electricity company joining electricity generation, transmission, and distribution under its aegis. Established as the prime mechanism for the industrial development of the province in the 1960s, it was designed to overcome the deficiencies of private-sector provision. It currently consists of three main divisions: Hydro-Québec Production operates Hydro Quebec's generation facilities in Quebec; Hydro-Québec Distribution supplies Quebec customers with electricity, by purchasing electricity from Hydro- Québec Production, at a regulated price; and TransEnergy operates Hydro Quebec's transmission system in Quebec.

The difficulty is that HQ is not the only public hydro company in the area, and its province-building design clashes directly with that of Newfoundland and Labrador Hydro and others in Atlantic Canada. Nalcor Energy is the parent company of Newfoundland and Labrador Hydro, the Churchill Falls (Labrador) Corporation—CF(L)Co and the Oil and Gas Corporation of Newfoundland and Labrador. In 2008 Nalcor also assumed ownership of the Bull Arm Site Corporation, the entity entrusted with building the gravity-based structure for the Hibernia offshore site (Newfoundland and Labrador 2013).

HQ engages in a policy of low residential, commercial, and industrial rates subsidized by the profits from the Upper Churchill (Churchill Falls) hydro development (Garcia 2009). This development is owned jointly by the two hydro companies (Newfoundland's at 65.8 and Quebec's at 34.2 percent) in a company called Churchill Falls (Labrador) Corporation, CF(L)Co. Most of its product is sold to Hydro Quebec, which reaps windfall profits due to a contract poorly negotiated by CFCLo/Brinco; Newfoundland and Labrador gets very little and will until the contract is said to expire in 2041. Terms on which wheeling[1] can occur are in dispute.

The frustrations of Newfoundland were not at an end in the new century. Newfoundland's attempts with TransEnergy to obtain energy wheeling rights through Quebec on reasonable terms for exploitation of the Lower Churchill

---

[1] The transfer of electricity from one utility area to another through transmission and distribution lines, allowing utility areas with excess supply to transmit excess power to others with supply shortages.

were unsuccessful. The failure led Newfoundland and Labrador Hydro to launch complaints in 2009 and 2010 with the Quebec regulator, the Régie de l'énergie, complaints still unresolved.

In addition, Quebec refuses to negotiate directly with NL over the Old Harry prospect straddling the Quebec-Newfoundland boundary located in the Laurentian Channel in the Gulf of St Lawrence. The so-called "Stanfield Line" was agreed to by Quebec in 1964, but Newfoundland and Labrador has rejected it.

Newfoundland and Labrador is not the only province to see a clash between its economic designs and those of Quebec. In 2009, premiers Shawn Graham of New Brunswick and Jean Charest of Quebec announced a deal that would have seen Hydro Quebec acquire most of the power generation assets (hydroelectric installations and Point Lepreau nuclear station) of the province's hydro crown, Énergie NB, for $3.2 billion, and the distribution network for $4.8 billion, the amount of its accumulated debt, with distribution remaining in the hands of New Brunswick. The benefits touted for the deal were a five-year rate freeze for residential ratepayers, a 15 percent power rate cut for medium-size industries, and a 23 percent cut in power rates for large industrial customers.

The deal raised a number of issues that were never concretely resolved in the minds of New Brunswick taxpayers and neighbouring provincial premiers. The first was that the Graham government had been elected in 2006 with a promise that NB Power would not be sold. Another was the issue of finances. HQ was to sell bulk electricity to New Brunswickers at a locked-in rate regardless of the market; business's rate was better than that of consumers; the deal seemed more for HQ's benefit that NB Hydro's; and there was a possibility that the agreement could affect NL/NS access to the New England electricity market, as premiers Williams and Dexter complained. Williams said that New Brunswick would feel the brunt of policies like those that had disadvantaged his own province for decades (CBC News New Brunswick 2010).

Not only had the people of the province second thoughts about the deal, but so too did Quebec itself. Charest called it off in March 2010, citing unforeseen costs not apparent at the time of the 2009 MOU (Radio-Canada 2010). However, the deal was already dead politically. The episode had shown that Quebec drove a hard bargain with neighbouring provinces. It was one thing to work in partnership with a fellow Crown, but still another to take it over completely and leave the province-building for Quebec as the standard by which to manage another province's energy affairs.

Are such histories fatal for future New East alliances? Not necessarily. Bad history wasn't enough to prevent premiers Bouchard and Tobin from inking the Lower Churchill-La Romaine hydro deal of 1998, the terms of which would have turned back some of the disadvantages of the 1969 deal. Furthermore, it is virtually inconceivable to imagine transmission of energy from a future Gull Island project—which could produce 2,250 MW, three times Muskrat Falls—except through Quebec, at mutually beneficial rates. Even a less exploitative HQ/NB Hydro deal can be imagined.

ATLANTIC CANADA: A MODEL OF INTERPROVINCIALISM

Available to Old Canada, however, is a model of cooperation and interprovincialism. The Atlantic provinces of Old Canada tend to combine or cooperate on the matters that affect them most. For example, faced with declining political influence, the premiers combine to form Maritime and Atlantic "Councils." Faced with declining population, they participate in the Atlantic Population Table (2006). Faced with decline in economic matters, they ramp up energy alliances. Faced with decline in working-age population, they cooperate on immigration and human capital initiatives. Table 3 provides a historical review of these multilateral Atlantic area initiatives:

In short, there have been five to six decades of cooperation amongst these provinces, which have been brought together by the logic of shared political, social, and economic circumstances of the sort chronicled at the beginning of this chapter. Yet these forms of cooperation, while valuable, are on lower-level matters and do not concern the big-ticket policies that could make Old Canada more competitive.

THE LOGIC OF THE NEW EAST

There is a logic of cooperation that looms larger as time goes on for the provinces of Old Canada. It speaks to a larger sphere of interaction and expanded institutional relationships in a new framework we call the New East.

The first element of the logic promoting potential intergovernmentalism in Old Canada is the changing federal environment. The change is toward simultaneous disengagement by Ottawa and Quebec. This is what the demise of the Laurentian axis looks like in practice. Ottawa announces it will play no future policy role in setting health policy after 2014, that will it continue its commitment to a classical federalist "Open Federalism" (Dunn 2008) and download selected federal responsibilities to the provinces. Quebec has been leaving Canada for years and is still in the process of cutting ties. Ottawa has no current specific strategy for engagement of Quebec to counter the trend. The New East would, however, be one.

However, there are signs that the net effect of recent federal policy is to download federal responsibilities on to the provinces. Quebec estimates its out-of-pocket costs for Bill C-10, the federal Crime Bill, at $750 million for new prisons, and at up to $80 million a year for application of the new rules, and is bitter that the new bill was introduced without provincial consultation (Canadian Press 2012). There were hints on other fronts of abandonment of federal roles to the provinces. For example, on 13 March 2012, the *Globe and Mail* reported, " the Conservative-dominated Commons environment committee on Tuesday recommended downloading much of the job of environmental assessment to the provinces and imposing timelines so

Table 3: Atlantic Area Initiatives

Name	Date Established	Purpose(s)
Atlantic Provinces Economic Council	1956	Economic intelligence
Council of Maritime Premiers (CMP)	1972	Ensure maximum cooperation between provinces and their agencies by: 1) creating regional agencies, 2) harmonizing policies, and 3) forming common positions vis-à-vis other governments. First such interprovincial body
Common procurement agreement	1989	Bid on government contracts for goods and services <$25K and construction tenders <$100K, designated services >$50K
Council of Atlantic Premiers (CAP)	2000	1) Promote Atlantic interests nationally by developing common positions to COF and FMM and others; 2) coordinate joint activities like trade promotion, fiscal arrangements, social and economic cooperation; 3) undertake joint analysis and review of range of public policies that affect Atlantic Canada, e.g., have agreements on Atlantic energy framework, aquaculture development, transportation
New England Governors and Eastern Canadian Premiers' (NEG-ECP) Annual Conference	1973	Undertake initiatives of common interest to the six NE States and five easternmost provinces, including Quebec. Has adopted action plans in many areas of trade, energy, transportation, and air quality, and the environment. Has four standing committees relating to these.
Maritime Provinces Higher Education Commission(MPHEC)	1974	An agency of the CMP. A renewed mandate was established in 1997 and a new MPHEC Act passed in 2005. Aims to provide best possible PSE environment
Maritime Provinces Education Foundation (MPEF)/ Council of Atlantic Ministers of Education & Training (CAMET)	1982 2004	1) Improve Atlantic educational systems 2) Undertake regional initiatives that transcend borders
Atlantic Population Table	2006	A cost-shared CIC, ACOA, the four Atlantic provinces, and HRSDC project to counter problems of aging and declining populations and to encourage immigration, youth retention
Atlantic Provinces Harness Racing Commission, Atlantic Veterinary College, Atlantic Lottery Corp		Special purpose bodies of regional benefit
Atlantic Energy Gateway	2007	Federal initiative to encourage provinces to develop renewable energy in the region and reduce greenhouse gas emissions. Provinces use this program to explore how to integrate their transmission systems.
Atlantic Procurement Agreement, 2008 and Harmonized Standard Terms and Conditions, 2007	2008	Builds on 1989 Agreement. Lowers interprovincial trade barriers and removes forms of discrimination between the four provinces. It also lowers the tendering thresholds for provincial government purchasing in Atlantic Canada for goods and services from $25,000 to $10,000.

Source: Author's compilations.

the development of big projects won't be delayed" (Galloway 2012). One month later, Minister Oliver announced, "The government will move to a 'one project, one review' policy on environmental projects by recognizing provincial reviews, as long as they meet the requirements of the Canadian Environmental Assessment Act" (Davidson 2012).

A second element of the logic is that a New East intergovernmentalism would make economic sense. Pierre-Olivier Pineau notes in a Federal Idea study that integrating electricity sectors (in Old Canada) could improve reliability, reduce investment costs, improve load factors, lead to economies of scale in new construction, and use lower-cost, but distant, power sources (Pineau 2012). One can imagine analogous fields with similar economic advantages.

Provinces, at EU insistence, joined in the Canada/EU Comprehensive Economic and Trade Agreement (CETA) talks because provincial concerns in labour, procurement, and resource matters affected the discussions. Accordingly, there may also be an opportunity to draft a New East "European Rim" approach analogous to the "Pacific Rim" strategies of Western provinces.

The third element relates to the implications of diminishing federal transfers. Federal transfers are important in Old Canada, and they are becoming less generous as Ottawa engages in its budget-balancing in the 2010s. Federal transfers made up 38 percent of the revenues of the Maritime provinces in 2010–11, and 22 percent of those of Newfoundland and Labrador; and federal health and social transfers paid for about a fifth of Atlantic Canada's health and social spending (APEC 2012). However, faced with the prospect of increasing deficits for most of the decade, federal authorities decided on a course of fiscal austerity that included cuts in the growth of transfers. Nationally, the Canada Health Transfer (CHT) was to grow at its historical rate by 6 percent per year until 2016–17, after which it would increase by a three-year average of nominal GDP growth; in 2014 it would change to an equal per capita entitlement. The Canada Social Transfer (CST) was to continue at a 3 percent growth rate annually, and equalization growth was to be related to nominal GDP.

The Parliamentary Budget Officer noted that the changes to the CHT escalator will reduce federal net debt relative to GDP, resulting in a sustainable federal fiscal structure. The implications for Atlantic Canada, and indeed for all provinces, are serious ones. Said the PBO, "provincial-territorial net debt relative to GDP is projected to increase substantially over the long term from 20 percent in 2010–11 to over 125 percent in 2050–51 and to over 480 percent by 2085–86" (PBO 2012, 2). The report let these stark figures speak for themselves.

And Old Canada is, well, older, so health costs there will be higher per capita than in the rest of the country. Having both the CHT and CST entitlements allocated on a per-capita basis does not lead to a sense of optimism for provincial treasurers. A more cooperative New East approach may help.

These developments on the transfer front are compounded by the likely effects of the federal government's four-year austerity program. APEC estimates significant negative fallout from federal program reductions. The long-term prospects for the Old Age Security program in the Atlantic area, where the population is older and more dependent than anywhere else on OAS entitlements, are of considerable concern (APEC 2012, 2).

The fourth aspect of the logic is that the provincial governments of Old Canada have significant debt structures. Even Newfoundland and Labrador, which posted several surpluses in a row and saw its economy outpace those of all the other provinces in 2011, announced it was slipping into deficit in 2012 and 2013 due to the end of Atlantic Accord payments, reduced volume of oil production, and the taking offline of two offshore platforms, and in "periodic deficits" for the next ten years (Newfoundland and Labrador 2012).

The other provinces are currently in deficit. Nova Scotia in December 2011 forecast a $365 million deficit and a $13.736 billion debt. New Brunswick's forecast was a $546 million deficit with a $10.3 billion debt. PEI foresaw a $73 million deficit with a $1.9 million debt (APEC 2012, 4-6).

Thus the economic health of the Atlantic provinces is not robust enough for them to engage in more functional area initiatives by themselves, but with another partner—Quebec—they may be better placed to do so. Such cooperation could take in many areas, the most pressing of which are big-ticket items like health care, procurement, and energy developments.

The fifth element in the logic is that most provinces want a National Energy Strategy and, if it is to be truly national, it needs Old Canada to reach an accord on it. Versions differ. Industry emphasizes matters like streamlining regulatory reform, the seeking of new markets, and establishing new infrastructure (Energy Policy Institute of Canada 2011). Conservationists tend to call for increased safeguards in the production, transportation, and consumption of energy (Canadian Renewable Energy Alliance 2013). Table 4 outlines an amalgam of such approaches. Whatever it turns out to be, without the needs of the five eastern provinces factored in, it isn't going to happen. And at present, there is no mechanism to promote all five talking to each other. The New East would be one mechanism.

Many of the suggested initiatives could be spearheaded by intergovernmental cooperation in a New East alliance. There is, for starters, a Council of Atlantic Environment Ministers, and regularized meetings of Atlantic Energy Ministers have begun functioning. There are 17 universities in Quebec, but more (20) in Atlantic Canada, many with expertise in energy matters. Intergovernmental inefficiency and disagreements can threaten potential markets (CBC News 2011a).

The sixth point in the logic is that the area is very familiar with regional inter-governmentalism. In addition to the many examples of multilateral Atlantic or Quebec-Atlantic relations (NEG-ECP meetings and initiatives) we have covered, there are many examples of bilateral relations involving provinces in Old Canada. (See Table 5.)

There is thus a history of intergovernmental relations which could be built upon, seven out of 11 involving the government of Quebec. Quebec is no stranger

Table 4: National Energy Strategy Action Items, 2012

Demand Side	Supply Side	Knowledge Base	Government Roles
• Streamline regulatory project reviews, e.g., have fewer joint reviews and one review per jurisdictional clarifications • Collaborative searches for new markets and international trade • Intensified interaction with US on electric grid issues, like smart grids, electricity reliability, and security • Collaborative development of infrastructure to diversify and expand energy markets away from US • Connect East and West by pipelines and/or national electricity grid • Include international commitments such as export development of Canadian RE technologies (through EDC) and official development assistance (through CIDA) to support the utilization of renewable energy to reduce poverty • Develop short- and long-term carbon-pricing regimes	• More exacting model energy codes • Improve product energy efficiency • Improve home energy rating systems • More efficient freight transportation (to reduce carbon emissions) • Increase use of low-impact renewable energy resources such as wind, solar, biomass, hydro and earth energy • Provide that overseas development and other international commitments connect renewable energy use and elimination of poverty • Develop alternate sources of electricity	• Develop lower-carbon emission economy technologies like carbon capture and storage, smart grids, marine renewables, electric vehicles • Develop collaborative action plans to market new energy technologies • Benchmark against the energy innovation of global competitors • Increase collaboration in development of energy labour force and consumer energy awareness • Increase research on ways to balance energy security, economic development, and reducing climate change	• Ensure energy strategy has federal-provincial-territorial-municipal elements • Federal-provincial collaboration in regulating pipeline projects • Reduce conflict and overlap in of federal and provincial climate change targets • Improve federal role in the sector – international energy agreements, approving foreign investment and pipelines, research and infrastructure funding/ loan guarantees, setting environmental standards • Municipal design of energy efficient building codes for housing, office and industrial buildings, and urban design, infrastructure, and transportation • Include framework for engagement with Aboriginal peoples • Participate internationally and bilaterally on energy efficiency or renewable energy treaties • Make renewable energy development a national priority, and in legislative form • Provide transfers to provinces for public transit and high speed rail corridors

Source: Author's compilations.

Table 5: Bilateral Agreements in Old Canada (Quebec/Atlantic Canada)

Bilateral Agreement	Date	Nature of Agreement
The New Brunswick-Québec Agreement	1969	Access for French-speaking New Brunswickers in various programs of study in Quebec, primarily in the health field
New Brunswick/Québec Cultural Cooperation Program Agreement	1969	Provides Quebec and New Brunswick cultural organizations, artists, and groups of artists with financial assistance for exchanges between the two provinces.
Newfoundland & Labrador–Quebec Agreement on Labour Mobility and Recognition of Qualifications, Skills and Work Experience in the Construction Industry	1999	Workers who reside in New Brunswick may work in all regions of Quebec and in all construction industry sectors if they are certified or else exempted by Quebec regulators.
Memorandum of Understanding Concerning Medical Education between the Province of New Brunswick and the Province of Newfoundland and Labrador	Began in September 2000	The Medical School at Memorial University reserves 40 seats for the full undergraduate medical program annually.
Agreement between Quebec and New Brunswick Concerning Transboundary Environmental Impacts	13 November 2002	The two governments share information on environmental problems of common interest, as well as expertise and mutual assistance on environmental matters, and will jointly study air quality, acid rain, surface and groundwater management, reduction of pollution in transboundary watercourses, and pollution from agricultural sources.
Newfoundland and Labrador/Nova Scotia/Dalhousie Rehabilitation Disciplines Agreement		A funding transfer from the Province of Newfoundland and Labrador to allow a maximum of 24 seats in Occupational Therapy and 30 seats in Physiotherapy to be reserved for students from that province in the rehabilitation disciplines at Dalhousie University.
Dalhousie-UNB Medical Education Program Agreement	June 2008	The agreement creates the Dalhousie University undergraduate medical education program in New Brunswick at the University of New Brunswick – Saint John campus, beginning in 2010–2011, allowing 30 New Brunswick students into the first year of the program annually.
Agreement between the Government of New Brunswick and the Government of Quebec on Labour Mobility and the Recognition of Qualifications, Skills and Work Experience in the Construction Industry	October 2008	Workers who reside in New Brunswick may work in all regions of Quebec and in all construction industry sectors if they are eligible to receive either a "certificat d'enregistrement" or an "exemption to hold an occupational competency certificate" issued by the Commission de la construction du Quebec.
Agreement on the opening of public procurement for New Brunswick and Quebec (replaces 1993 agreement)	October 2008	QC and NB premiers agree to streamline and modernize the original agreement signed in 1993, and which served as a model for the Agreement on Internal Trade (AIT) and the Atlantic Procurement Agreement.
New Brunswick-Nova Scotia Partnership Agreement on Regulation and the Economy (PARE)	2009	The two provinces agree to work collaboratively on matters affecting trade. PARE provides guiding principles for regulatory harmonization and standardization and aims at broader trade liberalization initiatives nationally.

Source: Adapted from Quebec and Atlantic provincial government websites, and trade enhancement arrangements, http://www.marcan.net/english/article1800table.htm.

to cooperation in the Atlantic area. It is possible to envisage new initiatives—an eastern TILMA, expanded energy cooperation—building on these.

Critics might be tempted to argue that the most of the agreements concern matters on which it is relatively easy to agree, overlooking the potential for issues of larger scope. Nicolle Bolleyer, for example, has observed that "Canadian regional intergovernmental agreements are "characterized by a 'bottom-up logic' driven by power-concentrating [parliamentary] governments which tend towards solutions of the smallest common denominator of only limited scope (in terms of concessions and territory)" (Bolleyer 2009, 104). If this is true—and there is some accuracy to it—it is not a damning point. If larger issues are not included, it is time to include them, and to make a difference. This was the intent of initiatives like the Council of the Federation; but the COF is not meant to attend to regional matters. However, Bolleyer is not completely accurate in the case of Canada. There are two large-scale intergovernmental agreements of a regional nature, the NWP and Muskrat Falls. They prove that large-scale interprovincial cooperation is possible.

The New West Partnership (NWP) is a wide-ranging regional agreement of significant depth. It began life as a two-province accord. The British Columbia-Alberta Trade, Investment and Labour Mobility Agreement, or TILMA, was explicitly designed to knit the two provinces into an economic unit that would balance off the economic strength of central Canada. Comparing it to other economic cooperation agreements in Canada, APEC head Elizabeth Beale saw TILMA as a "significant step up, in terms of the comprehensive nature of the agreement and the commitment to a fixed timetable for implementation. Unlike the Agreement on Internal Trade (AIT) ... TILMA covers all sectors and barriers unless explicitly excluded [some resource industries, water, social policy and Aboriginals], and has a viable enforcement mechanism similar to NAFTA and the WTO" (Beale 2007, 3). The agreement commits the governments to the principle of non-discrimination, to the mutual recognition of standards, regulations and professional credentials, to the elimination of trade, investment, and labour-mobility barriers and to effective dispute resolution.

The two became three in the New West Partnership Trade Agreement of 2010, which was to be fully implemented in 2013. The NWP carries on the essential elements of TILMA but has some modifications to accommodate the inclusion of Saskatchewan. Whether Manitoba will be included in future is an open question.

Another notable large-scale regional cooperation is the Muskrat Falls project, a bilateral NL/NS deal which has the possibility to become an Atlantic energy alliance, one from which other provinces in the region will likely benefit (see Table 6).

So there are some meaningful examples of regional intergovernmental agreements that are not simply lowest common denominator. There can be more.

A seventh and related point in the logic is that provincial regional intergovernmentalism is common in many federations from which Old Canada could learn. For example, Swiss regional intergovernmental arrangements are numerous (there are over 30 regional conferences in areas of cantonal responsibility), marked by

Table 6: Muskrat Falls Development: An Example of Constructive Interprovincialism

Description	Newfoundland and Labrador Role	Nova Scotia Role	Possible PEI and New Brunswick Roles
$6.2 billion project, announced between NS and NL on 18 November 2010.* The project has five components: the Muskrat Falls generating plant ($2.9 billion); transmission line to Churchill Falls and the Strait of Belle Isle; 30 km subsea Strait of Belle Isle crossing; Island transmission system to Soldier's Pond (all adding up to $2.1 billion); and 180 km Cabot Strait crossing (aka Maritime Link, $1.2 billion).	Newfoundland and Labrador will reserve 40 percent of the power for its own use, will raise $4.4 billion to pay for its share; 8,600 person years of work.	Emera, a private company serving Nova Scotia, gets 20 percent of that energy: 170 megawatts/yr (10 percent of its energy needs) for itself for a term of 35 years and constructs the underwater link.	PEI has asked to participate as part of the other provinces' request for proposals for their cables in the Muskrat Falls project, so there would be a third cable from PEI to New Brunswick. NB's geographic location and transmission infrastructure positions it as the energy gateway to New England and the US eastern seaboard.

*Since that date the estimate has increased to $7.7 billion.

Source: Author's compilations from various news reports, e.g., Gushue (2010).

voluntary power-sharing in policy-specific rather than generalist areas, and designed to yield collective positions to balance the power of cantons against the national government (Bolleyer 2009, 104-5).

The United States also has several regional groupings. The Council of State Governments (CSG) has four regional conferences of state legislators, state courts, and most regional governors. Regional groupings, especially those of regional governors, tend to specialize in matters specific to their region. The Eastern Regional Conference of the CSG, for example, tends to specialize in matters associated with the Eastern Canadian provinces, including agriculture, criminal justice, education, energy and environment, health, and transportation.

Another category of regional grouping involves the states and provinces that are engaged in North American trade, environmental, and economic matters. Earl Fry (2004, 5-6) has listed these and the memberships straddling the US-Canada border (see Table 7).

Table 7: North American Border Commissions and Groups

Border Commissions and Groups	Members
Border Governors' Conference	Arizona, California, New Mexico, Texas; Baja California, Chihuahua, Coahuila, Nuevo Léon, Sonora, Tamaulipas
Border Legislative Conference	Arizona, California, New Mexico, Texas; Baja California, Chihuahua, Coahuila, Nuevo Léon, Sonora, Tamaulipas
Chihuahua–New Mexico Border Commission of the Californias	California; Baja California Norte, Baja California Sur
Council of Great Lakes Governors	Illinois, Indiana, Michigan, Minnesota, New York, Ohio, Pennsylvania, Wisconsin; Ontario and Quebec (associate members)
Idaho–Alberta Task Force	Idaho, Alberta
Montana–Alberta Bilateral Advisory Council	Montana, Alberta
New England Governors and Eastern Canadian Premiers	Connecticut, Maine, Massachusetts, New Hampshire, Rhode Island, Vermont; New Brunswick, Newfoundland and Labrador, Nova Scotia, Prince Edward Island, Quebec
Pacific Northwest Economic Region (PNWER)	Alaska, Idaho, Montana, Oregon, Washington; Alberta, British Columbia, Yukon Territory
Sonora-Arizona Commission	Sonora, Arizona
Western Canadian Premiers and Western Governors' Association	Four provinces, 21 states

Source: Fry (2004, 5-6).

Fry's conclusion is that "the three federalist systems in North America present a new paradigm for regional economic integration-by-parts which is not captured in current fixations on the Ottawa-Washington-Mexico City diplomatic axis ... subnational governments, through their increased cross-border activities and their power for both cooperative and unilateral action, have a significant potential to shape North American integration that far outweighs the attention currently paid to them by scholars and the media." The potential Fry refers to has been largely overlooked in the case of Mexico and the United States but more employed in the case of Canada and the FTA/NAFTA talks, in which provinces played a relatively important part. Provinces are again involved, this time in the Canada-European

Union Comprehensive Economic and Trade Agreement (CETA) negotiations, because of EU insistence and because CETA involves provincial jurisdictions.

There are also some special-purpose regional groupings. These are very common in the United States; examples include the Western States Contracting Alliance, involving 15 states, which promotes cooperative multistate purchasing. Another is the Northeast Recycling Council organized by the Eastern Regional Conference of the Council of State Governments in 1989 and involving 10 states. Still another is the Western States Climate Initiative, formed in 2010 and composed of 11 states and Canadian provinces, to develop a cap-and-trade initiative to reduce greenhouse gas emissions by 15 percent by 2020 and designed to trade an estimated $21 billion worth of allowances annually (Wall 2011).

Some subnational or international groupings, although not regional in the sense we have been using the term, may have lessons for regional interprovincialism. One is the environmental record of the Council of the Australian Federation (CAF) as compared to Canadian provinces. The Australian Commonwealth and States were able to establish by 2009 an agreement on a coordinated plan of action on climate change emissions reduction, whereas Canadian governments have relied on unco-ordinated, unilateral action and a lack of action by first ministers. A crucial key to agreement was the 2007 commitment by the Council of the Australian Federation (CAF) to go ahead with a joint plan regardless of whether the Commonwealth agreed to or not. David Gordon and Douglas Macdonald conclude a case study on the issue: "What our analysis suggests is that strong institutions of IGR, those with participation rules that mandate inclusion of first ministers, codification of rules and procedures, and permanent secretariat, create a context that enables the emergence of collaborative norms and joint expectations and can create the conditions under which actors remain at the table long enough to negotiate coordinated outcomes as regards the substantive issues outlined above" (Gordon and Macdonald 2011, 22). It also helps, say the authors, that there are both vertical and horizontal linkages in Australia (i.e., federal-provincial and interprovincial) whereas the vertical links in Canada have atrophied over time. This is our argument in a nutshell. It is what the New East needs, especially on the Quebec-Atlantic cooperation front.

WHAT IS TO BE DONE? IMAGINE A NEW EAST, FOR STARTERS

So the picture is relatively clear. Historic alliances are dissolving. The provinces of broader Eastern Canada—Old Canada—are becoming more similar than dissimilar. The federal government is changing the game rules and making fiscal realities somewhat starker for the region than they were before.

Meanwhile a model of common fronts and intergovernmental cooperation beckons from the Atlantic area, pointing to a more formal intergovernmental arrangement in the New East. Intergovernmental collaboration, as national and international examples show, is helped along by involvement of first ministers, permanent secretariats, and codification of decision-making rules. These common fronts point to (or at least do not discourage) a more formal intergovernmental arrangement in the east of Canada.

What is to be done? Let me suggest a number of steps.

- Name the entity. If the "New East" is too figurative, provinces may prefer options like the Council of Eastern Canada, the Council of Eastern Canadian Premiers, or the Eastern Premiers Conference.
- Have a non-aligned think tank do a study on the economic trade and political connections and possible synergies between the provinces of the Quebec/Atlantic Canada area. The idea would be to aim higher than the current lower-level partnerships currently practised in the area—bigger-ticket items, if you will. On certain issues, other provinces, notably Ontario, might be brought into the fold, but the New East is a viable entity all on its own.
- Publish a consultation paper on the New East examining problems and pros-pects that greater cooperation could address. One would expect that energy, transportation, subsidies, trade, labour mobility, health services rationalization, Aboriginal affairs, and demographic policies would rank highly as candidates for discussion. A critical examination of the federal government's role (or in some cases, lack of one) would also be discussed. Options for institutional-ization—the role of first ministers, the advisability of a secretariat, and what decision rules are advisable—would emerge. Institutionalization, as we sug-gest, leads to collaboration.

These steps are for the long term. In the interim, some medium-term wins: com-mon fronts on Senate reform, fiscal negotiations, or dairy supply management in the face of Trans-Pacific Partnership talks.

Something like what is proposed here will be an accomplished fact in ten years. We have spent the past 50 years digging ourselves into the hole we are in now; we don't want this to continue for another 50. That is why we need a New East.

REFERENCES

Atlantic Provinces Economic Council (APEC). 2012. "A Pre-Budget Fiscal Update for Atlantic Canada." *Atlantic Report* (Winter). http://www.apec-econ.ca/files/pubs/%7BA8374716-3141-4948-BF26-B4AD68579A25%7D.pdf?title=APEC%27s%20Pre-Budget%20Fiscal%20Update%20for%20Atlantic%20Canada&publicationtype=Atlantic%20Report.

Beale, E. 2007. "Creating a Single Economy in Atlantic Canada: Will Our Provincial Governments Follow the Western Lead?" *Atlantic Report* 41 (4): 3.

Bolleyer, N. 2009. *Intergovernmental Cooperation: Rational Choices in Federal Systems and Beyond*. Oxford, UK: Oxford University Press.

Bott, R., and D.M. Carson 2007. *Canada's Evolving Offshore Oil and Gas Industry: Energy Today and Tomorrow*. Calgary: Canadian Centre for Energy Information.

Cameron, D. 1994. "Modern Ontario and the Laurentian Thesis." In *The State of the Federation*, edited by D.M. Brown and J. Hiebert. Kingston, ON: Queen's University Institute of Intergovernmental Relations.

Canadian Press. 2012. "Quebec Vows to Limit Clout of Conservative Crime Bill." 13 March. http://www.ctvnews.ca/quebec-vows-to-limit-clout-of-conservative-crime-bill-1.781342.

Canadian Renewable Energy Alliance. 2013. *National Strategy*. http://www.canrea.ca/site/national-strategy/.

CBC News. 2011a. "Clock Ticking for Hydro Deals, Canada Told." Canadian Press, 12 July. http://www.cbc.ca/news/canada/newfoundland-labrador/story/2011/07/12/nl-cp-hydro-premiers-governors-712.html.

—. 2011b. "Royal Military Renaming Slammed as Colonial Throwback." 17 August. http://www.cbc.ca/news/canada/story/2011/08/16/royal-army-navy.html.

CBC News New Brunswick. 2010. "Quebec Balked at NB Power Sale Costs." 24 March. http://www.cbc.ca/news/canada/newbrunswick/story/2010/03/24/nb-nbpower-graham-1027.html.

Creighton, D. 1972. *Towards the Discovery of Canada*. Toronto: Macmillan.

Davidson, A. 2012. "Ottawa to Slash Environmental Review Act." CBC News, 17 April. http://www.cbc.ca/news/politics/ottawa-to-slash-environment-review-role-1.1158340.

Dunn, C. 2008. "Canada's 'Open Federalism': Past, Present, and Future Tense." In *The Federal Nation: Perspectives on American Federalism*, edited by I.W. Morgan and P.J. Davies. New York: Palgrave Macmillan.

Elections Canada. 2013. "Past Elections." http://www.elections.ca/content.aspx?section=e le&dir=pas&document=index&lang=e.

Energy Policy Institute of Canada. 2011. *A Strategy for Canada's Global Energy Leadership*. http://www.canadasenergy.ca/wp-content/uploads/2011/01/Framework_Document_JAN_14.pdf.

Environmental Effects Monitoring (EEM). 2008. *Study of the Hydropower Potential in Canada*. Reproduced in *Hydropower in Canada, Past, Present and Future*. Ottawa: Canadian Hydropower Association.

Fry, E.H. *The Role of Subnational Governments in the Governance of North America: Mapping the New North American Reality*. IRPP Working Paper Series No. 2004-09d, 5-6.

Galloway, G. 2012. "Ottawa Wants to Bow out of Regulating Fish Habitat, Documents Show." http://www.theglobeandmail.com/news/politics/ottawa-wants-to-bow-out-of-regulating-fish-habitat-documents-show/article535218/.

Garcia, C. 2009. "How Would the Privatization of Hydro-Québec Make Quebecers Richer?" Montreal Economic Institute Research Paper. http://www.iedm.org/files/cahier0209_en.pdf.

Gordon, D., and D. Macdonald. 2011. "Institutions and Federal Climate Change Governance: A Comparison of the Intergovernmental Coordination in Australia and Canada." Paper presented at the Annual Meeting of the CPSA, 2011.

Gushue, J. 2010. "Historic Hydro Pact Signed between N.L., N.S." CBC News, 18 November. http://www.cbc.ca/news/canada/newfoundland-labrador/historic-hydro-pact-signed-between-n-l-n-s-1.883078.

Ibbitson, J. 2011. "The Collapse of the Laurentian Consensus." *A Literary Review of Canada Online*, 5 December. http://reviewcanada.ca/essays/2012/01/01the-collapse-of-the-laurentian-consensus/.

Institut de la statistique du Québec. 2011. "Interprovincial Comparisons, Table Set 5, Personal Disposable Income Per Capita, 2001–2010." http://www.stat.gouv.qc.ca/statistiques/economie/comparaisons-economiques/interprovinciales/chap5.pdf.

Kennedy, M. 2011. "Canada Consensus 2011: Harper Could Reap the Benefits as Census Suggests New Ridings." *National Post*, 8 February. http://news.nationalpost.com/2012/02/08/canada-census-2011-tories-could-reap-the-benefits-as-census-suggests-new-ridings/.

Leuprecht, C., and N. O'Conner. 2005. "Demographic Change and Federal Systems." In *Spatial Aspects of Federative Systems*, edited by G. Färber and N. Otter. Deutsches Forschungsinstitut für Öffentliche Verwaltung Speyer.

Mallory, J.R. 1984. *The Structure of Canadian Government*. Rev. ed. Toronto: Gage.

Mendelsohn, M., and S. Choudry. 2011. *Voter Equality and Other Canadian Values: Finding the Right Balance*. Toronto: Mowat Centre for Policy Innovation.

Newfoundland and Labrador. 2012. Speech from the Throne, 5 March. http://www.exec.gov.nl.ca/thronespeech/2012/speech2012.htm.

Newfoundland and Labrador, Department of Natural Resources. 2013. "Electricity" backgrounder. http://www.nr.gov.nl.ca/nr/energy/electricity/.

Nova Scotia Finance Department. 2011. "Tax Rates across Canada: Comparative Tax Rates for 2011 Tax Year (Updated as of April 26, 2011). http://www.novascotia.ca/finance/site-finance/media/finance/comparitave_2011.pdf.

Parliamentary Budget Officer of Canada (PBO). 2012. *Renewing the Canada Health Transfer: Implications for Federal and Provincial-Territorial Fiscal Sustainability*. 19 January. http://www.parl.gc.ca/PBO-DPB/documents/Renewing_CHT.pdf.

Pineau, P.-O. 2012. "L'intégration des secteurs de l'électricité au Canada : Bonne pour l'environnement et logique sur le plan économique," L'Idée fédérale: réseau québécois de réflexion sur le fédéralisme. http://ideefederale.ca/documents/Electricite_fr.pdf.

Quebec. 2011. *Budget Plan*, 2011–12. D17. www.budget.finances.gouv.qc.ca/Budget/2011-2012/en/documents/BudgetPlan.pdf.

— . *Budget Plan*. 2012. A29. http://www.budget.finances.gouv.qc.ca/Budget/2012-2013/en/documents/budgetplan.pdf.

Radio-Canada. 2010. "La vente [d'Énergie NB] ne tient plus." With La Presse Canadienne and CNW. 25 March. http://www.radiocanada.ca/regions/atlantique/2010/03/24/002-NB-energie-fin.shtml.

Statistics Canada. 2005. "Population Projections for Canada, Provinces and Territories 2005–2031." Catalogue no. 91-520-XIE, page 58.

—. 2008. "Federal Electoral District (FED) Profile, 2006 Census." Statistics Canada Catalogue no. 92-595-XWE. http://www12.statcan.ca/census-recensement/2006/dp-pd/prof/92-595/p2c.cfm?TPL=INDX&LANG=E.

—. 2010. "Gross Domestic Product Per Capita, Canada, Provinces and Territories, 2002/2003 to 2008/2009 (in Current Dollars)." Table A32, 42. Publication No. 81-595-M. http://publications.gc.ca/collections/collection_2010/statcan/81-595-M/81-595-m2010088-eng.pdf.

—. 2011a. "The Canadian Population in 2011: Population Counts and Growth." http://www12.statcan.gc.ca/census-recensement/2011/as-sa/98-310-x/98-310-x2011001-eng.cfm.

—. 2011b. Census. http://www12.statcan.gc.ca/census-recensement/2011/as-sa/98-310-x/2011001/fig/fig4-eng.cfm.

—. 2011c. "The Canadian Population in 2011: Population Counts and Growth." Catalogue No. 98-310-X2011001. http://www12.statcan.gc.ca/census-recensement/2011/as-sa/98-310-x/98-310-x2011001-eng.pdf.

—. 2013. "Gross Domestic Product Expenditure-Based by Province and Territory." Accessed December 2013. http://www.statcan.gc.ca/tables-tableaux/sum-som/l01/cst01/econ15-eng.htm.

Wall, A. 2011. "Interstate Relations Trends." Prepared for the Council of State Governments. 1 July. http://knowledgecenter.csg.org/drupal/content/interstate-relations-trends-0.

Queen's Policy Studies
Recent Publications

The Queen's Policy Studies Series is dedicated to the exploration of major public policy issues that confront governments and society in Canada and other nations.

Manuscript submission. We are pleased to consider new book proposals and manuscripts. Preliminary inquiries are welcome. A subvention is normally required for the publication of an academic book. Please direct questions or proposals to the Publications Unit by email at spspress@queensu.ca, or visit our website at: www.queensu.ca/sps/books, or contact us by phone at (613) 533-2192.

Our books are available from good bookstores everywhere, including the Queen's University bookstore (http://www.campusbookstore.com/). McGill-Queen's University Press is the exclusive world representative and distributor of books in the series. A full catalogue and ordering information may be found on their web site (**http://mqup.mcgill.ca/**).

For more information about new and backlist titles from Queen's Policy Studies, visit http://www.queensu.ca/sps/books.

School of Policy Studies

The Multiculturalism Question: Debating Identity in 21st-Century Canada,
Jack Jedwab (ed.) 2014. ISBN 978-1-55339-422-8

Government-Nonprofit Relations in Times of Recession, Rachel Laforest (ed.) 2013.
ISBN 978-1-55339-327-6

Intellectual Disabilities and *Dual Diagnosis: An Interprofessional Clinical Guide for Healthcare Providers,* Bruce D. McCreary and Jessica Jones (eds.) 2013. ISBN 978-1-55339-331-3

Rethinking Higher Education: Participation, Research, and Differentiation,
George Fallis 2013. ISBN 978-1-55339-333-7

Making Policy in Turbulent Times: Challenges and Prospects for Higher Education,
Paul Axelrod, Roopa Desai Trilokekar, Theresa Shanahan, and Richard Wellen (eds.)
2013. ISBN 978-1-55339-332-0

Building More Effective Labour-Management Relationships, Richard P. Chaykowski and Robert S. Hickey (eds.) 2013. ISBN 978-1-55339-306-1

Navigationg on the Titanic: Economic Growth, Energy, and the Failure of Governance,
Bryne Purchase 2013. ISBN 978-1-55339-330-6

Measuring the Value of a Postsecondary Education, Ken Norrie and Mary Catharine Lennon (eds.) 2013. ISBN 978-1-55339-325-2

Immigration, Integration, and Inclusion in Ontario Cities, Caroline Andrew, John Biles, Meyer Burstein, Victoria M. Esses, and Erin Tolley (eds.) 2012. ISBN 978-1-55339-292-7

Diverse Nations, Diverse Responses: Approaches to Social Cohesion in Immigrant Societies,
Paul Spoonley and Erin Tolley (eds.) 2012. ISBN 978-1-55339-309-2

Making EI Work: Research from the Mowat Centre Employment Insurance Task Force,
Keith Banting and Jon Medow (eds.) 2012. ISBN 978-1-55339-323-8

Managing Immigration and Diversity in Canada: A Transatlantic Dialogue in the New Age of Migration, Dan Rodríguez-García (ed.) 2012. ISBN 978-1-55339-289-7

International Perspectives: Integration and Inclusion, James Frideres and John Biles (eds.) 2012. ISBN 978-1-55339-317-7

Dynamic Negotiations: Teacher Labour Relations in Canadian Elementary and Secondary Education, Sara Slinn and Arthur Sweetman (eds.) 2012. ISBN 978-1-55339-304-7

Where to from Here? Keeping Medicare Sustainable, Stephen Duckett 2012. ISBN 978-1-55339-318-4

International Migration in Uncertain Times, John Nieuwenhuysen, Howard Duncan, and Stine Neerup (eds.) 2012. ISBN 978-1-55339-308-5

Centre for International and Defence Policy

Afghanistan in the Balance: Counterinsurgency, Comprehensive Approach, and Political Order, Hans-Georg Ehrhart, Sven Bernhard Gareis, and Charles Pentland (eds.), 2012. ISBN 978-1-55339-353-5

Institute of Intergovernmental Relations

Canada and the Crown: Essays on Constitutional Monarchy, D. Michael Jackson and Philippe Lagassé (eds.), 2013. ISBN 978-1-55339-204-0

Paradigm Freeze: Why It Is So Hard to Reform Health-Care Policy in Canada, Harvey Lazar, John N. Lavis, Pierre-Gerlier Forest, and John Church (eds.), 2013. ISBN 978-1-55339-324-5

Canada: The State of the Federation 2010, Matthew Mendelsohn, Joshua Hjartarson, and James Pearce (eds.), 2013. ISBN 978-1-55339-200-2

The Democratic Dilemma: Reforming Canada's Supreme Court, Nadia Verrelli (ed.), 2013. ISBN 978-1-55339-203-3